AUSTRIA

(Frontispiece, overleaf) *1   Bruck an der Mur: the church and square*

Virginia Waite

AUSTRIA

Hastings House, Publishers
New York, New York 10016

First published in the United States of America 1970
© Virginia Waite 1970
8038 0343 5

Text printed in Great Britain by Northumberland Press Ltd., Gateshead. Plates printed and books bound by Richard Clay (The Chaucer Press) Ltd., Bungay, Suffolk

To Vera as promised

Contents

	List of illustrations	9
	Acknowledgments	10
	Map of Austria	11
1	Introduction	13
2	Vorarlberg	37
3	Tyrol	45
4	Land Salzburg	78
5	Upper Austria	98
6	Lower Austria	114
7	Vienna	129
8	Burgenland	163
9	Styria	171
10	Carinthia	186
	Index	199

The Illustrations

1	Bruck an der Mur: the church and square	frontispiece
2	Innsbruck: St Anna's Column in the Maria-Theresienstrasse	17
3	Innsbruck: the Helbling House	18
4	Innsbruck: the Herzog-Friedrichstrasse	25
5	Mayrhofen, seen from a cable car	26
6	Skating at Seefeld	35
7	Ascending the chair lift above Lermoos	36
8	Sölden in the Ötztal valley	53
9	Skiers above Kitzbühel	54
10	Salzburg: view of the city and castle	71
11	Salzburg: a fountain	72
12	Salzburg: the staircase in the Mirabell Palace	89
13	The Abbey of Melk, above the Danube	90
14	Vienna: Schönbrunn	107
15	Vienna: St Stephen's cathedral	108
16	Vienna: Chinese room in Schönbrunn	125
17	Vienna: the Karlskirche	126
18	Vienna: the Spanish riding school	143
19	Graz: the river front and castle	144
20	Rein, near Graz: the monastery church	161
21	Band playing in a small village near Velden	162
22	The Wörthersee	179
23	Natters church in Tyrol	180

Acknowledgments

My grateful thanks are due to the following: Fremdenverkehrsstelle der Stadt Wien; Amt der Burgenlandischen Landesregierung; Amt der Steiermarkischen Landesregierung; Fremdenverkehrsverband in Linz, Oberösterreich; Amt der Niederösterreichischen Landesregierung; Landesfremdenverkehrsamt in Salzburg; Landesfremdenverkehrsamt fur Kärnten; Fremdenverkehrsverband in Lienz, Ost-Tirol; Landesfremdenverkehrsamt für Tirol; Landesverband für Fremdenverkehr in Vorarlberg; and particularly to Dr L. Oberrieder of the Austrian National Tourist Office, London.

The Publishers wish to thank the following for supplying photographs reproduced in this book: the Austrian National Tourist Office for plates 15 and 18; J. Allan Cash for plate 14; Feature-Pix for plate 10 (by Eric Jelly) and plates 21 and 23 (by Gerry Brenes); A. F. Kersting for plates 1-9, 11, 12, 16, 17, 19, 20 and 22; and Helga Schmidt-Glasner for plate 13.

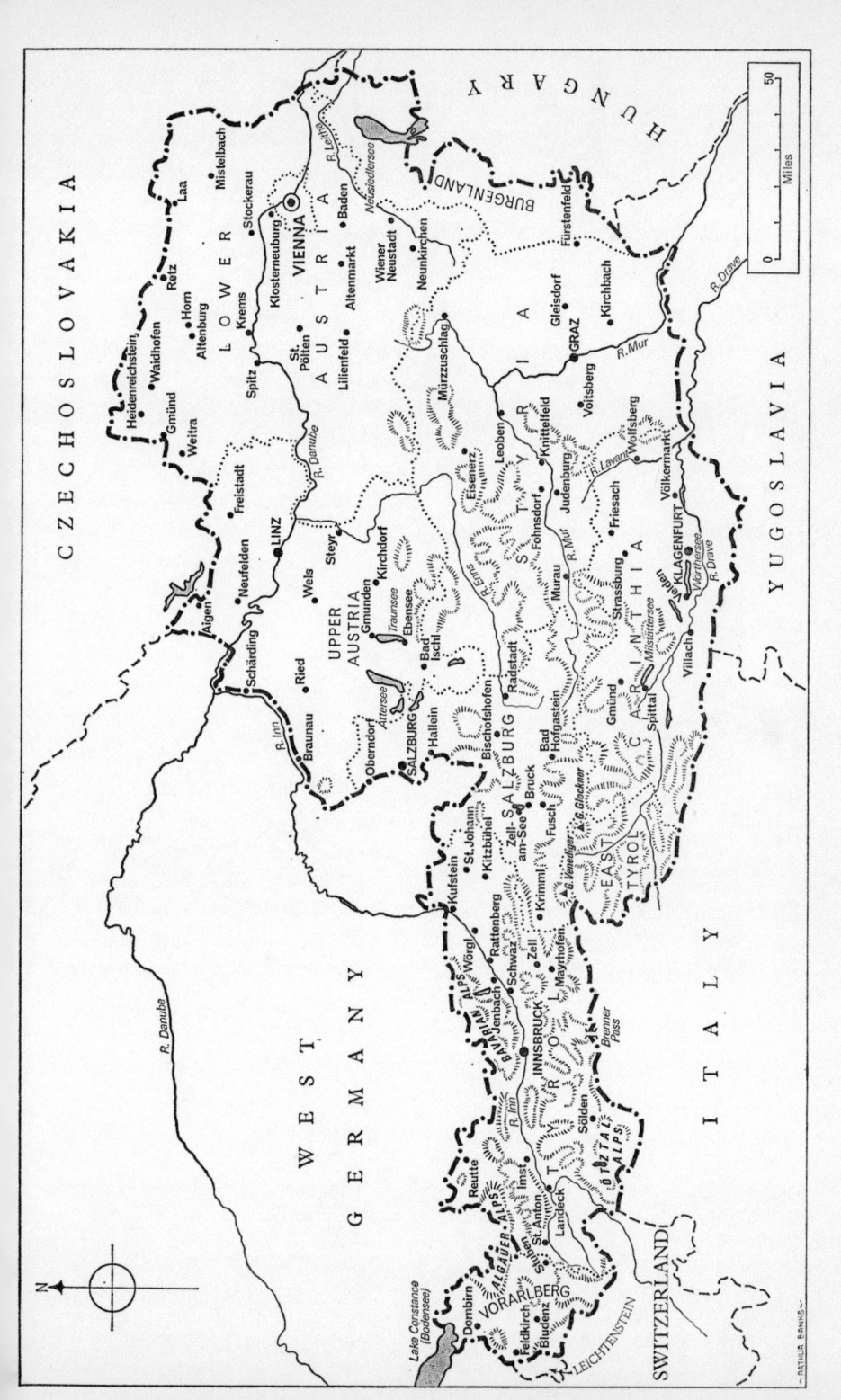

1 Introduction

Taken at its face value, Austria is a federal republic a little larger than Ireland and occupied by seven million people split between nine provinces, one of which is the capital tucked away on the right-hand side of the map. But even the most naïve traveller has to look beyond the surface, beyond the dirndl skirts, brass bands, immaculate villages, pretty rivers and dramatic mountains that make up a cosy, provincial country; for the monuments are too large and too numerous for this small-scale picture, the battle scars too obvious.

The nationalism of its people is not due to its lack of size, nor to its uneasy borders, but is a hangover from the old days, first the golden years when it was the centre of its empire and its people were justly proud and confident; then the crumbling years when it lost that empire, and each time the map was redrawn a different and smaller shape appeared; and finally, its sharp dissolution with a painful annexation to Germany followed by ten years of occupation by four foreign powers.

From ruling a vast slab of Europe to perpetual neutrality has been its adjustment and it has made it bravely and so quickly that a teenage visitor not forewarned would have difficulty in imagining its former status and power, were it not for those scars. After the very early Celts followed by the Romans, its history divides into four major periods—the Babenbergs; the Habsburgs and their expansion of territories; the loss of those lands; the formation of the republic and the struggle to a new position in the world.

The Babenbergs had quite a long slice of power, nearly 300 years in fact, from 976 when they were made Margraves of

Ostmark, which included Vienna. Their most noted emperor was Leopold III who stood on a hill outside the capital with his bride, a duchess from Constantinople, and let float away her veil. The gesture was more than a romantic one, because they had married amidst opposition and, if the veil should later be recovered, it would be a sign that they were forgiven. It was found, in an elderberry bush in a valley in the woods, and in gratitude Leopold founded the Augustine monastery of Klosterneuburg, six miles from Vienna.

The end of their dynasty was a sad and sordid affair. The last of the male line, Friedrich the Quarrelsome, had been killed in 1246 in the battle of Leitha, so his old sister was brought out of retirement and forced to marry in order to keep the line going. Her unwise choice was the king of Bohemia, 25 years her junior, who as soon as he became emperor dispatched his wife to a nunnery and remarried a young woman. Fortunately for Austria, the chances of an early death being what they were in the thirteenth century, the Bohemian King Ottakar was also killed, in the battle of Marchfeld. His opponent and victor was the first Habsburg, Rudolf I, whose rule began in 1278.

A few years later Rudolf bequeathed Austria and Styria to his sons and established the domains of the house of Habsburg which were to last more than six centuries until the end of the first world war. These hundreds of years of rule by one dynasty, which incidentally littered the country with castles, palaces, museums, memorials and so forth, had a threefold aim. Primarily, the Habsburg power had to be maintained and expanded, which was accomplished by marrying off the heirs and heiresses to suitable rulers and would-be rulers elsewhere and reaping in the new countries as a result—like Hungary, Bohemia, Spain, France, the Netherlands and much of Italy.

Secondly, the rulers had to keep the Turks out of Hungary and south-east Europe (hence all those castles), which involved perpetual skirmishing if not perpetual battle somewhere along some border most of the time. Thirdly, they defended the Roman Catholic church, although they were not always on the pope's side. The Holy Roman Empire had begun with the coronation of Charlemagne on Christmas Day in 800 and was to continue with the Habsburgs until the nineteenth century. The empire's ideal king was Christ, his deputy on earth was emperor.

By the fifteenth century Vienna had become one of the most important capital cities in Christendom. The Austrian domains were combined into one country by Maximilian 1, who married Maria, heiress to Burgundy, first of all acquiring the Low Countries as a result and then Burgundy itself after the Burgundian Charles the Bold was killed in the battle of Nancy. Maximilian's son, Philip the Handsome, though he was anything but, married Joanna, and added Spain to the empire's lands. The double wedding in 1515 of Maximilian's grandchildren, Ferdinand and Maria, had an even more spectacular and unexpected result.

Ferdinand married Anna, heiress to the throne of Hungary and Bohemia, Maria married Anna's brother Louis, heir to the same throne, and the two houses came to an agreement that if one of the lines should die out the other would have the right of succession. Louis was killed in the battle of Mohacs only 11 years later, leaving no children, so Ferdinand acquired Bohemia and Hungary, though most of the latter was then in Turkish hands.

The next century was not such a successful one for the Habsburgs. The Turks had made one effort to take Vienna and failed. While the Counter-Reformation began to win the country back to the church it was followed by a revolt in Bohemia, opening the Thirty Years War, and Swedish troops had occupied part of Austria. Rome and the dynasty breathed freely again when the Turks were finally driven out and back from their second siege of the capital in 1683.

Once the dangers of protestantism and of Turkish aggression had at last disappeared a new epoch began, that of baroque, first appearing in architecture, but eventually stylised in furniture, in weapons, in music, even coffins. The final victory, both in a military and a religious sense, was the excuse, if ever the Austrians needed one, to blossom forth.

Of course it was not the end of the wars. The beginning of the eighteenth century saw the war of the Spanish Succession in which the Habsburgs lost that throne to the Bourbons (but gained part of the Netherlands and Italian territories in compensation), and not long afterwards was the war of the Austrian Succession, despite Charles vi's efforts to secure his daughter's throne by pragmatic sanction.

The golden rule of Maria-Theresia, who was safely enthroned throughout the empire after she was married to Franz Stefan of Lorraine, is always considered the best that the Habsburgs offered to the world. It was certainly a time of peace and of reform and progress. Come the nineteenth century the picture was very different. Napoleon twice occupied Vienna and under French pressure Franz ii in 1806 declared the Holy Roman Empire dissolved, having two years before assumed the title of Emperor of Austria (as opposed to his previous title of Archduke).

This emperor's lands included that part of Austria above and below the River Enns, the patrimonial dominions of Styria, Carinthia, Gorz, Krain, Tyrol, the possessions in south-western Germany (the remainder of which is now Vorarlberg) and the kingdoms of Hungary and Bohemia. Although Napoleon married Austria's Marie-Louise, one of Maria-Theresia's large brood of children, this did not help him in the final war of liberation when Austria joined Prussia, Russia, England and Sweden to defeat him.

The Congress of Vienna, in 1814, redrew the map of Europe after the fall of Napoleon, and the Italian provinces that Austria won back were combined into the kingdom of Lombardy and Venetia. Prince Metternich, who a few years earlier had been made foreign minister, became the power behind the throne. He was responsible for giving Austria, for the last time in its history, great status in the world. He was also responsible for introducing the most repressive police system it had ever known. Sadly, the revolutionaries of 1848 who tried to end this internal tyranny only succeeded in bringing more oppression to Vienna.

Ferdinand I abdicated and it was left to Franz Joseph to re-establish order and royal authority. He took over a vast empire, but when he died, having ruled for 68 years, it was on the point

2 Innsbruck: St Anna's Column in the Maria-Theresienstrasse

3 Innsbruck: the Helbling House

of collapse. Austria lost Lombardy, then Venetia. It left the German alliance, was neutral in the Franco-Prussian war, then, in the way of history, changed its mind in 1882 with the formation of the triple alliance of Germany, Austria and Italy. On a personal front Franz Joseph had seen the death of his son and heir, Rudolf; the assassination of his wife; the assassination of the next heir, Franz Ferdinand, and his wife in the streets of Sarajevo, capital of Bosnia, in June 1914.

Less than a month afterwards Austria declared war on Serbia, fighting alongside Germany, Bulgaria and Turkey. Two years later Franz Joseph died and his grand-nephew, Charles, took over for two more short years, presiding over the dissolution of the Austro-Hungarian empire. The Habsburg reign was over and its passing and final end was, like the end of the Babenbergs, a sad and humiliating affair. There was no final blaze of glory for Charles. He signed away the empire and renounced its powers, though not its crown, then with his wife fled from Schönbrunn to his private shooting lodge north-east of Vienna in November 1918.

Early in 1919 the newly formed republic, consisting of about one-eighth of the population and territory of the empire, held the first elections and the Social Democrats just scraped in, with Karl Renner, a former imperial civil servant, as the first federal chancellor. Shortly afterwards the government gave the emperor two alternatives: formal abdication or exile. In fact Renner had tried to force Charles' hand before this but had been foiled by a British officer who had been sent by George v to give 'moral support' to the emperor and empress.

In the spring of 1921 Charles made a bid to regain at least his Hungarian crown, and argued, unsuccessfully, in Budapest with the Regent who was his ex-aide-de-camp and admiral. Later that year he made a second and more dramatic attempt, flying in, then taking a railway journey which turned from triumph into an armistice into treachery into ruin. The emperor's final trip into exile was under the British flag, by ship down the Danube into the Black Sea and then via Gibraltar to Madeira.

Although it had been arranged that Poland, Czechoslovakia, Yugoslavia and Rumania should each make an annual contribution to Charles, they gave nothing. His empress Zita went to Switzerland in 1922, to collect their children and the personal jewellery supposed to be in safe-keeping. She found the family all right, but the bank vault empty and the keeper of the jewels fled. Charles could no longer afford the prices at Madeira's big hotel and moved, thankfully, to a small villa which was lent, rent free, high on the hill. But the climate cost him his life; in the damp and the rain and the mist Charles caught pneumonia. The last Habsburg emperor died, penniless, in exile, at the age of 35.

Meanwhile back in Vienna the new political party was in trouble with constant crises and disturbances, culminating in the assassination in 1934 of Engelbert Dollfuss who only a year earlier had become Christian Socialist federal chancellor. A few years later Hitler's ultimatum changed Austria's name, back to what it was when the Babenbergs first began to rule. It was to be known, henceforward, as Ostmark, part of the great German Reich. The annexation was forcible, with the help of the Gestapo and concentration camps.

Everything Austrian, as well as the name, was obliterated, and ever since Austrians have been trying to explain away Anschluss, why a plebiscite approved of it, why Hitler was given a triumphant reception in Vienna. Their country, they say, was in such desperate straits that professional people were working as labourers. Germany promised them a better standard of living —and prospects. By the end of the second world war both promises were in ruins and those who had earlier proclaimed Anschluss as the only salvation, kept silent.

In July 1945 the Allied zones of occupation were agreed. Russia was to have Lower Austria, excluding Vienna, all of Upper Austria north of the Danube, and Burgenland. The United States took over Land Salzburg and the remainder of Upper Austria. Great Britain had Carinthia, East Tyrol and Styria. France was given Tyrol and Vorarlberg. Each of the four powers had a quarter of Vienna and by September of that year they were installed in the capital.

In December Karl Renner was elected president of the Austrian republic and about a year later put into words the growing feeling about his country's prospects and its future role as a neutral mediator between east and west, when he wrote: 'Just as Switzerland is surrounded by the three great countries of western Europe, so Austria is surrounded by the five peoples of central Europe, whose lines of communication traverse her territory. It is in the common interest of all Austria's five neighbours that their communications should be free for all, and remain so; that no one country should monopolise them for itself against the others, let alone utilise them as a springboard for military operations. . . .'

Austria's full sovereignty was not restored until the State Treaty in 1955; even so, the proclamation of her permanent neutrality was postponed until the last of the occupation forces had withdrawn in October of that year. The republic needed to make it ultra-clear that her decision was a voluntary one. She faced two international problems. First, the question of how she was to integrate with Europe, given that almost 750 miles of frontier was shared with eastern countries under Communist control. Relations with Hungary certainly suffered after the 1956 uprising, when Austria had to cope with something like 170,000 refugees who fled across the border.

Secondly, she had to cope with the vexing question of South Tyrol. During the first world war a secret treaty had been signed in London by Great Britain, France and Russia, giving South Tyrol to Italy if she joined the war on the Allies' side. There were bitter protests at the handing over of the region, stretching south from the Brenner Pass to the Salurn Gorge, for in 1919 it contained only about 7,000 Italians in a total population of a quarter of a million.

In June 1939 the Hitler-Mussolini agreement offered the inhabitants the option of taking German nationality and moving to new homes in that country. In fact, this was a 'thank you' from Germany to Italy for her benevolent attitude at the time of the Nazi occupation of Austria a year previously. There was not much of an option about the offer, either. Any German-speaking people who elected to stay on in South Tyrol were threatened with dispossession and removal to southern Italy.

After the second world war Austria and Italy tried to get together on a formula for the region, now known as the Italian province of Bolzano, and talks have been going on intermittently ever since. Though great progress has been made, there are still occasional outbreaks of violence when each country accuses the other of inflaming the situation. But internal problems were even more pressing than external ones in 1945. The vast empire with more than 50 million inhabitants had been able to supply all its own raw materials and be virtually self-supporting. The new republic added up its daunting losses, then looked at what was left on which it could build anew.

There was still the Danube, of course, flowing for more than 200 miles from west to east of the country. But although there had been iron foundries, cotton, paper and woollen mills, and breweries, in the rare non-mountainous regions, these were more in the nature of large handicraft enterprises than efficient big companies. Timber there was in plenty (Austria is the third most heavily forested country in Europe) and this proved invaluable to both home and export markets.

By far the largest new industry was that of tourism, whose earliest beginnings go back to the second half of the nineteenth century. In 1884 there was a 'meeting of delegates for the promotion of tourist traffic in the Austrian Alpine regions' and 107 municipalities attended. By 1909 there were already 530 shelter huts in the mountains, but mass holidaymaking did not set in until after the first world war.

Geographically, the country could not be better suited, containing as it does all the ingredients (except the sea) to appeal to a wide variety of tastes and pockets. Most of Austria is taken up by the eastern end of the Alps falling away to the Danube in the north and the Hungarian plain in the east. Horizontally, it is scored with great river valleys—from the Drau and its attendants in Carinthia to the Mur and the Enns in Styria; from the Salzach in Land Salzburg to the mighty Danube which cuts through the middle of Upper and Lower Austria.

But the Alps have permitted only two all-weather road passes, the Brenner in the west and the Semmering in the east, and these have been supplemented by at least two tunnels cut painfully through the mountains, so that some of the provinces need not remain cut off from their neighbours during the winter months. A colourful booklet introduces the country to intending visitors with these words: 'It is easy to fall in love with Austria—with its landscape, people, atmosphere, music and art, its whole way of life. Anyone who comes for the first time senses this . . . the warm-hearted welcome, the joy of living created by an atmosphere in which you feel at ease from the very first moment.'

Atmosphere is a key word, for it is the one thing in which the Austrians excel, as an extra ingredient to whatever is your particular fancy. Some visitors have made up their minds in advance to seek out just a single facet that they know will make them 'fall in love'. Perhaps it is music, the spirit of Vienna with its waltz, the floating stage at Bregenz with its operetta festival, or Salzburg, city of Mozart. I remember arriving there for the first time one snowy Sunday afternoon, to find all the statues carefully barricaded with wood against the frost, and how coffee and cognac seemed at that moment more important than the hidden monuments.

The café was not one of those smart places for tourists, but dark brown and full of locals who had draped their green loden coats and feathered hats on to a Victorian stand. As I sat down the orchestra (a full symphony one by the sound of it) struck up from an interior room playing, naturally, Mozart overtures. But when the faded, tasselled green velvet curtains eventually parted they revealed only a handful of musicians, each with several instruments grouped around his feet. The concert was non-stop and fortissimo, in order to compete with the conversation around the café which was also non-stop and fortissimo. Hours later I wandered out at dusk, the blizzard still blowing, and warmed as much by the music and the atmosphere as by the refreshments.

Perhaps the magic key for other visitors is therapy of a different kind, at thermal spas and baths of which there are more than a hundred scattered through the lowlands, the highlands, the forests, the lakeland. You do not joke about 'taking the cure', for every Austrian seems to have seriously studied the subject and be an expert upon the value of brine, sulphur, mud or iodine. Even a quick tumbler of the magic water in the Kursaal of a morning is a solemn moment.

The technical data in the many brochures is absolutely terrifying and, I suspect, so is the reality if you are 'buried' deep in the healing galleries, once a mine, near Bad Gastein. But this famous spa is also very discreet about its water, by piping it straight from the springs into some hotel bathrooms. The local guidebook states authoritatively: 'The secret of a successful cure lies, of course, in the combined effect of the actual treatment with the experience of scenic beauty, a pleasant climate and the right amount of entertainment and sport.'

The scenery and climate alone would be enough to make most of us feel a little better. But for the active visitor Austria has as many lakes as she does health resorts, sandwiched between Lake Constance in the west which shares its circumference with Germany and Switzerland, and the Neusiedler-see in Burgenland whose southern tip belongs to Hungary. In between are dozens of smaller brothers to these and two large pockets of lakeland, down in the south in Carinthia, and, most famous of all, the Salzkammergut, largely Upper Austrian territory.

The mountains (and you are never far away from them anywhere) spell solitude for the climbers who tour with local guides staying overnight in a choice of several hundred huts. Many of us find just being in the Alps is sufficient, sitting in a sunny Alm with a picnic lunch, counting the varieties of flowers and watching the farmers—and all the family—haymaking. They are

4 Innsbruck: the Herzog-Friedrichstrasse
5 (overleaf) *Mayrhofen, seen from a cable car*

always working against the clock because winter transforms the landscape and there is little to be done except climb upon the roofs of their houses to shift the heavy white mass before it 'avalanches' off by itself.

For many visitors, the snow is the reason for their journey, particularly to Tyrol and Vorarlberg, to stay in old gasthofs with creaking boards or modern annexes or de-luxe castles now run as fancy hotels. Whatever the style and price of the accommodation, the building is sure to contain lots of wood, the rooms will be comfortable and always warm. My holiday home in Saalbach (one of Land Salzburg's more popular resorts) was once the wood carver's cottage because there was no room at any of the inns.

The room was tiny, the bed reminiscent of dormitory schooldays, but every day I got back from skiing to find that the wood carver had lit my fire, and a huge box of logs took up any spare space between stove and bed. If the weather was fine he would delay putting a match to the wood until late afternoon, but if there was a blizzard he seemed to know, instinctively, when I would return to hang up my wet clothes on the rickety line above the stove, and there was always a cheerful blaze. I did not pay for the logs, nor for the electric heater that warmed me in the mornings, and this cosy niche cost all of eleven shillings a night.

What Austria does splendidly are the smaller resorts, the intimate villages where the skiing is necessarily limited but where you will know everybody, holidaymakers and natives, and even if there is a comparatively long walk to the nearest chairlift how can you grumble when Franz in the ski-hire shop describes his village as the one 'where the sun dances round the whole of the mountain'.

The native zest for living seems more pronounced in the Alps, even if they may overestimate the skill and fitness of their visitors! I arrived too late for skiing at one tiny village, to be told that we would all go toboganning instead. I did not see, then, why one sport was impossible and the other not, but obediently got into a Land Rover, while protesting my total ignorance of the toboggans strapped to its roof, and was taken to a little hut at the top of the nearest mountain. Several schnapps later, and in Austria you have a choice of accepting a double or a triple of this lethal liquor, a torch was tied around my neck and I was pushed off, in the moonlight, down what appeared to be the local equivalent of the Cresta Run. Laughter and schnapps got me to the bottom in one bruised piece.

Skiing events arranged especially for holidaymakers can be just as much of an endurance test. Carnival time comes to the mountains in the form of fancy-dress ski races, with much muttering and making of curious costumes the night before, and a draw, for the gentlemen only, before the start, in which their lady partners for the festivities are selected for them. Then the pairs sort themselves out: one of the 'Beatles' with a crinolined lady; the Laughing Cavalier and a scarecrow; a night-shirted sleepyhead complete with lighted candle and a sleek black pussy cat with long tail. As the only entry rule is that you should have had a few days' skiing, the couples are invariably a wild contrast in skills, and lucky the first-year skier who draws an instructor for a partner.

The start of the race is a brisk, official affair, each pair disappearing through the slalom gates to the speediest of their ability. The end is a shambles! For in between, the competitors have made a compulsory stop at a schnapps halt and for every glass each consumes so many seconds are knocked off their total race time. The really speedy skier with an iron stomach and strong legs can arrive at the bottom with a minus time—to be faced by the obstacle course, over the barrel, through the tunnel and what-have-you to the finishing line. The winners receive a magnum of champagne to be drunk on the spot, the last pair home (who usually took a wrong turning somewhere after the schnapps halt) get a bottle of schnapps, also to be finished there and then.

It is a dishevelled and wavering bunch of people who finally return to the village, to be indulged and cosseted by the hoteliers. Mountain inns, particularly, are family businesses, and you should expect to be introduced to 'my brother who runs the keller bar, my sister who handles the accounts, my mother who keeps the chef in order'. The cooking is simple, with the exception of the pastries, which are on a par with the waltz as Austria's contribution to civilisation, the helpings invariably gargantuan.

Woe betide the traveller with a poor appetite for it is something the easy-going natives find hard to tolerate. I have helped myself from the cold buffet, filled my platter to a reasonable height and had it removed, in horror, by one of the family, who has then begun all over again to make her choice, at least double the quantity, of what I should eat. Plead illness or a weak stomach and you are liable to be put to bed as a fragile invalid!

For those visitors in search of more spiritual aspects of Austria, its heritage encourages specialisation to a fine degree, with the temptation to lose oneself in a certain period of history and to follow its course, as far as is possible, within the confines of the present map. The treasures left behind from romanesque and gothic times are considerable. The Cistercians built several abbeys, the most notable being Heiligenkreuz near Vienna. The capital's cathedral, scarred and wounded though it has been, is restored to glorious gothic. Down in Carinthia, the crypt of Gurk Abbey remains for me, though I cannot explain why, the most exquisite example I have ever seen.

After this period there was a lull, architecturally speaking, until the Turkish foes were forever banished, and then began baroque, firstly by Italians, then by native artists, overlaid on to gothic, and later standing on its own. Finally, there is the nineteenth century, cosy and comfortable under the influence of Biedermeier, plus a rash of 'neo-cisms', reaffirming the Austrian passion to imitate, though it seems to me that their personal taste and their own architectural geniuses are quite capable of presenting models for others to ape.

On this sort of journey into history, it is even more tempting to align oneself not with inanimate buildings but on the side of a particular Habsburg and see the country through his or her eyes. The 'stars' of the dynasty, for deeds or personalities or both, include Maximilian I, Maria-Theresia, her son Joseph II and Franz Joseph. Emperor Maximilian, so dashing and brilliant, used the arts and sciences to ensure that he would be remembered by his people. Last year the four hundred and fiftieth anniversary of his death was celebrated by special events and exhibitions in Innsbruck, where he is remembered as the royal who was boldest in battle, in hunting and in politics.

Maria-Theresia's personal taste and influence lies delicately on a large number of Austrian buildings, and her brood of children become almost close friends of your own family as you follow their lives through their innumerable portraits. Her femininity and love of pretty things come over strongly, as do her benefactory ways. The sharpest contrast between this empress and her son is in their tombs in the imperial vaults. Hers is exotic and complex, his, starkly simple and austere.

Joseph II's advisers and the aristocracy were appalled when this reforming monarch opened the imperial game park in the Prater to the public, but he said tartly to his critics worried about the dangers of him coming into contact with the common people: 'To be as exclusive as you wish, I should be obliged to retire to the Habsburg vault of the Capuchins and never leave it.'

To follow Franz Joseph's long rule you need to immerse yourself in the thermal spas, to visit his hunting lodge at Bad Ischl, to realise that though he now seems buried deep in history, a similar iron bedstead to that on which he always slept can still be bought in Viennese shops. It is not so long ago after all, just that events afterwards moved so fast. My own preference is not to cultivate, exclusively, either the past or a favourite emperor, but to take Austria, capriciously, as she presents herself, in a sort of all-round education, dipping a little into this era, a little into that; dabbling in one period, then another; and above all, finding out that the Austrian, patriotic as he is, does not in fact exist!

When it comes down to it he is a Styrian or a Carinthian or a Tyrolean or a Viennese, particularly a Viennese who is different from all the others as a result of his city's history as a frontier fortress between east and west. Federal is the key word that has helped to retain the variety between the nine Länder. Vienna is, of course, not only a province in its own right but the capital of the country and the city from which Lower Austria is administered. It is no accident that the ministry of education foots the bill for every Austrian child to spend at least one week here. If nothing else, the experience must prove quite an antidote to their regional upbringings.

The Viennese seem to remain astonishingly unaware of the eastern frontier which is so close, but it is much more obtrusive in Burgenland, south of the capital, a province occupied only to its capacity at weekends when the population has returned from its working stint in Vienna. It is the newest addition to Austria and a look at the empire map explains its poverty and the fact that only one castle has remained intact. For it was constantly in the firing line over the centuries and is struggling to catch up economically. Tourism is an intriguing thought rather than a fact. The local authorities are well aware of its value but cannot as yet invest in large numbers of places where the visitor might stay.

Its mysterious lake, the Neusiedler-see, is visited largely by the Viennese and ornithologists. The splendid lidos in the south of the province have been built for the Burgenlanders rather than for prospective long-distance travellers. Yet its charm is considerable because its past is so haunting. Pockets of Serbo-Croats live here, the Slavonic face appears instead of the Germanic one and there's an untamed feeling in the air despite the monotonous Hungarian plain and the watch towers marching down its eastern flank.

Lower Austria, which surrounds Vienna as well as stretching in all directions from there, is the largest province, cradle and burial places of the Babenbergs. Woods and wine are the two words which sum up its contribution, scenically and commercially. The Wienerwald, so near to Vienna, is immortalised in music by Beethoven and Strauss; the wine, thousands of gallons of it, comes from south of the city and from the banks of the Danube.

The new wine is drunk in places called the Heurigen (literally, of today). If the rendezvous of the intellectuals and the businessmen is the coffee house, then the Heurigen are second home to the sentimentalists. They come in their hundreds, looking for the pine branch hanging on a long pole outside as a sign that wine is available within, and bring with them cold sausages and picnic fare. The rollicking songs and fun are a light-hearted contrast to Lower Austria's quartet of beautiful monasteries, two in the countryside and two near the Danube, all worthy of at least a day of your time.

Upper Austria, which shares the Danube with its twin neighbour, is responsible for promoting the largest proportion of the Salzkammergut, but to get anywhere near the salt after which the region is named, you need to travel deep inside the mountains. Otherwise the 'white gold' is invisible and the visitors' view one of gentle lakes and hills and in summer hordes of people clamouring to hire boats or deckchairs or a place at one of the lidos. It would be easy from the map to assume that one lake is much like another, and it would be quite wrong, for all are individuals, with a speciality and a flavour all their own. The Danube in this province plays second fiddle, except in Linz, whose commerce has depended for centuries on the waterway and whose industrial smoke tends to obscure its contribution to the heritage.

The twin provinces south of the previous pair are Styria and Carinthia, both sharing part of their borders with Yugoslavia. Styria's name comes from the twelfth-century count who was put in charge here by the emperor of that era. Like its neighbour, it is something of a bridgehead, geographically, and it is almost impossible not to get off the beaten track. The province's contours discourage a logical straight journey from A to B, and would much rather have you curl and twist, like the rivers do. The capital, Graz, is sited in a commercially important place, but talk to the people who live in mountainous Upper Styria and they may never have made the journey to this pleasant city.

Carinthia, as befits the most southern province, is the least Germanic of all of them and the Austrians flock here in search of warmth and sunshine. The climate is certainly more reliable than either Tyrol or the Salzkammergut, yet it has both the mountains and the lakes that these other regions possess. The highest peak in Austria is open in summer to motorists who drive up to nearly 8,000 feet before walking upon the creaking glacier with the Grossglockner summit above. The lakeland district is benign and welcoming and able to accommodate thousands of visitors in its lively resorts.

In this province, baroque has not overwhelmed the architecture and the eye tunes in, restfully, to romanesque and gothic. What completes one's conversion to Carinthia is that all its delights are within easy reach of one another. You can stay on the Wörthersee, for example, and see the whole of the province from here, the only point of no-return being the high alpine route into Land Salzburg.

For many people this province is the city of Salzburg and nothing more. They crowd in to worship at Mozart's shrine, disregarding the high prices for the privilege of being here when the music festival is on. They are right to believe there is nowhere like it anywhere in Austria, for the city is an Italian one, never under the wing of the Habsburgs but always ruled by the archbishops, largely ambitious wealthy men who donned priest's robes and then proceeded to live as they had always done.

The citizens were angry enough about Archbishop Dietrich who built a palace and named it after his mistress, but his nephew Marcus Sitticus went one better. His summer mansion, a little out of the city centre, included all sorts of eccentricities and, the Salzburgers, suspected, more than one lady. 'Wolf Dietrich, who had one mistress, we drove away,' they muttered, 'but his successor has doubled the establishment.' Nevertheless, despite their worldly ways, or maybe because of them, the religious rulers evolved a style and a civilisation in Salzburg which is unique. Should you have time to dally elsewhere in the province, then the choice must be at Bad Gastein, a spa as famous for its incredible situation as for its waters, and as popular in winter with skiers as in summer with cure-takers.

Tyrol is the province that has made its name among the British as a winter-sports paradise and it is only when you arrive in Innsbruck on a February weekend morning that you realise the natives are after the same goal as yourself. Trying to make your way through the crowds at the railway station, every one of whom is carrying a pair of skis, is a boisterous start to any visit. Even during weekdays you get the impression that the inhabitants of this Alpine town are on the point of setting off for the mountains.

Most of them are clad, as a matter of course, in ski-wear. If the skis are in the rack outside their shop or office, you can be sure that the lunch-time rush hour to the nearest lift and the snow will be on. This province is certainly the most long-winded to investigate, for the river Inn is its main artery and to this river you must constantly return after each detour into the many secret valleys that lead off it.

Its baby brother, East Tyrol, could until a few years ago be reached only by driving over the Brenner pass into Italy first. Now a tunnel links this remote region to Land Salzburg, with a short drive from there into Tyrol. The most westerly province of all is Vorarlberg, and we will begin our journey here, for no other reason than that it makes a cameo curtain-raiser to what comes after.

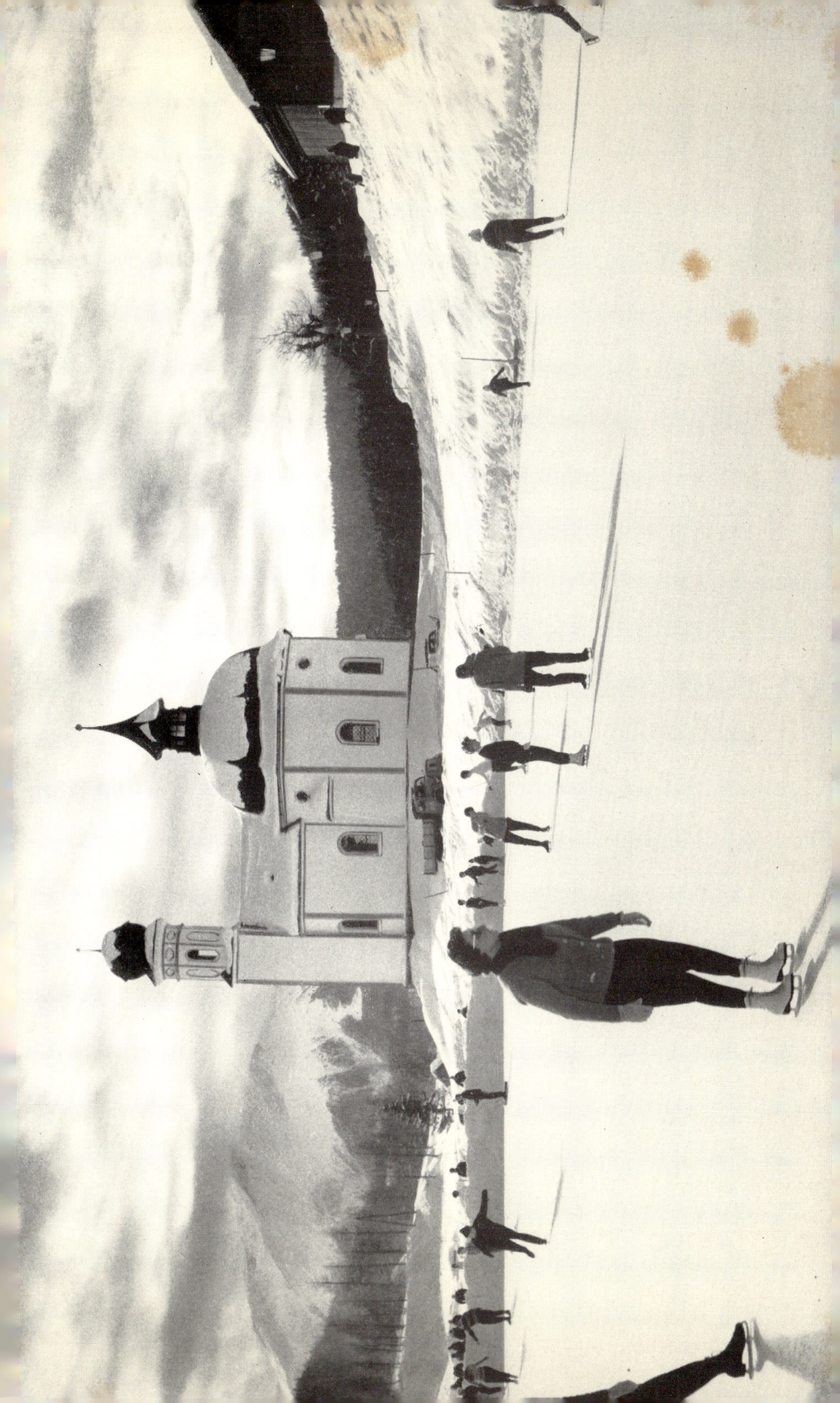

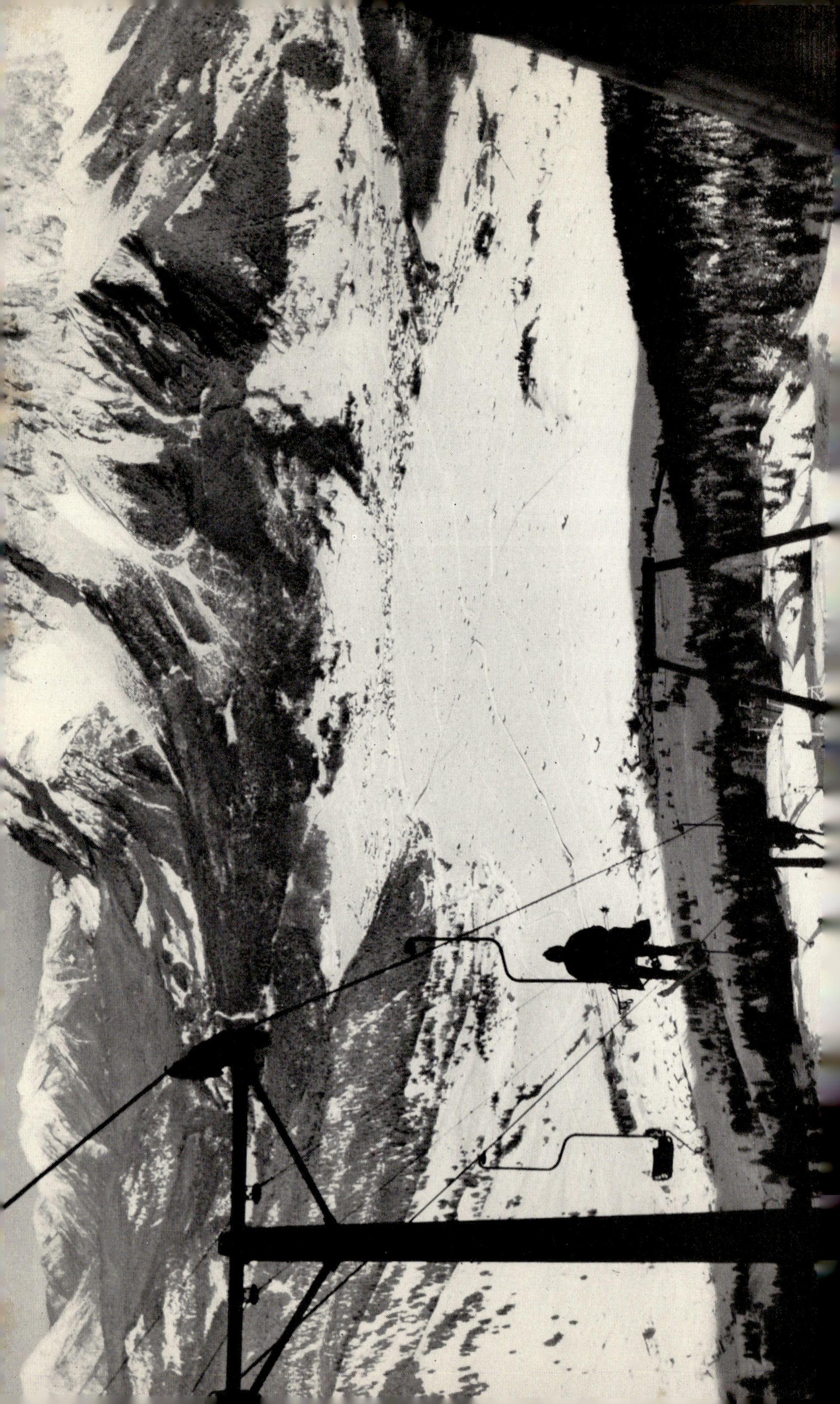

2 Vorarlberg

From Bregenz, the capital of Austria's smallest province, it is all of three miles to Germany, nine to Switzerland and 22 to Liechtenstein. But despite Vorarlberg's obvious ties and proximity to its western neighbours (or maybe because of them), the fact that numbers of its population originally came from over those borders and its difficulty in communicating with the rest of Austria (only one road east to Tyrol is open throughout the year), it retains a flavour which is entirely its own.

Because of the geography and the native pride, it is a region where change comes slowly. Whatever has happened and whoever has taken over in its history has tended to stay. Even now much of its outlying districts seem distinctly old-fashioned in dress and customs and way of life; the twentieth century simply has not percolated or penetrated that deeply.

The Celts were the first known inhabitants around 100 B.C. on the Lake of Constance, which was then much marshier and much larger than its present considerable expanse of 40 miles long and nine miles at its widest. The Romans followed on until A.D. 400 and renamed the territory Räthla and its capital, Brigantium. But after that, with the exception of two Swiss monks, Columbine and Gallus, who brought Christianity a couple of hundred years later, Vorarlberg was left to its own devices for centuries. And even when the Counts of Bregenz and Montfort embarked on feudalism it was a benevolent dictatorship and much of the population was in effect self-ruling.

This freedom was one of the attractions for Swiss emigrants and to a certain extent Germans, too. There had been persecution of the Swiss catholics by the protestants in the thirteenth

7 *Ascending the chair lift above Lermoos*

century, and the persecuted fled into Vorarlberg to set up communities in the Montafon and elsewhere, where to this day they continue to speak a dialect that their Swiss neighbours understand. The German influx settled in the Bregenzerwald and are a simpler, more austere people than the others.

The province became part of Austria when Count Montfort sold it to the Habsburgs. Its capital sits on the lakeside nudging Germany, and with 25,000 inhabitants it is not even the largest town; that honour goes to Dornbirn, the centre of the important textile industry which supplies nearly half of the entire country's production. But Bregenz has the historical feeling and background to befit a provincial capital, and part of the old Roman walls in its upper town remain.

In the new town, at lake level, is the See Kapelle, now centrally situated, but marking the spot where the lake originally came to before the natives began reclamation in the thirteenth to fifteenth centuries. The town suffered badly during the Thirty Years War with Sweden, most of it being destroyed in 1647 with the exception of its precious landmark, Martinsturm (St Martin's Tower), built by the Montforts as a vegetable warehouse, among other things, to which a chapel was later added containing frescoes. Today the tower is a museum, reached by a covered outdoor wooden stairway and containing a miscellaneous selection of relics.

Now that the lake has been reclaimed there is little room to expand the capital, for behind it is the Pfaender mountain, whose 3,500-foot summit is reached by a cablecar in seven minutes, and the Gebhardsberg, also nudging the back of the town, with, as you would expect, the castle Hohenbregenz, or what remains of it, sitting on the top. Although it, too, was destroyed by the Swedes, some of the old walls are still there and once a year, on 27 August, there is an open-air mass in the courtyard near the church celebrating the baptism of St Gebhard. On weekdays the restaurant is a rendezvous for businessmen and tourists to look down over the town while having lunch.

To reach the lakeside itself, you need to cross the railway line, built behind the promenade, and apart from an occasional café and gardens there is no development on the actual waterfront. Bregenz has a few modern innovations, including a couple of fine churches to add to its parish church, St Gallus, which is baroque and renaissance, lacking great height but with ornate ceilings and walls and inlaid wooden choir stalls. The Kolumbankirche was built only a few years ago in a semicircular amphitheatre shape with two panels of modern stained-glass windows stretching from floor to ceiling.

Just outside the town, the seventeenth-century Cistercian monastery of Mehrerau rebuilt its church some 20-odd years ago, and it is surprisingly harmonious externally with the monastery and school buildings. Inside it is stark, perhaps too stark, with the vaulted wood ceiling from the old church, white knobbly stone walls, dark-wood plain pews and a black altar with a small golden cross. The old crypt remains beneath.

Apart, then, from its modern architecture, its lake and one or two historical buildings, Bregenz has little else to offer except for four weeks of the year in July-August when it proudly presents its operetta festival on a floating stage on the lake. When in 1946 the manager of the local theatre first had the idea of a summer festival on Lake Constance, the opening production took place on what was little more than a glorified raft.

A year later a larger stage was built and a year after that came the first of the lavish productions that attract up to 80,000 people. The audience remains on dry land, and the stage and its machinery sit on pylons off-shore. The only worrying problem, apart from teeming rain, is high wind, when up to 36 microphones come into use to bring the sound of Viennese operetta to those seated in the bankside amphitheatre.

Vorarlberg has only three main valleys, their rivers producing the second major industry, electrical power. The Rhine marks the border with Switzerland, and provides the concentrated industrial zone; the Ill leads eventually to the Silvretta region with its high alpine road; the third valley, in the north, has the Bregenzernach. This last area is probably the least visited part of the province because its communication artery, the Hochtannberg alpine road, was opened less than 20 years ago and the natives are modest enough not to shout loudly about their splendours.

The Hochtannberg runs west from the Tyrol border at Warth and it is strangely bare, for which there is a very good reason. Early natives so deforested the land that avalanches successfully removed the remaining trees. What is left is rounded green hills and nothing much in the way of townships until Bezau, an Alemmanic settlement which ruled its own affairs in a very democratic way, although the area belonged to Count Montfort.

The freely elected aldermen of the Bregenzerwald laid down their laws in a wooden town hall built on stilts outside Bezau on a hill called Bezegg. They had one rigid regulation: every decision had to be unanimous, so a leather door to the building was kept firmly shut until the aldermen managed to agree, and this form of local government lasted from the thirteenth until the nineteenth century.

Not far away is the little village of Reuthe with a very old church, but so restored that you would never realise it until you reach the chancel and see the fourteenth-century frescoes discovered beneath the whitewash during the renovation a few years ago. The people in this district were once famous bricklayers and carpenters, called upon to help build the baroque churches around Lake Constance. Their timber industry is, along with fruit and cattle, the major occupation, apart from making schnapps.

They use their wood to insulate their homes with a scaly outside layer; they use it to make huge water troughs; they use it to carve a tree trunk, polish it and lay it horizontally outside their houses as a pleasing decoration. The farmers close down their village estates for the summer and with their cattle go up into the hills to their charmingly titled Maisäss (May seats). Everyone comes back down the mountain on 25 September.

Although they grew no crops, there were, luckily, scythes in every farmyard which the young girls of the Bregenzerwald borrowed one terrible night. They pretended to be ghosts, in their nightcaps and white gowns, with the aim of repelling the invading Swedes. Incredibly the ruse worked and today the young women on Sundays put on their Schwedentracht (Swedish costume) in remembrance. National costume is worn almost as a matter of course by the older folk. It is not so rich or expensive as the golden glittering costume of Bregenz itself, but has blue sleeves, a plain black bodice and voluminous skirt. If the old ladies are not wearing this, they are in everyday gear of plain black, the skirts modestly down to their ankles.

A few miles back from Bezau is a winding fearsome road to a hamlet called Damüls, founded by five Swiss families who fled over the mountains into free Austria. These people speak a dialect which the Swiss can understand—but not their Austrian neighbours!—and greet foreigners who have made the remote journey to visit them with a warm-heartedness and an eagerness personally to show them the only sight (apart from the view). It is indeed worth the drive to visit the lovely chapel, with a gothic chancel, a flat wooden ceiling and one section covered in sixteenth-century frescoes which, if you have visited Switzerland, will seem reminiscent of those in the Valais region.

The second of Vorarlberg's valleys, the Rhine, is not as wide as its concentration of people and industry suggests, but it lacks the high mountain backcloth of the other two, so seems larger because of its open scenery. On a trip along it south from Bregenz, the first halt must be at Dornbirn, for the famous seventeenth-century house in the main square, once the mayor's residence, and on Sunday morning the meeting place for the male population who stand chatting outside it.

It is called the Red House because it is supposed to be repainted with oxen blood every few years, though sceptics claim that common old paint is used nowadays. The present owner is a textile merchant who has used his imagination to keep the olde worlde interior complete with sleigh, cowbells, spinning wheel, carved-wood chairs and oxen yokes as lamp standards in a charming restaurant.

The road south from Dornbirn is not particularly interesting until just before Feldkirch (do not drive too fast otherwise you will find yourself in Liechtenstein!), when a side turning leads to Rankweil and a fortress-turned-church sitting on a rock. There is a circular stone gallery, reached by steep steps, around what seems to be the tower, but in fact the entrance to Liebfraven church is at this high level.

Feldkirch itself, if you have only ever seen the railway station as a customs halt, is quite a surprise, for sections of it have the charm of Innsbruck with galleried old streets. The town hall is not officially open to the public, but ask the policeman inside nicely and he will unlock the council chamber to reveal its wooden carved ceiling, of the mid-fifteenth century, portraits of worthies looking down from the walls and in one corner a harmonious ceramic stove in dark brown, matching the rest of the room.

The fifteenth-century parish church, St Nicholas, produces surprises, too: it has a winged altar by Wolf Huber, dating from 1520, the four panels so delicate they really do not fit the gothic style of the church or the modern stained-glass window behind the altar. Although the town was plundered and burnt by the Swedes and went through several sieges before this, at least one of the old round towers is still there, the Katzenturm, with, lying wisely on the floor and not suspended, Austria's largest bell, weighing nearly eight tons and cast in 1665.

Naturally Feldkirch has a castle, Schattenburg, the oldest sections dating from the thirteenth century, with a fine courtyard surrounded by wooden balconies, a fountain and pretty plants, which is the setting for chamber-music evenings in the summer. The remainder of the castle has a series of restaurants and, (horrors) mini-golf outside the walls, but the building has a good deal of charm because it is authentic; the rather dilapidated exterior is real, not rebuilt.

Bludenz, another well-known train halt, sits at the cross-roads between five valleys, so it is clearly a parting of the ways for the motorist, who has to choose from several alternatives, the two most dramatic routes being either to Stuben and the Flexenstrasse, up to Lech, or the Silvretta high alpine route. Both lead into Tyrol. The five valleys—Walgau, Grosswalsertal, Brandnertal, Klostertal, Montafon—and the setting they give to Bludenz are rather more important than the town itself.

It is a cosy little place with arcades as in Feldkirch and a sturdy stone gateway, Friedrich Tor, named after the prince of that name who took refuge here after he had lost a battle with another prince in the fifteenth century. The two royals, Johann and Friedrich von Tyrol of the Empty Purse (because he never had any money), met near Lake Constance with their followers. Johann was the victor, poor Friedrich ran away and found Bludenz the first friendly town to open its doors to him.

To reach this far you have travelled the first of the valleys, the Walgau; to the right of Bludenz is the Brandnertal with a glacier at the end, to the left is Grosswalsertal through Ludesch to Raggal and branching straight ahead are the two most famed—Klostertal and Montafon. The Klostertal will deliver you at Stuben, with the choice of changing provinces or staying in Vorarlberg to drive the galleried, awe-inspiring Flexenstrasse into one of the world's most famous skiing regions, the White Ring Circuit, a linked system of lift installations that joins up four resorts, St Anton, St Christoph, Zurs and Lech, these last two being in Vorarlberg.

None of the quartet can be described as cheap, unassuming villages. The expert skiing fraternity drop in at Lech to have their boots handmade, and the chances are that the bootmaker already possesses their personal foot-last because they will have worshipped at this skiing shrine before. Both Lech and Zurs are about as well equipped for winter sports as is imaginable, both get very crowded and there is a certain cachet about being at either at the right time—but only if you are a skier.

Unlike some sophisticated resorts this pair are for expert participants, not spectators, and the evening post-mortems on the day's runs are likely to prove rather boring for someone who has not even tried the 'bunny' slopes. The Flexenstrasse is nearly always kept open, though in an occasional bad year avalanches may temporarily close it. The train through from Stuben to St Christoph into the Arlberg is sometimes Vorarlberg's only winter link with Tyrol.

The other valley from Bludenz, the Montafon, provides good skiing from less crowded resorts like Schruns, Gargellen and Partenen, but is better known for its summer motoring route, the Silvretta high alpine road leading up to the Vermunt and Silvretta reservoirs and the Bieler Höhe. The cold glacial scenery is highlighted by the 10,943-foot Piz Buin, on whose glacier is a summer skiing school.

Piz Buin, by the way, is only 50 miles as the crow flies from Lake Constance, another indication of the compactness of the province. The Silvretta road is nothing like so dramatic for motorists as the Grossglockner, but its terrain has some beautiful walks up to the snow level and beyond, with mountain huts in which to stay overnight. The other side of the pass, down into the Paznaun valley in Tyrol, is comparatively gentle.

3 Tyrol

Maximilian I could not have foreseen that more than 400 years after his fifteenth-century reign, the Landlibell army he formed in Tyrol would still be in existence. For almost everything else in this province changed, or was changed by, events and history. Innsbruck, for instance, the capital city, lost its power and importance in the seventeenth century, and large areas of land were taken over and administered by 'foreigners'. Yet the home guard survived not only centralisation away from regional government, but every other stage of history—and there were some turbulent times—until the outbreak of the first world war.

The potential of Innsbruck in the middle ages was enormous. It was served by gold, copper and silver mines, and the old trading route ran through it from Nuremberg to Venice. Maximilian realised, and rightly, that this western centre of the empire was a much safer base than Vienna, so exposed to attack from the east. The obvious theme of its commerce should be making weapons and its defence was to be left to the Landlibell. The town was not in fact the original settlement on the River Inn when the Germanic countries began trading with Italy over the Brenner Pass.

The Romans founded Vieldidena (today the Wilten quarter of Innsbruck), fortified it against teutonic invasion and it survived remarkably well below the Bergisel hill in the shadow of its ancient monastery. But it was not a satisfactory home for the early Bavarian counts of Andech, one of whom chose the south bank of the river, built a bridge across in 1187 or thereabouts and called the place Innsbruck.

Because of the bridge the new settlement soon overtook Wilten in importance and in 1239 was given the status of a town; less than 200 years later it was the capital of Tyrol, then a much larger province than it is today, and having been bequeathed at Meran to Rudolf IV by the famous Tyrolean Countess Maultasch (a free translation of which might be 'big mouth'). She was said to be a very ugly lady, but she cared deeply about Tyrol and devoted her life to ensuring that it fell into Austrian hands.

Countess Margaretha was originally married to a Bohemian prince from Luxembourg when she was 13 and he was eight. Such a small boy could not have been hated for himself, but he was loathed by the Tyrolese because he was from Luxembourg, and with the emperor's help they managed to have him expelled in 1341. Margaretha wasted no time on her exiled bridegroom but was remarried to Ludwig of Brandenburg the following year.

Though she conveniently 'forgot' that her first husband was still alive others, particularly the church, did not, and it was only when Rudolf IV intervened that the excommunication ended and the countess's second marriage became legalised. In gratitude, and for safety's sake because the plotters were still trying to take over Tyrol, she bequeathed the province to Rudolf and handed it over to him in September 1363.

The capital was then Meran and remained so for 100 or more years until in 1490 Archduke Sigismund abdicated in favour of his cousin Maximilian I, and Innsbruck's position as imperial and cultural metropolis for the Habsburgs and their western possessions was established. It was even more assured by the creation of the Landlibell in 1511, decreeing that every adult was entitled to carry arms. The corps was based on the principle of self-defence and exempted the Tyrolese from any obligation to take part in a war beyond the borders of their own province. In return for their pledge Maximilian agreed to consult them about any possible frontier disputes and not to use the levy they paid him for warfare outside Tyrol. They repaid him handsomely with their support, and continued to do so, to the region's benefit, for four centuries!

As the first major reigning prince in Tyrol, it fell to Maximilian to set the style of luxury and pomp, of expansion and court festivities, and like other royalty he was helped by master builders, artists, craftsmen and musicians from various countries whose imprint can still be seen today. One of his most curious and frankly rather pointless extravaganzas was to order his tomb and a glittering collection of statues to stand about it.

He never got round to building the church in which to put them, numbers of the statues were never completed and the emperor himself is actually buried in Wiener-Neustadt—not in the Hofkirche obligingly built by his successor to take what was finished of the statuary and the tomb. Maximilian envisaged his final resting place amidst rows of enormous bronze statues, 40 of them, including not just relatives but historical characters like King Arthur. On the face of it Innsbruck, as a sixteenth-century weapon-manufacturing centre, was just the place to handle the job, but unfortunately the craftsmen who made cannons had no experience of figure design.

Master Gilg Sesselscreiber was called from Munich to start the collection and the first statue was cast by Peter Loeffler in 1509. There were endless production problems because the casting took so long, and endless financial ones, too, because copper and tin were expensive. Sesselscreiber constantly asked for more money (as it turned out, not for the work but to pay his debts) and was eventually imprisoned. In all 28 statues were produced (more were finished but never cast), most from Innsbruck but two from Nuremberg, the final one not being completed until 1550, 30 years or so after Maximilian's death.

As well as these giant statues the emperor also planned 100 saints, small ones, and a series of bronze busts of Holy Roman Emperors. Stephan Godl from Nuremberg was given the order for these, but following Sesselscreiber's collapse gatecrashed his way into producing the giants, too. After Maximilian's death this expert founder was sponsored by the new governor of Tyrol, and in the 25 years until his death in 1534 Godl finished 23 small and 17 large statues.

If you look closely at them you can see how many designers

had a hand and how crude was the work of some of them. The miniature saints are ranged along the gallery of the church, the giant statues in two rows either side of Maximilian's empty tomb, with marble reliefs showing, naturally, the life and times of the emperor. Here the designer is not Germanic, but Flemish.

This emperor left behind another gem which has become the landmark of Innsbruck, and that is the golden roof (goldenes Dachl), though one legend attributes its expensive veneer to Friedrich of the Empty Purse demonstrating how he eventually made his fortune! In fact it was probably Maximilian who added the copper gilded roof to the royal theatre box from which they watched open-air performances in the courtyard below. Certainly the gilding was to commemorate his second marriage to Maria Bianca Sforza of Milan, and though there is no theatre now, the building still has a romantic flavour, for it has become the registry office and young couples can study the outside frieze showing Tyrolean coats of arms before or after the ceremony.

Ferdinand I succeeded Maximilian and built the Hofkirche to house tomb and statues, but it was Ferdinand of Tyrol who followed who really carried on the promotion of Innsbruck. Before making it his headquarters this lively fellow sent a message from Prague where he was then living, that he needed a country house—quite a reasonable order in those days, except that Ferdinand forebore to mention that it was to be a belated wedding present for his wife. No one, not even his father, knew of the secret marriage, nor that the young bride was a commoner, a merchant's daughter from Augsburg. Eventually Philippine Welser, the bride, was acknowledged, but her two sons had to be reared as though they were foundlings.

The home Ferdinand chose for Philippine was Schloss Ambras, only a few miles from Innsbruck, which had been the fortified residence of the Counts of Andech until it went up in flames in 1133. In 1564, after he was appointed governor of Tyrol and the Vorlande (Vorarlberg and the Swabian possessions of the Habsburgs), Ferdinand began the modernisation and extension of the house. But its new and interesting career did not last long. Philippine died in 1580 and two years later Ferdinand remarried to gain a lawful heir.

By this time the bridegroom was 53, the bride, the 16-year-old Duchess of Mantua. It was not a happy liaison and, although they had three children, all of them were girls. Soon the young duchess confined herself to an Italian-style life with her courtiers, and her husband became more and more absorbed in his curious collection, the remnants of which are still housed at Ambras. Ferdinand had begun the collection in Bohemia and brought it with him to Innsbruck. The original emphasis was the armoury, a picture of the former owner accompanying each piece.

Today's display, while depleted, shows the governor's passion for the odd and fanciful, like the miniature armour for his children and court dwarf, and the giant outfit for his court giant. There is a stag with 24 antlers grown into a tree trunk which was mentioned in an inventory as early as 1596; books in which members of the Bacchus Cult wrote their comments; mechanical clockwork toys; beautiful miniature ivory-handled tools for his children; ivory and mother-of-pearl items; a Chinese golden singing bell; hideous portraits of human deformities; in fact an extraordinary mixture of the ghastly, the farcical and the beautiful.

The Bacchus memories date from when there was a lake and cave in the grounds of Schloss Ambras to which the novice was brought for his initiation, being given spicy dishes to start with, then being asked to empty a tankard containing five pints in one gulp. If he failed he was forced to begin, more drunkenly, all over again, and there is a unique chair with a capturing mechanism which must have played a part in this merry-making.

Although Ferdinand's will firmly stated that 'everything and all should remain in this castle of Ambras' his 'foundling' son, Charles of Burgau, sold the collection to Emperor Rudolf II in 1606, when the curiosity cabinet alone fetched 100,000 florins. In fact nothing was moved until 1665 when Leopold I 'borrowed' 500 books and manuscripts to take to Vienna. When Tyrol became part of

Bavaria in 1805 what remained was sent for safe-keeping to Lower Belvedere in Vienna.

Schloss Ambras never had another master like Ferdinand of Tyrol. After his death the castle became more of a burden than an asset and in the nineteenth century the dangerously decayed sections, like the building for ball games, the fourth armoury and the banqueting hall, were demolished. Charles Louis, brother of Franz Joseph I, made an abortive attempt to rebuild in the nineteenth century, but only succeeded in making matters worse. Today it is a shabby and silent house, with only a hint of those early days of feasting and luxury, like a splendid bathroom for Philippine, who would be seated on a stool wearing her bathing cap in the middle of a vast tub, while the servants stood around and threw water over her.

In the city of Innsbruck Ferdinand added his own delicate memorial to his wife, alongside Maximilian's statue collection in the Hofkirche; it is the silver chapel in which he and Philippine are buried, called silver because that is the material of which the sixteenth-century altar is made. It also contains a seventeenth-century Italian organ with cedar wood pipes to soften the sound, which is still played today, but only for music of that period.

After 1665 Tyrol no longer had a reigning prince living in Innsbruck, but the city was destined for one final blaze of royal glory when Empress Maria-Theresia chose it as the place where her son Leopold II should marry in 1765. Considering she was only here for about three weeks, and that short period marred by tragedy, she had an astonishing influence on the buildings and flavour of the city.

The main shopping street looking out towards the Karwendel range of mountains is named after her, and at one end is the famous archway half-built as a triumphant commemoration of the wedding when the bridegroom's father had a stroke after a theatre visit. They left one side of it joyful, with the bridal pair—Leopold and Maria Luisa of Spain—and their families, and redesigned the other as a mourning plaque for Franz Stefan of Lorraine, Maria-Theresia's husband to whom she was devoted (it is said she took the daring step of having her hair cut off as a mark of bereavement).

The empress's major alteration was to the gothic Imperial Palace, whose façade was changed and whose interior was so gutted that even the number of storeys was altered, resulting in the top of a gothic archway appearing at floor level in at least one of the corridors. The Riesensaal (Giant's Hall) has kept both its name and dimensions from Ferdinand's time, with the children of Maria-Theresia set in wall panels with smaller portraits of their husbands/wives above them. A ceiling painting here displays one of the first allegorical themes, the triumph of the rulers with the virtues represented by figures and horses. Maria-Theresia never saw the room like this; she merely ordered the changes, then left.

She also ordered the room in which her husband died to be turned into a memorial chapel, in delicate rococo white and gold with an Italian marble altar, which was restored a few years ago and nearly broke itself and the chapel in the restoration! When they tried to move the altar from its wooden base it nearly went through the floor, which has since been reinforced with steel. Behind the altar is an architectural semicircular painting in toning grey. The total effect of the chapel is gentle and harmonious.

It was a shame that Maria-Theresia's efforts were obsolete before they were completed, because in 1780, just after her reign, centralisation arrived and the local governors and dukes lost their importance, as did Innsbruck's palace. Today the state rooms are obviously unused, but there is some true historical interest because when Charles v of Lorraine, Franz Stefan's grandfather, first took over Tyrol, he commissioned a painter-reporter to accompany him to the wars and the resulting graphic pictures on the palace walls show some of the drama (the tapestry versions of the same scenes can be seen in Vienna).

The earlier impetus to Tyrol's economy was mining. Maria-Theresia promoted agriculture and education and by the end of the eighteenth century the shape and style of the provincial capital was firmly established. Hemmed in so closely by mountain ranges, it has altered comparatively little since those days, except that the old town and the original country palaces are now all part of the built-up area. Modern buildings and main roads have been kept strictly on the outer ring, leaving two distinctive inner segments untouched and enchanting.

The city's oldest district, on the north bank of the river, is Hötting, with its gabled houses backed by mountains and fronted by the Inn flowing fast and grey. Most people quickly cross the river from here to a compact cluster of gems so tightly knit that to walk more than a few paces without consulting the guidebook means you miss one of the famous monuments!

For a start you could take up a central position facing the famed golden roof on Herzog-Friedrichstrasse and simply swivel your head: there is the city tower, 185 feet high, in which sat the watchman to blow his trumpet if he spotted a fire. It originally had a pointed spire which, like so many others in Austria, was changed to a domed copper cupola in the mid-sixteenth century. Turn the other way and there's the Helbling House, first of all gothic, now eighteenth-century ornate stucco with pink walls. Across the street is the oldest inn, the Goldener Adler, which has been around since the fourteenth century and numbers Wagner, Prince Eugene of Savoy and Gustav of Sweden among its guests.

Both shops and inns, in fact almost every building along this street, have gothic arcades, the most northerly examples of this kind of architecture you are likely to see in this part of the world. The end of Herzog-Friedrichstrasse was the first city limit. The archway marking it has now disappeared, but the semicircular moat has been filled in and called Markt and Burg Graben, and takes you up to the court church with Maximilian's statues, Ferdinand's silver chapel and Andreas Hofer's grave.

Behind this is the Imperial Palace, Leopold's fountain, a lovely park and Innsbruck's favourite and famous church: St Jacob's, built in 1720 to replace the decaying parish church and sitting

8 Sölden in the Ötztal valley

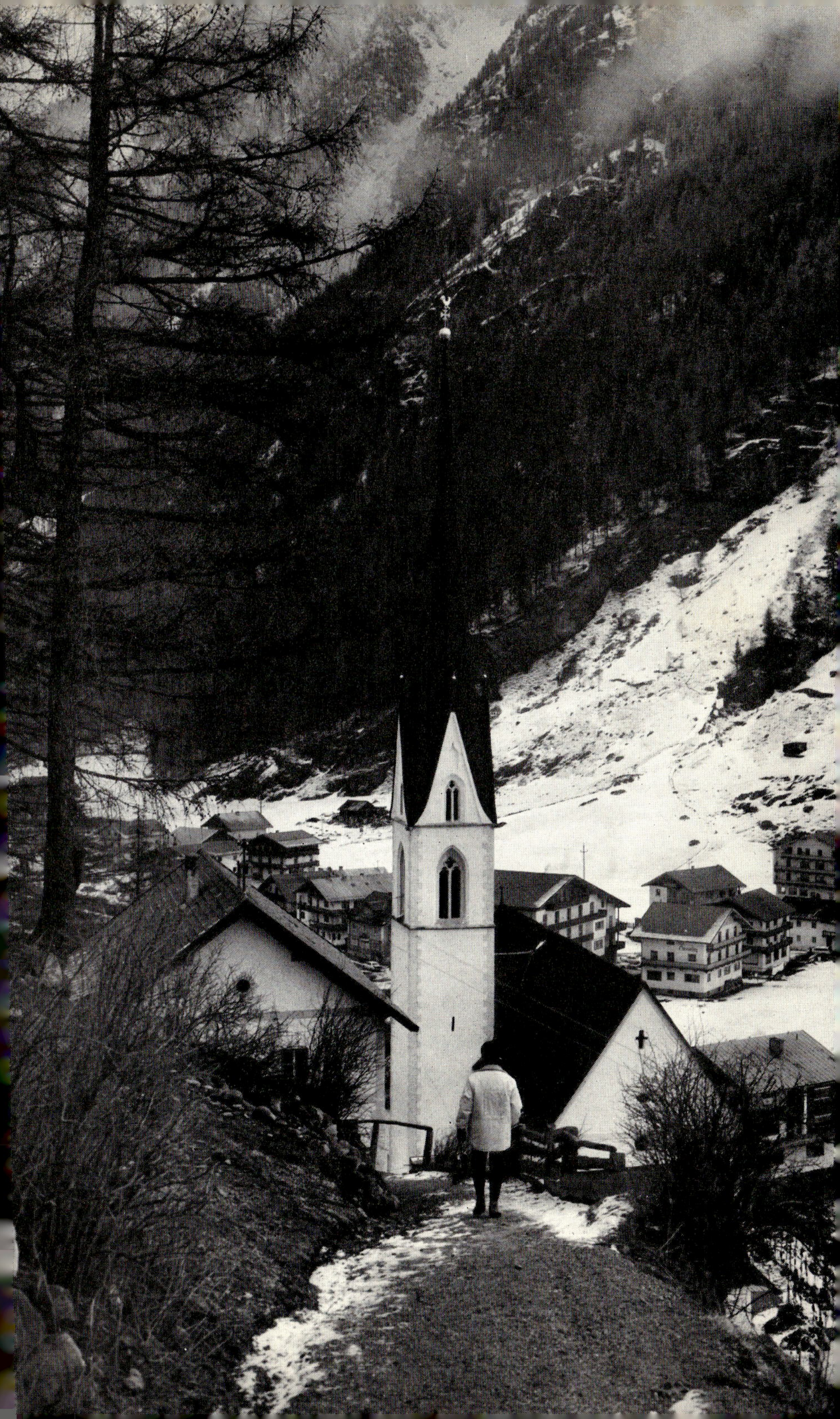

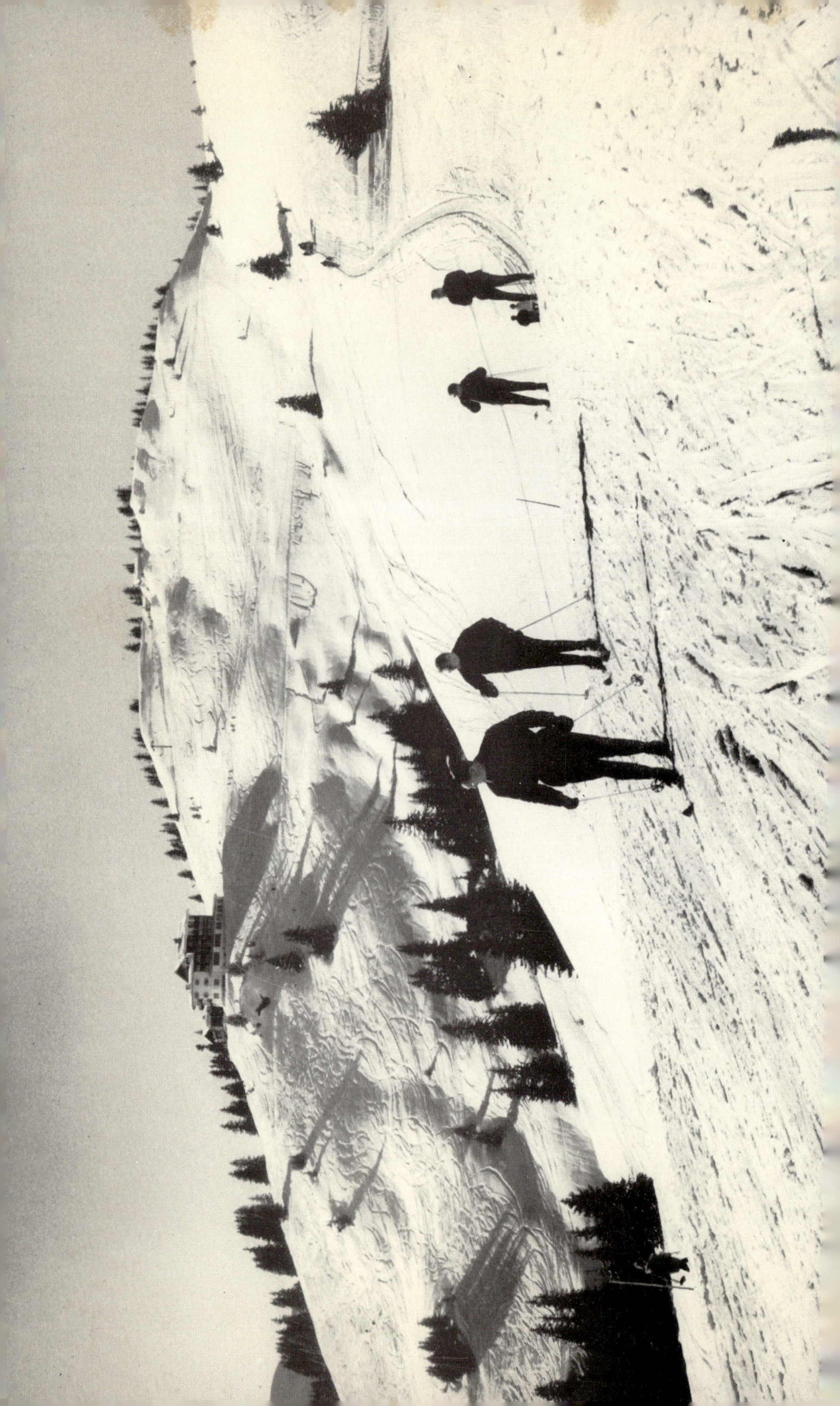

in a quiet square with round garden. It is late baroque, its interior rather crude and heavy, but has a beautiful gold pulpit and altar on which is one of Lucas Cranach's finest Virgin Marys. All the houses in this area are fifteenth- and sixteenth-century with gothic archways, and there are some tiny courtyards, to be discovered only by the determined walker, where the wooden balconies of the houses have been glassed in against the weather. In nearby Hofgasse is an eye-catching giant set into the wall of one of the houses. This rich collection of sights completes the first inner segment.

There is no sign of Innsbruck's outer wall, pulled down around 1850 when the whole place was enlarged, but the line between the original city and country is still sharply defined. A short stroll down Maria-Theresienstrasse is St Anna's Column commemorating 26 July 1703, when the Bavarian troops withdrew, and nearby is the most famous of the 'country' palaces, the eighteenth-century Landhaus, seat of today's regional government, its gracious stairways and courtyards retaining some of the old aristocratic flavour.

It is worth a small detour to Boznerplatz to see Rudolf's fountain, commemorating the joining of Tyrol with Austria, before returning to the main street and its final landmark, the two-faced archway, representing joy and grief, set against the mountain backcloth. All this can take a day or a week, depending on your historical inclinations, and I have made no mention of Innsbruck's major museums, the most important of which is next door to the Hofkirche and quite irresistible as an insight into the development of the province's culture.

Any influence or style, like in Vorarlberg, took time to spread through Tyrol and, once there, stayed longer than in Austria's more eastern provinces. But as the Tiroler Volkskunstmuseum, begun at the turn of the century in a converted monastery, shows, the farmers and peasants evolved their own culture which is surprisingly delicate and ornate. There is nothing crude about the fine milling stools, scythe shields, pewter and ceramic ware, cowbells with leather embroidered handles. Workaday items were all given more than a utility look: you did not just slap butter on a plate, it was turned out of a pretty mould; the stocking leg cast is finely carved, though the hose would be plain.

Almost every valley in Tyrol designed its style of house and the examples in the museum show that in this, too, the regions were independent and imaginative as well as practical. Naturally the models of the mountain farms reflect a more closed-in look than, say, the welcoming Kitzbühel one in which animals, stores and people occupied one building; the Ötztal valley, on the other hand, separated the farming community, housing maize and animals in one building, humans in another. Nearly all the farms show the big bell which summoned the workers from vineyards or fields to eat; nearly all have small windows designed to reflect as much light as possible; and under the eaves is a carved wooden dragon to ward off the evil spirits.

As well as these charming models the Volkskunstmuseum also has life-size room interiors, such as a fifteenth-century inn with gothic carved ceilings and walls, which was in use until 1908 and looks remarkably like some of the inns still around. The major difference between the farmhouse living room and that of the prosperous merchant is the stove—plain in the former, ornate ceramic in the latter.

Innsbruck has two other major sights both connected with the same event and sited at opposite ends of the town. Bergisel, where the Tyrolese fought against Napoleon to win town and country in 1809, is marked with a statue of the hero of that battle and a memorial chapel; at the northern end of the town is a circular painting telling the story of the one glorious day. And if you have never heard of Andreas Hofer you should conceal your ignorance from the locals, who still glow with pride at the mention of his name. He epitomises their independence, their fight to remain free, the remarkable success of the Landlibell.

In fact it was by no means the first nor the last success of this volunteer corps of sharpshooters. They had already proved invaluable in the war against the Swedes and, when Innsbruck's regular army troops were defeated by the Bavarians in 1703 and the local government accepted the new sovereignty, the Landlibell upped and defeated the professionals. When Maria-Theresia introduced a system of conscription, Tyrol was exempted and towards the end of the eighteenth century there were as many as 100 companies in continual service as frontier guards or in open battle. In 1805 Austria had to cede the north of Tyrol to Bavaria and the south to Italy, which was the beginning of the rebellion that burst four years later.

The Tyrolese refused to credit their new overlords with any benevolence or progressiveness, so the Bavarian plans for roads, agriculture, cattle breeding, postal services were seen merely as a wish to rule the province completely. The fact that Bavaria wished to centralise the government further and perhaps abolish even the name Tyrol certainly did not help friendly relations, but above all the Tyrolese, under the Bavarian system of conscription, feared they might be called upon to take part in a war against Austria.

It was an intolerable thought for these most passionately devoted subjects of the Habsburgs. They had been promised they would be reunited with Austria after liberation, so they set about as early a liberation as possible and were probably helped by the fact that although the Bavarians found out that an uprising was to take place, Napoleon did not believe it would be significant enough to warrant both the French and Bavarian armies. He was confident that the individual garrisons of regular troops already in Tyrol would hold out against the Landlibell.

At the head of the rebels was an innkeeper called Andreas Hofer, nicknamed the Sandwirt, who first led his own compatriots from the Passeier valley, then the whole of south Tyrol, then became supreme commander, despite the fact that he was known more for commonsense and vigour than military skill. The army genius was a farmer from Rinn called Josef Speckbacher, who as a youngster used to go poaching for chamois in the Karwendel mountains and died from wounds at Hall. The most fiery of the leading quartet was a red-bearded Capuchin monk, Father Joachim Haspinger, and another innkeeper, Peter

Mayr, completed the group.

Both Mayr and Hofer died before firing squads, the former at Bozen after he had been court-martialled and refused to lie to save himself despite pleas from his wife and friends; the latter at Mantua. The favourite hero is buried with the 'greats' in the Hofkirche, and naturally is a prominent figure in the magnificent circular painting about the one-day battle. There are more than 10,000 square feet of hand-woven Irish linen, 30 feet high and 300 feet around. It was painted by a German in 1896 and so cleverly housed that you are convinced there is hidden artificial light to point up the drama. But there is not, just pure daylight shining on Andreas Hofer, with black beard and green hat, the monk, Haspinger, the French being shot, women giving wine to soldiers and so on.

When Emperor Franz II returned to liberated Tyrol in 1816 he arranged for a gala shooting contest that went on for several weeks and was attended by several thousand riflemen. This Tyrolean hobby goes back to the middle ages when all towns of any size had Zielstätten, or shooting ranges. Franz must have been pretty keen on the sport, for he arranged an even bigger gala when he brought his ally, Czar Alexander of Russia, to Tyrol in 1822.

The targets, by the way, were not the plain ones we are accustomed to today, but very fancy indeed. The centre target at the Russian celebrations shows 'the genius of Austria emptying the cornucopia of his bounty over the country', the country being represented by the Castle of Tyrol. Sometimes the targets might be the blossom of a gigantic flower or, comically, a gentleman soaring upwards surrounded by money bags or, topically, a scene depicting the day's event with all the riflemen drawn up on parade.

The Brenner Pass, the only road leading over the Alps, was transformed by Maria-Theresia in 1774 from a cart track into a fashionable carriageway, at a time when the Tyrolean roadside inn was on its second 'reincarnation', having first disappeared along with the Roman empire and been replaced by monasteries giving hospitality to travellers. The development of trade helped to bring back the inn business, which in those days had to offer a good deal more than just bed and breakfast. The hostelry provided medicines, washerwomen, tailors, cobblers, saddlers, blacksmiths and entertainment; and this may well have been the birth of tipping. A Venetian travelling through Austria wrote of the gratuity he left to the inn servants and of the maid 'who kindly kept me company in the night'.

The prosperity of the inn around here lasted until the railway was built in 1867, but it has taken another century for the road to catch up with the ever-increasing cars upon it. The 22-mile Brenner Pass from Volders in the Inn valley to Brennersee just before the Italian frontier used to be a weekend nightmare in the summer, traffic jams stretching almost its entire length. Now the road has been finally finished, including 42 bridges and viaducts, and the driving time halved.

Modern Innsbruck gained a valuable boost to its economy and tourism when it was host to the Winter Olympics in 1964. Its 100,000 inhabitants, 4,000 of whom are university students, and uncountable visitors, can take advantage of the Olympic ice stadium, ski jump, bobsleigh and toboggan runs. It has always called itself the town of the cableways, and in winter it is nothing unusual to see crowds of workers heading to the hills for a skiing lunch hour. The local bus and tram services link easily with mountain installations to bring the countryside even closer to Innsbruck's doorstep.

The Nordkettenbahn, from the district of Hungerburg, for instance, takes the visitor up to the Seegrubbe, at more than 6,000 feet, and into the middle of the Karwendel range for walking tours. South of the city are a trio of possibilities: the farthest at Lizum, all of 12 miles away with lifts up either the Birgitzköpfl, at well over 6,000 feet, or the Hoadl, 1,000 feet higher. Nearer still are the quaintly named villages of Natters and Mutters, where there is a cableway to the Mutterer Alm and a chairlift up above to yet another summit.

The most famous of Innsbruck's 'home' resorts is Igls, reached by a narrow-gauge railway puffing past the tiny tranquil Lanser See before reaching the village with its Patscherkofelbahn to the 6,000+feet summit of that mountain. Igls is a lively bustling place, splendid to visit if you are based in the big city half an hour away, not so good to stay in, unless you can bear with equanimity the visiting crowds, particularly during winter lunch hours and summer weekends.

The River Inn meanders its way through the centre of Tyrol, forming the backbone of a leaf; the veins are its tributaries and the aching decision is which of the numerous valleys to investigate—some steep-sided and sinister, others wide and gentle, some forested and rocky, others meadows and pastures. Driving west from Innsbruck and retaining the north bank of the river, it is a short distance to the sunny plateau on which sits Seefeld, its bland open flavour an incongruous contrast to the fearsome legends about it told with relish by the natives.

The most dramatic (and the unlikeliest) tale is of a simple and good-hearted giant, Thyrsus, who one day fought, and lost, a terrible battle with a sword-swinging giant from Innsbruck. The country ogre crawled wounded up the hill to Seefeld leaving a trail of blood behind him and saying: 'Go, innocent blood, be for man and beast good.' They later found tar deposits in the area which are used for medical purposes and giant-lovers claim it is, symbolically, the blood of poor Thyrsus.

The little lake just outside the village centre called Wildsee, embellished for tourism with a man-made swimming pool alongside, has, naturally, its own dragon who, on another terrible day in Seefeld's history, got so hungry it rose from the depths and swallowed a passing horse and rider. Twentieth-century visitors are anything but frightened at this sunny resort, which until the second world war devoted itself to summer traffic and only afterwards began the business of attracting skiers. Today's twin amenities—the fine indoor swimming pools, a projected golf course, dozens of ski lifts, an ice rink—jostle for position and popularity.

It is not, as you will gather, a place of great historical interest, but guests at one of the hotels may wonder about the courtyard and the frescoes in the vaulted corridors. The answer is that, like many other hotels in Austria, this was once a monastery and was closed in the mid-eighteenth century by Joseph II. The monks fled, many treasures were stolen, and during the Napoleonic wars the building was used as an army headquarters and occupied by Marshal Ney for several weeks. After the Bavarians sold it, Klosterbräu began again, not as a monastery, but as an hotel.

In the portal of the gothic church is a relief telling the story of one of the most famous (or infamous) characters to pass through Seefeld. He was a fourteenth-century Scot named Oswald, who as an arrogant knight refused the small host at communion, saying it was not big enough for him. The priest gave him a larger one, but as soon as Oswald took it he began to sink into the ground, saved only when the host was removed. The now-repentant knight went off to the monastery at Stams to take the orders, and a curious hand-shaped dent in the altar is pointed out as the place where he saved himself. As soon as this story got around the pilgrims came flocking, a larger church was built and the old altar retained in it.

From Seefeld you can take to the by-roads and stay in the same gentle scenery, going north towards Germany via Leutasch, certainly the longest village in Austria, which stretches through various hamlets for more than ten miles. But there is only one overall mayor and come election time a close-fought battle between the hamlets to push their own special candidate. The woods and curling lanes continue into Germany where you need to switch to the main road and virtually drive round the bottom of the craggy Zugspitze through Garmisch-Partenkirchen and back into Austria again, tossing up whether to lunch at Ehrwald or Lermoos, two pretty villages nodding to each other across a flat plateau; Lermoos overlooks the mountain, Ehrwald is overlooked by it.

From here another decision has to be made, either to go south over the Fernpass with its icy green lakes and thick pine woods back to the main Inn valley, or to head north-west to Reutte, then south through the Lechtal, one of the most remote and least inhabited valleys in Austria. It has no direct communication with the Inn valley and can be reached only from Reutte, near the German border, or Warth at its western end and on the way into Vorarlberg. The farmers here must be the envy of all their fellows in Tyrol, for theirs is a broad open valley, they gather their crops on level ground and only near Warth do the mountains close in.

After the tranquillity of this top left-hand corner of Tyrol, the main road west from Innsbruck will seem busy indeed, but it has many opportunities to explore the veins or valleys south of the river, and not so far along is Telfs, whose baroque houses have bay windows with stubbly glass and wooden statues set into window frames. Nearby is the monastery of Stams, not so fine as those in Lower Austria, but meriting a quiet wander around. The church is the largest baroque one in Tyrol, and sunk in the floor of the nave is the seventeenth-century vault in which are buried some famous counts and countesses—Countess Maultasch's father and Maximilian's second wife among them.

A few miles from Stams is the turn-off into Tyrol's most well-known valley, the Ötztal, rich, wide and fertile at its beginning, then narrower and dramatic as it climbs to the mountains, glaciers and Austria's highest parish. Not far from the village of Ötz which gives its name to the valley is the tiny Piburger See, where the car park is wisely situated outside the hamlet (all of half a dozen houses smothered in flowers) and there is a short walk to the lakeside. The woods that circle it are deep and quiet with moss-covered rocks around the tree-roots, and on a grey day there is no one swimming from the natural lido, only walkers in the little café overlooked by mountains drinking chocolate with freshly sifted icing sugar on top.

The valley road passes through Maurach gorge and the largest village, Längenfeld, before rising to an alpine pasture with straggly Sölden stretched along it and its little brother Hochsölden perched in the upper meadows. Both resorts are famous for winter sports and linked by a chairlift as well as the highest cableway in Austria, rising 5,000 feet in two sections to the

10,000 foot summit of the Gaislachkogel. At Zwieselstein the valley becomes two-pronged, one fork leading to the quiet undeveloped village of Vent, the other to Ober-gurgl and the Timmelsjoch toll road to Hoch-gurgl and towards the Italian border. Some day, they say, the link will be completed between the two countries.

Hoch-gurgl claims Austria's highest chairlift to its summer skiing grounds at 10,000 feet just below the summit of the Wurmkogel. The lift starts then at 6.30 a.m. for the early birds, but in winter it is three hours later so that skiers will not freeze to the chairlift that wafts above the glacier. Ober-gurgl is Austria's highest parish and even in summer there is a nip in the air at more than 6,000 feet. Be here a few days and you would know most of the inhabitants and the other visitors. It is not particularly picturesque, architecturally, but people come for its backcloth of glaciers and peaks and the magnificent skiing.

Back down the Ötztal valley to the main road, and westwards a few miles is Imst, the most commercially important junction between Innsbruck and Landeck. For tourists it comes to life once every four years, usually the Sunday before Ash Wednesday, with its famous Schemenlaufen, like most traditional dance forms, of heathen origin now overlaid with Christianity. Several hundred inhabitants take part, all of them men, and all from Imst—a 'foreigner' from a neighbouring village who once tried to infiltrate had a very rough time indeed.

The two main characters are Roller, who wears a bright cummerbund with lots of little bells rather like an English Morris dance ensemble, and Scheller, who wears a wide leather cummerbund, also with bells. There may be up to 35 of each character, plus the same number of witches and hundreds of other minor parts. You tend to inherit your role from your grandfather, and the costume to go with it. These are terribly expensive, because of the heavy and ornate headdresses, and the ones not privately owned are locked up in the town hall for the long period between each performance. A local man carves the masks, some of which are several hundred years old, and any bells needed are made in Germany.

What it is really all about is difficult to discover. The teacher who has lived in Imst a mere 20 years and so is not yet eligible to participate, says he has been researching all this time and has not come up with an answer. But everyone can describe what actually happens. About a fortnight before the great event, the women go off into the woods and meadows to collect the flowers, leaves, branches and so on to weave into the high headdress frames. On the day itself they sew their menfolk into the costumes and the procession assembles outside the parish church, whose bell tolls the start at noon.

The parade goes on for around six hours, the Roller and Scheller couples dancing, the witches lashing out with their broomsticks at anyone they regard as having been dissolute during the previous four years, and the watching crowd of some 20,000 or 30,000 kept in their places by costumed characters using big soft balls attached to handles. As the Schemenlaufen makes its way through the several squares in town, it stops to dance in each, and onlookers are likely to be 'kidnapped' by the performers and held 'hostage' until they make a small contribution to the funds.

The following day, far from being exhausted, the villagers do the whole thing again, just for themselves, and without some of the heavier paraphernalia. The Imster Schemenlaufen is one of four similar events that climax the carnival season. The Nassereither Schellenlaufen is more intimate, the Schleicherlaufen in Telfs is dominated by masked dancers followed by goatherds, poachers and bear-baiters, the Mullerlaufen of Thaur features enormously heavy headdresses.

The Tyrolese have always loved pageantry, dressing up and folklore, and their annual calendar of these events is a long and impressive one, meaning that the visitor is almost certain to strike at least one of them on his travels. It might be a simple rural caper on St George's day, with the youngsters of the village tying cowbells to their waists. Or it could be the Gauderfest, with Gauder beer and sausages, at Zell in the Ziller valley in early May. Or the wood-chopping contest in Innsbruck when the champions split a 10-groschen piece with their axes.

At Whitsun there is a graphic presentation of the spiritual descent of the Holy Ghost, often symbolised by a wooden dove lowered through a hole in the ceiling of the church and kept circling. Christmas cribs have been known for around 700 years and it is not considered gate-crashing for strangers to ask to see the examples in private homes. The visit of St Nicholas to Innsbruck on 6 December is a spectacular affair. He lights a Christmas tree in front of the golden roof, in preparation for the entry of Christkindl (Baby Jesus) accompanied by shepherds, angels and torch-bearers, all children, delivering a message of goodwill to the mayor.

On Corpus Christi day farmers in national costume on decorated horses take part in Antlassritt, commemorating the victory over the Swedish invasion and carrying green branches for sabres. No end of bonfires are lit in different places at different times, the most dramatic of the fiery displays being the originally pagan Scheibenschlagen, when birchwood discs are heated and stuck glowing on to hazel sticks before being hurled into the night. So if you are around in July at Landeck, Grins, Pinswang or Pragraten in East Tyrol, beware of flying torches!

Our Lady's Day, 15 August, sees women and girls taking to the attics of their homes with consecrated bunches of garden flowers, herbs and hazel twigs which are supposed to protect the house from thunderstorms. At Thaur, a 1,000-year-old village, a life-sized carved donkey is carried across the fields accompanied by youngsters with enormous poles decorated with ivy, pretzels and apples. In a chapel high above East Tyrol's capital, Lienz, newly baked loaves are given away to the congregation. Musically, Tyrol has more brass bands, at 276, than it does number of parishes, and naturally they celebrate a Day of Brass Band Music with a series of concerts.

Possibly the most charming procession of all is the Almatrieb, celebrating the cattle's return from the high alpine pastures in September/October. For the farmers this is the prelude to the long, hard winter and they pray for a warm extended autumn so that they can delay the moment when their herds have to be brought indoors. For the cattle, it is the end of an idyllic summer and the one moment in the year when they know they are the star performers. They have been decorated with spruce and pine, garlanded with ribbons and flowers and may even be wearing a one-legged milking stool as a headdress, perhaps one reason why the examples in the Tiroler Volkskunstmuseum in Innsbruck are so elaborately carved. The womenfolk have baked cakes and biscuits for the slow, jingling procession down the mountain back to the village.

In the old days the threshing after Kirchtag, harvest festival, in mid-October, used to take up the remainder of the year, and the farmers' wives would hold spinning get-togethers during the winter, the visitors bringing their own spinning wheels and flax or wool. Now you are much more likely to hear the click of knitting needles. Somehow the farmer has to provide fodder for his cattle for 200 days of the year. There will be three crops, the last one used for autumn grazing, but he may also have to bring down the hay from his high meadows before the first snows and any avalanche danger.

Occasionally the crop can be loaded on to an animal, but much more often the farmer himself is the carrier, pulling a sledge so tightly packed that he has to make a hole in the hay through which to poke his head and shoulders! In East Tyrol the job was often a cooperative effort, the farmers setting out together before dawn with lanterns in order to be safely down again before the midday sun softened the snow and increased the risk of avalanches. Straw by the way, is much too precious to use on the floor of cowsheds. Instead, ferns, moss, heather and pine needles are the carpet, and before timber-felling became controlled young men used to shin up the pines with spiked boots to lop off the lower branches and thus ruin the trees.

The traditional opening of the farming year is Candlemas in February, which used to be celebrated with a holiday and a mop fair, when servants were paid their annual wages and farmhands hired. It is the time when the mountain farmers are waiting for the snows to melt (and sometimes scattering earth and ashes around to hasten the process), then, eventually, clearing away the avalanche debris of boulders, branches, even fallen trees. Earth may need to be carried from the lowest furrows to the top of the field and sometimes sowing is by hand to ensure that the seeds do not 'slide' downhill. According to an old superstition everything that grows tall should be planted when the moon is waxing and everything beneath the ground when it is waning.

We left Imst to digress on Tyrolean festivities and farming. Back on the main road is Landeck, merely a communications centre for both rail and road—the latter leading south and giving you a choice of going to Switzerland or west into Vorarlberg via the Arlberg Pass and St Anton and St Christoph. There is one more enticing valley in Tyrol off the Landeck road, that of the Paznaun, narrow, quiet and sinister, opening out when it reaches Ischgl, then rising from Galtür over the Silvretta alpine road, drivable in summer only to the glaciers that form the border with Vorarlberg.

In winter, skiers take the lifts of Ischgl, walk over the ridge at the top and ski down into the Samnaun valley, a Swiss duty-free zone dating from special trading agreements when the two areas were dependent upon one another and there were no communications to link them with anywhere else. This no longer applies, but the special prices in the Samnaun still do!

The Paznaun completes the bottom left-hand corner of the Inn valley and to investigate the rest of Tyrol you need to retrace your steps to Innsbruck, and set off eastwards on the same arterial road, not going more than a few miles before halting at Solbad Hall, which in the tenth and twelfth centuries was more important than Innsbruck and until very recently was a salt-mining town. Although they work the mines no more, they keep up the customs of a mining community, with a museum, a miner's band and celebrations on the birthday of St Barbara, the miners' patron saint.

In the lower town is the round tower where Duke Sigismund

minted his own money (a rare mediaeval privilege) and up the hill in the very old quarter is the fifteenth-century town hall, whose outside wooden steps lead from the courtyard to the first floor council chamber. This has baroque wood panelling and doors, pillars of late gothic and a wondrous ceramic stove in the corner. The fireguard and wrought-iron chandelier look absolutely right in this setting, yet turn out to have been made in the twentieth century.

The upper town region contains lots of patrician houses with bay windows and in the tiny narrow alleyways the houses nearly touch window panes at first-floor level. The large gothic church has one extraordinary feature, an unsymmetrical altar due to its alterations and extensions. The effect is that the altar goes off sideways into an angled corner.

From Solbad the road takes you through what were once Tyrol's only trading communities, when river transport was vital and German neighbours were keen to do business. Wattens now makes glass beads and optical items, Weer has a timber industry and Schwaz has turned to the new industry of tourism. Just before reaching this town there is a baroque church called Kreuzkirchlein with a delightful story behind it.

The tale dates from the war of the Spanish Succession when in July 1703 the bridge over the Inn at Zirl, well westwards of Innsbruck, was burnt down and the crucifix that stood upon it was carried downstream to a point between Pill and Schwaz. A local man rescued it, and thoughtfully built a little wooden chapel to house it. The present church dates from around 1764 and over the door is a grand picture of the consecration with crowds of peasants, musicians, clergy and so on.

Schwaz was a mediaeval mining town, too, and in the second half of the fifteenth century they reckon there were 30,000 miners here, who contributed towards the magnificent copper-tiled roof (said to contain 15,000 tiles) on the gothic church. In fact silver mining was more important than copper, and the size of the church is explained by the fact that half of it was used for catholic services and half for protestant, though not at the same time of course. They still have two altars and two services, just the same. The most famous town family were the Fugger merchants from Bavaria, who virtually owned Schwaz during the sixteenth century and clearly helped to put the place on the commercial map. Their premises, with painted baroque exterior, are still a collection of shops—shoe-maker and tobacconist among them.

Jenbach is the next decision-taking junction and the Tyrolese would have you drive north from here to their only lake of any size, the 5½-mile-long Achensee with its one resort, Pertisau, stretching languidly through the meadows and backed by the Karwendel range across which walk summer mountaineers. South from Jenbach is the Zillertal, wide and pretty for most of the way with what the natives describe as an express train (because it is single-track, criss-crosses the road and goes at a speed which enables travellers to get off and pick flowers) taking you to Mayrhofen, which if you were asked to describe a typical Tyrolean village would fit the bill exactly.

The railway ends here, but the road becomes a winding lane to take you through Lanersbach to Hintertux and the head of the valley. The Zillertal is so picturesque and charming you might well spend an entire fortnight basking in its warmth and wish to return to the same spot the following year.

But travellers who keep on the move will have headed back to the main road and have arrived at Rattenberg, a mediaeval town, the smallest in Tyrol and so perfectly preserved it looks as though it has been reproduced for a film set. There was never any room to expand here, because it is sited close to the river and the rock rises steeply behind. Thus it became an obvious fortress town against Bavarian invaders who were finally defeated in 1505 during Maximilian's reign. Rattenberg's thin clustered houses have wonderful façades, red and white shutters and wooden balustrades. Most of the shops look like wine cellars with their gothic arches for entrances and stone-ceilinged interiors.

Almost anything would seem less than perfect after this, so

it is perhaps best to change the mood, drive on to Wörgl, then up to the pilgrimage church of Mariastein on the route north towards one of the main German border points at Kufstein. The chapel and tower date from the mid-fourteenth century and were later surrounded by other buildings, all of them protected by a defensive wall to safeguard the Tyrolese from the Bavarians.

A second chapel was added in the sixteenth century when Mariastein became open to pilgrims, not such a simple order as it sounds, for the pilgrims had to go up the stairs of the tower and past the living quarters of the owner, the public-spirited Count Schurff. During the next couple of hundred years something like 20,000 pilgrims passed through annually and among the offerings they brought (and exhibited today) were lambs, women's hair, brides' veils and wooden and bone spoons—these latter supposedly a defence against toothache!

From Wörgl there are two easterly routes by which to leave Tyrol, either direct through St Johann or south via Kitzbühel, in which case you certainly will not be leaving the province so directly, and especially not if you are carrying with you a little book, perfectly sweet and totally biased, about the resort. It begins: 'Kitzbühel is not a place, it is a condition. It is true that superficial characters stubbornly maintain that it is a town in Tyrol (population 7,000; height above sea level, 2,500 feet). For the connoisseur, however, for those madly in love with it—and only they shall count as experts—Kitzbühel is and will remain a condition, a disease, and an incurable one at that, which almost everybody tends to catch.'

It is not so over-stated as you might think, for Kitz, as aficionados call it, does seem to grasp the heartstrings. Other places are prettier; others have skiing just as good; others are equally sophisticated. And yet . . . today's resort is preparing to celebrate its seven-hundredth birthday in 1971 and looks as though it has always catered for the carefree, idle ones, except when you remember that tourism is a comparatively recent occupation. Clearly the Kitzbühelers had industry of a different kind once upon a time.

10 *Salzburg: view of the city and castle*

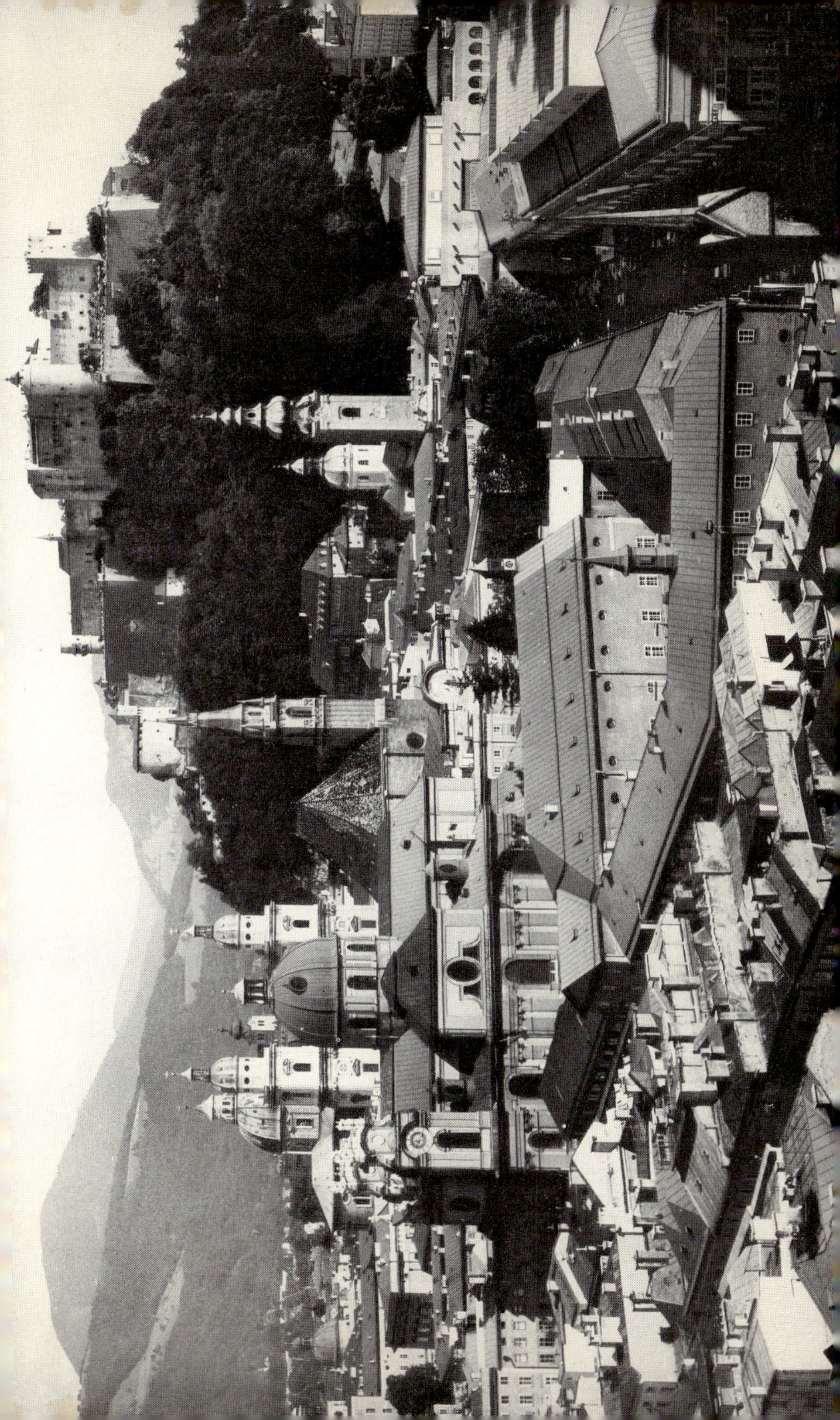

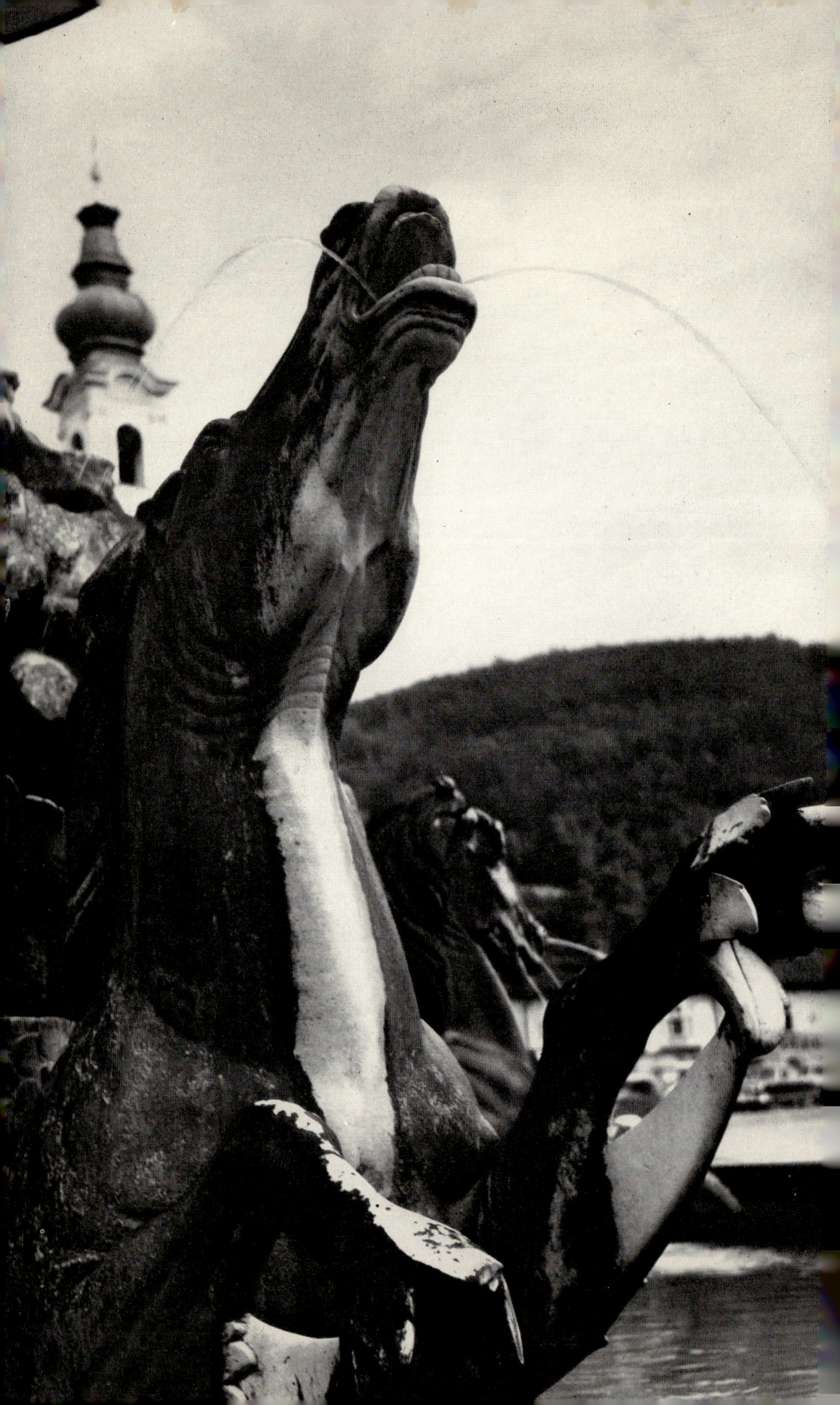

They were given a similar town charter to Munich from a Bavarian duke in 1271 and a few years later were presented with acres of pasture land by another duke as an incentive to fortify their town. He could not have known the natives very intimately, for they were notorious peace-lovers. They made the effort at fortification, apparently building walls that were thick and strong, except that they were hollow and stuffed with earth. They would never have stood up to a cannon ball, and luckily did not have to; eventually the natives calmly demolished the ramparts and built their own houses on top of the foundations. Three of the four old town gates remind visitors of these earlier sham defences.

Between the fifteenth and seventeenth centuries the town and surrounding area lived richly on its copper and silver mining. In 1500 there were 20 mines being worked and there is still the exit of one shaft behind the town sawmill on the Högl. The history books point to another shaft, 3,000 feet deep, as *the* engineering feat of 1540! The rich got very rich indeed on the proceeds; the great merchants and bankers like the Fuggers and Rosenbergs made themselves a clear profit of 700,000 guilders from one mine alone over a 15-year period. Eventually the silver mines had to be closed, when the battle against water made the operation too expensive and dangerous, but fortunately salt had already been discovered as a worthy and lucrative substitute.

The religious development of Kitzbühel went nothing like so smoothly. It was a catholic town which in the sixteenth century executed 68 anabaptists, probably because of their fanaticism to abolish private ownership. Today there are two churches worth visiting; both for their bells. St Catherine's probably existed in the mid-fourteenth century, built within the walls so that if ever there was a siege (though there never was) the townsfolk would have somewhere to shelter. The fireman sat at the top of its tower until 1875 and rang the bell if he saw smoke. Now there is a modern electric clock in the watch room which sets the timing for the 18-bell carillon that plays well-known folk songs twice a day and thrice on Sundays.

Kitzbühel's other famous bells, hanging in the tower of Our

11 *Salzburg: a fountain*

Lady, are enormous, together weighing 1,300 pounds, and the larger is a particular pride of the natives because of its clear rich A flat. It was originally made for a church in Innsbruck but in the casting was dented by a tile, so the prospective buyers refused to proceed with the purchase. The burghers of Kitzbühel bought it for its metal value alone in 1847 and it astonishingly survived several plots to be melted down throughout both world wars.

The story is told that one of the bells had earlier proved to be the most accurate weather forecaster in the district, ever since they reckoned its boom deflected and broke up banks of cloud. As far back as the sixteenth century there was an observation post way down the Inn valley which hung out a white cloth to warn the sacristan of Kitzbühel of approaching thunderstorms. Presumably he then rang the bell in the hope of 'persuading' the storm to by-pass the town.

The arrival of the railway line in 1875 began a new flourishing era for the resort, though twentieth-century visitors often find it difficult to get their bearings on this large-scale railway roundabout that almost circles Kitzbühel. Skiing, for which it is now famous, came a little later, when an enterprising mayor, Franz Reisch, sent off to Norway for a 7-foot 10-inch pair of skis and climbed the Horn with them. It didn't take long to produce the shorter, fatter Alpine variety and hotels sprang up to welcome the celebrities and high society who liked to spend part of their winter here.

Today's developments are getting more and more scattered as space runs out; skiers who cannot get on the slopes for the crowds during the day can carry on the sport under floodlights at night. Prices are aristocratic and courteous car-drivers tend to run slaloms around pedestrians wandering through the narrow streets. Summer visitors are almost as numerous as winter ones, and they go walking in the softly wooded Kitzbüheler Alps or swimming or taking a mud bath in the warm soft peat of the Schwarzsee.

There is a legend attached to this lake, of course, about two peasants who quarrelled for years for the ownership of a piece of forest. Eventually one put a curse on his neighbour that the disputed woodland might turn to water. It did, that night, and swallowed up not only the forest but the wicked peasant, too. On clear days, they would have you see the tips of the sunken trees on the lake's bottom.

South of Kitzbühel is the Thurn Pass over which itinerant weavers used to walk when the snow melted, carrying their dismantled looms on their backs and pushing the rest of their gear in wheelbarrows. They stayed with local farmers for weeks on end, until they had turned the flax given them by the inhabitants into linen. Today the route is a more prosaic exit from the province of Tyrol into Land Salzburg, or a short cut via the same road, straight on through a tunnel to reach that curious offshoot, East Tyrol.

The people in this corner of Austria are very independent. 'We prefer to spend hours going to Innsbruck because we are Tyrolese —we do not belong to Carinthia,' said one. Nevertheless this tiny pocket of land with 40,000 inhabitants did belong to Carinthia until 1945. As for the 'hours going to Innsbruck' via Italy and the Brenner Pass, it has not been necessary for the past few years, with the opening of the three-mile-long Felbertauern tunnel, to give East Tyrol a beloved link with its big brother after a short drive through Land Salzburg.

The only other road connections are, predictably, eastwards into Carinthia, and it is from the capital, Lienz, that motorists begin the long summer climb into this neighbouring province up the Grossglockner. It is, incidentally, the most charming entry into the town, which sits snugly on the sunny side of the valley opposite the serrated edge of the Lienzer Dolomites, a view that makes it even more easy to appreciate how the region has remained remote and cut off, though the Italian border is only 20 or so miles away.

Everything is scaled down here. The natives are very keen to promote skiing and indeed boast a cablecar and chairlifts, but unless the snow is abundant you cannot ski back to the capital for much of the season. But in summer they are the first to join the tourists in the alpine meadows, calling in at mountain cafés for refreshments or simply sitting and looking. They have their own lake, too, a couple of miles outside the centre. It is called the Tristachersee, is tiny, with green muddy water, a camping field at one end, a few row-boats and one hotel. Pine trees hug the shore protectively.

Lienz, then, can hardly be expected to have the hallmarks of a provincial capital. There is no besmirching of the air by industry, no grand platz, only two little squares. Any commerce is connected with natural resources, like processing the pines for oil, and modern treasure-seekers go to the Lienz mountains in search of adularia, garnets, malachite and rock crystal.

The mountain farmers breed chinchillas, and it is no surprise to discover that those itinerant weavers over the Thurn Pass left behind some sort of heritage. There is still at least one hand-weaver who uses the flax brought him by the farmers to produce a coarse cloth to be made into the lumberman's working suit. Poetically, the wooden frames on which the hay is dried are in this region called Heuharpfen, because, like real harps, they respond and vibrate to the wind.

East Tyrol, apart from its capital, boasts two villages, about 25 hamlets and two interesting sights. There is the ruined Roman town of Aguntum, scene of a clash in 610 between Bavarians from the west and Hungarians and Slavs from the east; and Bruck Castle, on the outskirts of Lienz. This latter began life as just a tower towards the end of the thirteenth century and by the beginning of the sixteenth had acquired dungeons, more towers, gates, walls, and so on. It had also become the local court and prison and remained the arsenal until 1780.

But then the owners, from Hall in north Tyrol, were banished by Joseph II, and nobody would buy the place because of its decayed condition. So they changed it into a military hospital and barracks and the mayor of Lienz in 1827 took over. Unfortunately he did not have much of a chance to revitalise or restore before his son was put in charge, in 1861, and obviously a lad for a lively life. He saw Bruck as a brewery and inn and in his efforts to convert it into such virtually ruined the original structure, dividing rooms, changing windows and generally messing about to such an extent that at least one circular tower had to be pulled down as it became unsafe.

Two more efforts were made at reconstruction, in 1911 and 1942, and the existing tower was divided into eight floors, the better to display its war trophies. What is in fact the most charming aspect of Bruck Castle today is its shabbiness. The setting is enchanting, up in the woods, with a little pond as part of the grounds, and the museum sections of folklore, history, war and ethnography have been done with logic and affection. It matters not that the building which houses them has been changed once too often; now it can rest, a dignified old gentleman, sure of its welcome and appeal.

4 Land Salzburg

Salzburg, unlike Vienna, invested in churches rather than palaces. For centuries it accumulated ecclesiastical property by donation, purchase and barter; the crucifix, rarely the sword, was used as the means of expansion. Today's city is a combination of the archbishop's residence and his churches and the burgher's town, which is a proper partnership, for without the copper mines at Mülbach and the gold from the Tauern mountains and the salt from the Dürnberg mines the archbishops would have been considerably worse off.

With their spectacular trading agreements the clergy were able to construct, reconstruct and add, and if at times it seems that they were simply trying to rival their predecessors in splendour and monuments, then perhaps this was their right. But in return their sponsorship gave Salzburg its cultural treasures and its sophisticated Italian flavour; in other words, an Austrian city that is unique and distinctive.

The all-powerful archbishops, beginning with St Rupert in the eighth century, had their seat here until 1816, so any investigation of the history and development leads easily through the ecclesiastical biographies. Before St Rupert arrived from Germany around 700, having been given the province by a Bavarian duke, the Celts and Romans had, as elsewhere, been around, living on the tops of the hills which surround Salzburg and calling the area Yuvavum.

Rupert, the patron saint, was the trend-setter on harnessing commerce to the needs of the church. He began the salt industry at Dürnberg and on the proceeds founded the city and built St Peter's. Behind the church are the catacombs where early Christians hid from Roman persecution, and in the tiny dark graveyard you will find, among the wrought-iron crosses, seven plain ones in a row, without identification, which are supposed to commemorate the seven wives of a carpenter who tickled each to death. The saint is buried here, not because it is 'his' church, but because there was controversy over whether his bones, then resting in the cathedral with the other archbishops, were really his. The argument still goes on and meanwhile Rupert's remains stay in St Peter's.

Quite a few of Salzburg's 36 Roman Catholic churches, its major fortress and a part of its residential quarter were already built before Archbishop Wolf Dietrich began a major reconstruction at the end of the sixteenth century. St Peter's had gained a romanesque basilica in the twelfth century, the Franciscan church on Sigmund Haffnergasse had begun to acquire its extraordinary layers of architectural styles and in the façade of the cathedral was the first of three dates that were milestones in its history.

The first date, 774, is the cathedral's foundation, but it had already burnt to the ground several times before Dietrich made public his grandiose plans. He wanted a church as big as a palace and undeterred by the lack of space on the site first pulled down some houses in the square that were in the way, then shifted the cemetery to St Sebastian's church, and finally demolished the cathedral itself to begin afresh with new materials. Like almost everything else this archbishop started, he never finished the job, the exception being his own mausoleum, St Gabriel's chapel, sitting in the middle of St Sebastian's cemetery surrounded by the 88 arches of the cloisters.

Mirabell Palace was another of Dietrich's extravaganzas, though when he began it in 1606 he called it Altenau, after his mistress Salome Alt by whom he had had 15 children. All that remains here as a reminder of him is the pavilion in the grounds in which he kept exotic birds (it is now a museum). He also had a hand in the Hohensalzburg fortress, which had been started in 1077 with just one wall and one building but was mostly completed by the sixteenth century, though every archbishop afterwards added his own particular bit and left his coat of arms upon it.

Dietrich's reign of construction came abruptly and hurtfully to an end when following a quarrel with Bavaria he fled to the Alps; his keen successor, Marcus Sitticus, had him captured and brought back and stalled all plots to be overthrown by keeping the unfavoured archbishop locked up in the fortress. Even Dietrich's last wishes about his funeral were ignored by naughty Sitticus. The imprisoned archbishop stipulated, according to the plaques inset into the brightly tiled walls of his mausoleum, a quiet modest affair; his successor immediately turned it into the opposite.

If Dietrich seemed an unsuccessful builder in terms of completion, Sitticus was anything but. In seven short years, 1612-19, he accomplished a good deal, starting with the cathedral. Naturally he disagreed with the way Dietrich had tackled the job, saying it was too big, so he began again in 1614, with master builder Santino Solari. But, like his predecessor, he didn't finish the job, either.

Sitticus had a rethink about the Mirabell, too, changing its name and then its style, conversely making this building bigger, although this is not the palace you see today. His builder was responsible for one other mammoth task, the palace of Hellbrunn, about five miles south from the city centre, begun in July 1613 and finished less than two years later. As early as this it included a zoological garden with fish ponds and aviaries supplying the double demands of entertainment and food.

Despite its subsequent history, when buildings were added or destroyed, it retains two unique features planned and promoted by Sitticus: the rock theatre where in the early seventeenth century was staged the first open-air opera performance this side of the Alps, and the waterworks, revealing a crude sense of humour from this archbishop. A favourite entertainment was to have the guests seated round the prince's marble table in the grounds and, if they got drunk or Sitticus got bored, to switch on the water sprays that came up through their seats (but not through his).

In those days the visitors would be led down a wide spiral staircase to the Wasser-Spiele (water toys) in the grottos in the palace itself; and they would go into the garden via Neptune's Grotto with its yawning mouth and, when you least expect it, 'rain' pouring down from the ceiling. Modern guests begin in the garden with a guide who seems to be a direct descendant of Sitticus. 'Wet surprises follow later,' he chortles. And indeed they do.

Among the grottos is a shell one with a painted stucco ceiling; a ruined one with walls full of bursting and gaping crevices; and a birdsong one, the 'voices' produced by the sounds of air escaping from organ pipes standing in water. Outside there is a water-bell under which flowers keep fresh for months and a fantastic figure theatre built by a Dürnberg miner in four years.

Its inscription states: 'For the visitor to admire, for youth as an entertainment, for the gardens as an ornament, and for posterity as a memorial.' The theatre shows dozens of figures doing different things—soldiers marching up and down, trumpeters blowing their horns from the balconies, every conceivable tradesman and craftsman busy in the courtyards. Although the mechanism is really primitive, because the wheels are wooden discs and the cogs are metal pegs, it all works so easily it can be moved by a child. Every item in the Wasser-Spiele works by water pressure only, a remarkable achievement.

The sole purpose of Hellbrunn was to glorify the ruling archbishop. The sculptures in the gardens depict classical gods and heroes and some are connected with the theatre. At least two—Orpheus and a Roman emperor—look very like Sitticus himself and this was probably deliberate. The interior of the house is rather disappointing, for what is left is pretty crude, but the stroll to the Stein Theatre through the beechwoods is enchanting and in 1968 you could drive up to it for the first time when they re-started, as a trial, a season of open-air performances once more.

Almost nothing has been changed or constructed here since Sitticus first had the walls hewn into the right shape after the natural amphitheatre had been formed by quarrying for material to build the palace. The first show was on 31 August 1617, and bravely titled 'Artistic play of the Holy Virgin Christine, an excellent work'. Sitticus made one other grand gesture here, when he promised Maximilian, governor of Tyrol, there would be a new house for him to stay in when he came to visit the following month. The overworked Santino Solari did it, in 1615, and the result is a nonsensical miniature castle called, naturally, Monats-Schlösschen (Month Castle).

You might imagine that after all this construction the next archbishop along the line would have little else to add, but Paris Lodron, whose coat of arms shows a lion with a comically curly 'pretzel' tail, did not think so. He finished the cathedral, and the date, 1628, is the second of the three inlaid into its façade. And as he ruled during the Thirty Years War he was responsible for many of the fortifications in Salzburg. The ramparts around the Mirabell, then the only building in this part of the city, were made in Lodron's time, and the remains can still be seen in the gardens; so was the gateway to the Hohensalzburg fortress, today looking very different from its garrison era up to 1860.

Walking up the hill to it gives you the real feeling of its strength as well as understanding why no one succeeded in raiding it. Hohensalzburg is enormous, but it has not had a very interesting past and only two things are worth noting: the little wooden organ called the Salzburger Stier, dating from 1502, which is the only open-air one in Austria, and the story of the bull-washing ceremony in the seventeenth century which gave the locals the nickname they still hold.

The legend begins during a civil war, when the peasants sat at the bottom of the hill and waited to starve out the townsfolk hidden in their fortress. When the castle inmates were down to their last bull they paraded him on the parapet for the benefit of the peasants below, then took him back inside, painted him another colour, and showed him again. They repeated this manoeuvre so often the foolish peasants believed the townsfolk must still have hundreds of animals left for food and so gave up the battle. The people of Salzburg are therefore nicknamed Stierwascher (bull washer) and a modern folklore group have chosen this as their title.

Despite the frenetic building activity of the early archbishops, the beautiful architectural gems of the province's capital came later, and luckily most of them survived the disastrous fire of 1818 which destroyed so much of the town. Salzburg was already showing its heavy Italian influence (if the archbishops were not educated there themselves, they sent for their builders and designers and craftsmen from Italy) with its five squares, a must in a mediaeval Italian town.

Today's count is more than five because Makartplatz (named after a nineteenth-century painter) had until the middle of the last century a house in its centre, so was never included. The golden era of Austria's most famous architects, Lucas von Hildebrandt and Fischer von Erlach, proved the real heritage left behind. Hildebrandt designed the present Mirabell palace in the early eighteenth century; von Erlach was responsible for the baroque gardens, the balustrades and the marble urns.

The Raphael Donner marble staircase, around 1726, is the palace's best-loved treasure, with cherubs sitting on the banisters and statues in niches by Donner's pupils. It is also probably the most photographed staircase anywhere, for a curious reason. The palace, now local government offices, includes on the first floor the registry office, a marble hall which doubles for chamber music. People come from all over Europe to wed here and afterwards have their picture taken at the bottom of the stairs, alongside the little cherub with his hand to his head in an attitude of despair!

The Mirabell gardens include the famous rose one, an open-air hedge theatre planted in the seventeenth century, and at the corner of the fountain stone statues of the four elements—water, fire, earth, air. The renowned marionette theatre plays Mozart, so the plaque in these gardens commemorating its founder, Anton Aicher, incorporates a miniature Mozart. There is light relief to be found in the dwarf garden, full of grotesque though funny dwarf statues showing the trades of Salzburg and collected from various parts of the province. No one, though, knows quite how old they are.

The nicest thing about the palace gardens is that they run into and are a part of the Kurgarten, which is full of lovely plane trees. The natives stroll around during their lunch hour and on summer afternoons it is a good beginning—or ending—to historical sightseeing.

Apart from the Mirabell there are only three other interesting items to be seen on this right bank of the river: St Sebastian's cemetery already mentioned; Makartplatz for Holy Trinity, the first of four churches built by von Erlach in Salzburg; and the house in the same square in which Mozart lived from the age of seven (not to be confused with the one in which he was born). It was badly damaged in the second world war and they decided not to reconstruct but simply left standing what escaped the bombs.

Across the river are more signs of war damage, but also the original old city where the Italian design really comes off. Getreidgasse, for instance, not open to traffic, is mostly fourteenth- and fifteenth-century houses, and though it is not a straight road because it followed the course of the river, there is always, somehow, a view to the end; it is a system the stone masons followed elsewhere to ensure that the eye could reach for something lovely. In Salzburg the eye does not need the bait, for at close range in this street are all those lovely wrought-iron painted gold shop signs, inside the Café Mozart are the older folk playing chess of an afternoon, and no. 9 is Mozart's birthplace, a spacious third-floor apartment.

Life must have been a little cramped for the inhabitants in this district, for if it was not the river running almost into your living room, then it was the rough rock face of the Mönchsberg behind where, in 1669, a landslide killed more than 200, and a grave in St Sebastian's cemetery tells the story of that tragedy in verse. It cannot happen again, for every spring the rock face is surveyed to see if any section has worked loose or if there are cavities needing filling. The fellows who tap for trouble like large-scale dentists are quaintly called Bergputzer (mountain cleaners).

The stage of the festival theatre, previously Dietrich's court stables, is hewn out of this face, and the summer riding school next door which is part of it has 96 rock loggias in three tiers for the spectators. The small new concert hall alongside is backed by rock, too, and has a sliding roof for wet weather, though customers complain that the deafening noise of rain upon the roof is worse than getting wet! The conversion was finished in the early 1960s after earlier plans to build a new Festspielhaus at Hellbrunn in 1924 fell through.

Despite Mozart's upbringing here, Salzburg began comparatively late in its history to cash in on the musical scene. Its festival, together with the Wagnerian one run by Herbert von Karajan at Easter, fills the town coffers and a street has been renamed in honour of the Vienna Philharmonic, not to the unqualified delight of the residents there who rather wanted to stick to the name they had grown up with.

Once embarked on an annual musical cavalcade with an image throughout the world of being a musical capital, Salzburg has let no opportunity slip to take advantage of the situation. Mozartian reminders, for instance, include those two houses, St Peter's where his Mass in C minor was first performed, the family grave in St Sebastian's and the Mozarteum music academy. The Glockenspiel, with 35 bells, in Residenzplatz, plays Mozart melodies three times a day, although it was bought from Antwerp 50 years or more before the composer was born, as part of an archbishop's trading deal. Unfortunately he forgot to 'buy' someone who knew how it worked and the bell stayed silent for its first few years until a Dutchman was called to manipulate it.

Part of the festival celebrations is a torch dance in national costume around the fountain in the centre of Residenzplatz, and when you settle the bill at a café here, try and believe that the horses blowing water so disdainfully through their nostrils on the fountain are not making a silent comment on your foolhardiness. For a drink at this point in Salzburg is a breathtakingly expensive to-do, nice as the view is.

Given that the weather record is not exactly encouraging, they struggle on with quite a number of open-air events (maybe festival-lovers do not believe they have gained the real flavour unless the performance is beneath the stars or clouds). Hofmannsthal's *Everyman* is the traditional curtain-raiser to the jamboree, since Max Reinhardt and Richard Strauss began the festival in 1920, and it is always performed against the backcloth of the cathedral whose third date, 1959, inlaid into its façade, is so modern that further investigation is essential.

The date marks the reconstruction following a bomb that fell straight through the cupola. Inside, the ceiling of the dome has been repainted copying from slides of the original. The elegant, beautifully proportioned shape remains, the font where Mozart was baptised has been given a modern cover, the new pulpit does not jar. The crypt where are buried all the archbishops except St Rupert and Dietrich, has been restored in modern style.

Salzburg is embarrassingly rich in churches and the visitor without weeks to spend here tends to be selective in those he sees. St Sebastian's, on Linzergasse, has already been mentioned for its cemetery and mausoleum. University Church, built at the end of the seventeenth century, is reckoned to be among the finest in Europe. But the real eye-opener is the Franciscan church, for the lot, in terms of architectural styles are all bundled up together. It began in the eighth century, acquired a romanesque aisle in the thirteenth century, a gothic choir in the fifteenth, baroque chapels during the seventeenth and a baroque high altar in the early eighteenth.

Astonishingly, it does not look a muddle but manages some sort of harmony despite its variegated history. When the cathedral was destroyed in the middle ages the Franciscan church was the most important in Salzburg. The archbishop lived alongside and actually built his house into the church, a sort of renaissance annexe so that he could stroll to the service without leaving home.

For such a civilised city, its university has had rather bad luck. It was founded in the seventeenth century, then closed, with the exception of the theology faculty, during the decline and depressions from 1810. It reopened for philosophy a few years ago in 1964 and the famous academy of music dates from 1953.

The 120,000 inhabitants should be grateful for that depression, for it is one reason why Salzburg has remained so harmonious and so little, architecturally, has changed. They not only have a compact, beautiful city, but above and around it are lovely places to visit, some within walking distance, or, for the lazy, a quick lift or funicular from the centre, as is the case with the Mönschsberg and the cablecar from the Festungsgasse to the fortress.

One of the towers up here, by the way, had a very accurate siting for its cannon balls: diagonally across the river into a gap left specially between the houses. Why there? Because any visitors to town from Linz or elsewhere had to pass the spot, and presumably the Salzburgers would lob over the ammunition on those they believed to be enemies.

If you feel the city hills are just too close to town for an evening's jaunt, then there is the road to the Gaisberg (4,245 feet), all the way to the summit since the middle 1920s, though most people halt at the hotel for the view halfway up, which is also the terminal for a chairlift that can take you back to the valley. Or only seven miles away is the Untersberg (6,100 feet) whose plateau is reached by cablecar. Combining a view with sightseeing could mean a short drive to Maria Plain, a baroque twin-towered pilgrimage church built around 1671-73, for which Mozart composed his 'Coronation' Mass.

Salzburg sits in the north of the province that takes its name. If you imagine Land Salzburg in the shape of a mountaineer's boot, then the capital is sited where the laces would knot high on the ankle, the toe points towards Tyrol, the sole is on the Tauern mountains that form the border with Carinthia and East Tyrol, the heel marks where Styria begins. The current borders date from the mid-nineteenth century, when an order issued by the emperor guaranteed the area the status of an independent province.

A third of the total population live in Salzburg itself, and apart from this there are only three other towns—Hallein, Zell am See and Radstadt—in the five districts, one of which, Pongau, was almost deserted in the eighteenth century, when 20,000 of its inhabitants were forced to flee following persecution of the protestants by Archbishop von Firmian. The persecuted had, prior to this, adopted the district as their own.

Only ten miles or so north of the capital is the birthplace of one of the world's most beautiful carols, 'Silent Night, Holy Night', a poem composed by the Rev. Joseph Mohr, curate of St Nikola in Oberndorf, who asked Franz Xavier Gruber, teacher and organist from Arnsdorf, to set it to music. The first performance was on 24 December 1818, at St Nikola, which has been replaced by a memorial chapel dating from 1937.

This area is called, appropriately, the Salzburger Alpenvorland, and it has warm lakes such as the Wallersee, Mattsee and Obertrumer See. Probably the most popular motoring tour from Salzburg is to the Pinzgau district, which has the Saalach valley, the limestone mountains providing gorges and caves and winter sports resorts of the calibre of Saalbach. It is reached by taking a short cut, called the Deutsche Eck, through Germany and over the tight Stein Pass, steeply wooded and rocky as its name suggests, back into Austria to follow the Saalach river.

The first of the many villages along the banks is Unken, with dilapidated castles dating from the defence of the Festnung Kniepass against Napoleon and a 500-year-old hotel painted a gay pink. Another village, Lofer, was described to me by a first-timer in Austria as 'like a lot of immaculate cuckoo clocks without the cuckoos', and it is from here that people walk through the woods to the von Erlach pilgrimage church of Maria Kirchental, built in 1701, in St Martin bei Lofer, and also reachable by a toll road.

Lamprechtsofen is one of the several caves on the road from

12 Salzburg: the staircase in the Mirabell Palace
13 (overleaf) the *Abbey of Melk*, above the Danube

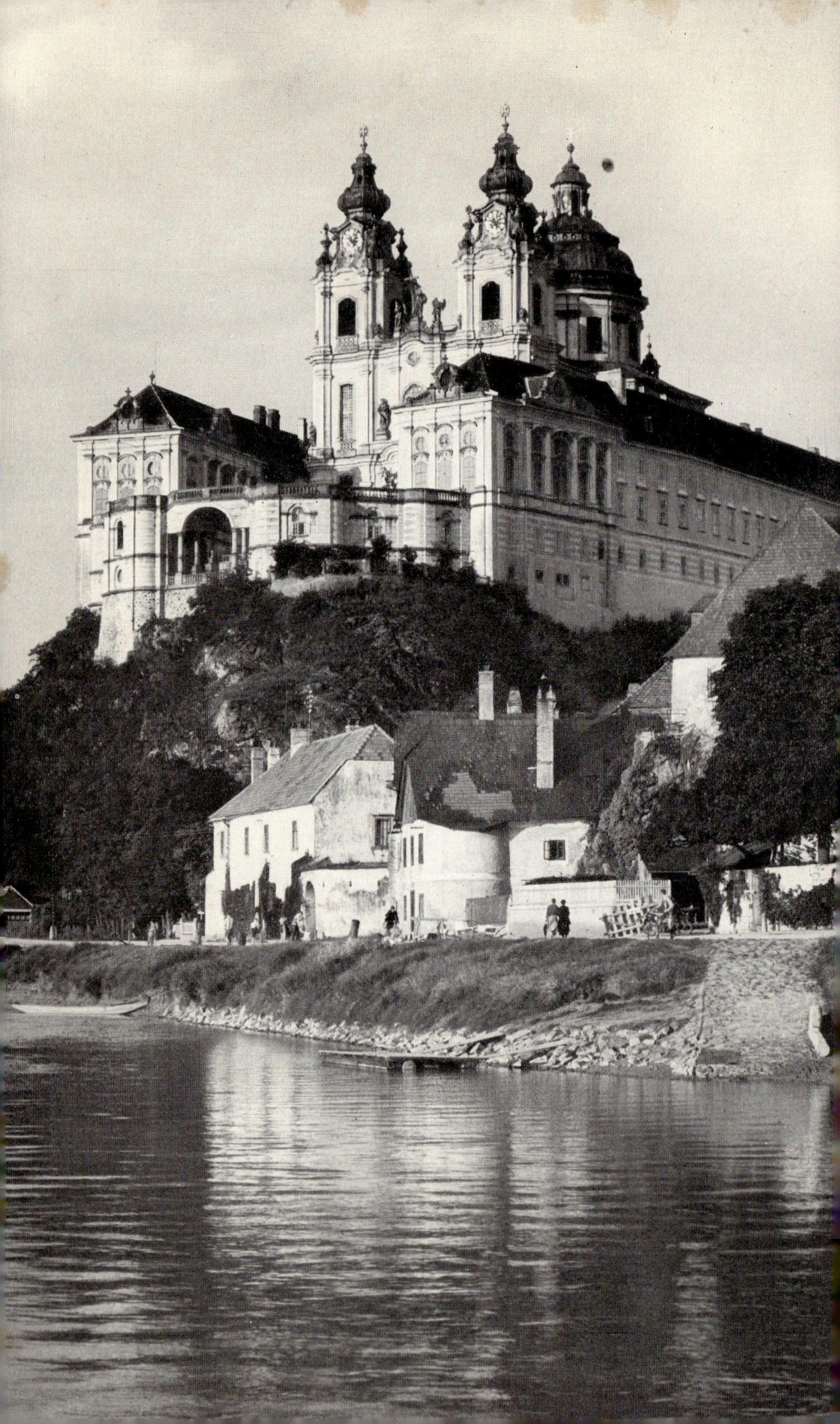

Land Salzburg 91

Lofer to Weissbach, and there is also a highly dramatic power plant, Diesbach, whose pipes run outside down the mountain. The original idea of hiding the pipes inside had to be abandoned when engineers discovered the rock formation would not stand the pressure.

It is soon after this that the valley widens into the basin of Saalfelden, a great area for cattle and horse breeding. The Noriker are big horses bred for farm work; the Haflinger have blond manes and tails, are sand-coloured, small and sturdy for mountain work. Either breed may have been born at Maishofen, where the houses, with flowers tumbling out of window boxes, are scattered through the village, each with its garden, usually in the form of a small orchard.

Here is also the turn-off point to the Glemm valley and Saalbach, which springs to life in the winter with cablecar and lifts leading up to wonderful skiing on the Kohlmaiskopf (5,400 feet) and the Schattberg (more than 6,000 feet). Just south of Maishofen is Zell am See, one of the most important traffic junctions. It is 35 miles north of the Grossglockner, eastwards is the turn-off for the Gastein valley and to the west is the recently constructed Felbertauern tunnel connecting the province with East Tyrol. Like the Grossglockner alpine road, you pay a toll to use the tunnel, and the tickets are interchangeable for either route.

For such a busy situation, lakeside Zell is surprisingly picturesque, with lots of little half squares off-centred so that they give views to the next one, and even the shop whose plaque shows it to have been built in 1968 harmonises with the old buildings. A splendid glass-screened swimming pool alongside the ice rink opened recently, and the natives are very proud of the ozonisation they have used in it in place of chlorine.

The little music pavilion in the park has thrice-weekly concerts, and they reckon the fish are living in the cleanest lake in Austria. Boat trips along its two-and-a-half miles and across its one mile to the little village of Thumersbach are in a fine Dutch boat with glass roof, taking a look at the camping site at one end, and at the other, more energetic pursuits like water ski-jumping and ski-flying with kites and little gliders towed off by light aeroplanes from a level strip. Overlooking the activity are the typical Austrian weekend houses, each with wooden balconies, red and white shutters, cascading flowers, swans and ducks gliding around the boat houses and small yachts.

From anywhere in the village the mountain you notice is the Kitzsteinhorn (10,570 feet) with its glistering glacier reached by a cablecar all the year round and particularly useful for summer skiers. The more modest Schmittenhöhe, at 6,600 feet, also has a cablecar, from which there is a pleasant walk to a chairlift and another cablecar. What visitors may not notice is the homely Hönigkogel, which because it is covered in trees, summit and all, tends to be dismissed as just a little hill, yet it rises to all of 6,000 feet.

Like many resorts in Austria, Zell's popularity dates from the installation of the railway in 1875. There is also a narrow-gauge one which runs westwards for 30 miles or more, linking up with the Upper Pinzgau, passing the Kaprun hydro-electric power plant (one of those cold reservoir lakes) and then to the Krimml waterfalls which drop 900 feet in three stages. At this far end of the valley you have almost left Land Salzburg, the exit to Tyrol being over the Gerlospass.

Eastwards instead of westwards from Zell the main road leads into the neighbouring Pongau district, its narrow valleys including the one to Bad Gastein, which peels off southwards towards the Tauern mountains; or northwards up the Salzach (not to be confused with the Saalach) valley; or eastwards again through the Enns via pretty St Johann to Wagrain, connected by a ski lift circuit to the village of Flachau. It is near here that one of the province's few towns sits, Radstadt, at the foot of the Tauern pass leading into Styria.

South is the Lungau, the quietest of the five districts, where all the resorts are above 3,000 feet, and to reach Carinthia there is the Katschberg pass to negotiate, not in the grand scale, but with enough avalanche galleries to be dramatic. But to stay longer in Land Salzburg you need to turn north from Radstadt through Eben, which proudly built a modern church ten years ago when it became a parish, and into the wide Lammer valley of meadows and trees to Abtenau, the protective range of the Tennengebirge standing off so that it does not overpower this sweet village.

There must be hundreds so very like it throughout Austria. Most will have, too, a Gasthof Post, the original coaching stop which in Abtenau's case is still run by the same family, pictures of the grandparents in the stage-coach days and the back end of a coach built into the hall. A couple of years ago the village opened its pride and joy, a magnificent open-air swimming pool, and points out its technical marvels—high diving board, competition length, fine changing rooms—while the visitors are more impressed by the rolling green countryside around and the dramatic mountain backcloth.

It is as good a place as any to take in a Schuhplattler evening, which is folklore at its most folkloric. The basic ensemble has a bass wind horn, a trumpet, clarinet, accordion and timpani. The dancers, either in breeches or short lederhosen, always represent various trades and crafts, and their dances always show the baker, miner, lumberjack, whatever, at work. Although it is a fairly crude dance form, it has a vitality and a liveliness and is more than likely to involve the spectators at some stage.

There are no other sights to be seen in Abtenau; for drama you need to change valleys from the Lammer back to the Salzach to visit the largest ice cave in the world, the Eisriensenwelt above Werfen, where legend says the ghost of Charlemagne still roams. Just south of here is the first of the three villages, Bischofshofen, in the Pongau, where every leap year in early January the Run of the Perchts takes place.

This exotic festival goes back to pagan days when the tribes idolised gods and goddesses, but no-one is quite sure how that evolved into today's ceremonies, which they believe are to expel the evil spirits from the farms, thus avoiding a bad harvest and ensuring a prosperous year. All the participants have to be local farmers, males only, and there are three main roles: King Herod as the judge, fining men and women for adultery or drunkenness; the Turk and the Moor, plus a vast chorus of Fair Ones, Ugly Ones, artisans, animals and clowns.

The early pagan star was Frigga or Bergtha, Wodan's wife, who displayed a schizophrenic personality, first of all appearing as a good woman distributing presents to diligent housewives, then as an ugly old witch causing mischief and disaster. Although it is called the Run of the Perchts, this is not strictly speaking accurate, because some of the participants would be hard put to it to run wearing headdresses weighing 66 pounds!

The movement is more like a slow waltzing step. The Fair Perchts are the weighted down ones, particularly in the Bad Gastein version where their tower caps are decorated with mirrors and paper flowers. The Bad Ones wear a devil's horned headdress with sheepskins and cowbells tied to their backsides which make a satisfactory clanking noise as they jump up and down.

The Perchts visit each farm led by the Percht Captain, who wishes the farmer a fertile year; all the Fair Ones, mindful of their hats, do a deep curtsy and then there is a bit of a caper from the chorus and the procession moves on to the next farm. Somewhere along the line a basketwoman carrying a dummy child in swaddling clothes will place it in the hands of a new young wife who, it is claimed, will then become pregnant that year.

If all the frivolity should put you in mind for a rest and a cure, then one of Austria's most famous spas, Bad Gastein, is near Bischofshofen. It is especially dramatic to arrive at dusk via the narrow, sinister valley, for the lights of Gastein twinkle deceptively close but the road switchbacks tantalisingly on for what seems an age before you are there. It has been known as a spa for 600 years, a legend saying that the magical water was discovered by two priests who gave it to a wounded deer who then recovered. Maximilian I was here for the cure around 1500 but the heyday of the spa was at the turn of the century into the early twentieth.

Royalty and aristocracy used Bad Gastein as an away-from-it-all spot, and Emperor Franz Joseph and Wilhelm 1 of Prussia signed a peace treaty in the 1860s in the Villa Solitude. A picture in the town reading room shows the resort as it was then—apart from the Villa, there were only a few other buildings like the Schwaigerhaus which built a special entrance for Bismarck so that he would not have to climb the stairs on his several visits from 1877 to 1886.

Though the town has naturally expanded a great deal since that picture, the flavour of Bad Gastein has not really changed at all since the railway line was built, opening up the valley to large numbers of travellers. They began the line, from St Veit and Schwarzach, in 1902 and on 20 September 1905, Franz Joseph made the first ceremonial journey into town by train.

The old prints showing the splendid scene do not include the tricky bit, which was that the inexperienced train driver failed to halt so that the emperor would descend on to the red carpet laid out on the platform. For a few panic-stricken minutes officials, with no knowledge of the locomotive engine, did not know whether to ask the driver to move up a bit or shift the carpet! They wisely decided to move the latter.

The local authorities regard the station, still exactly as it was then, as an eyesore, but to visitors it puts Bad Gastein in its right perspective. Many of the hotels date from this time, too, and the Hotel d'Europe to this day hands you a price list including the charges for your servants. Franz Joseph favoured the Hotel Straubinger and stayed in a wood-panelled room with his Empress. Schubert liked the old coaching inn, too, and composed the Gasteiner Symphony here in August 1825.

The hotel has been run by the same family for 300 years and its emblem, a post horn of course, also has the symbol of the spa, a water jug, after the 17 springs which gush out water at a temperature of 42° Centigrade and have a daily capacity of 4.6 million litres, though only about a third of this is piped round the town and down to Hofgastein. One would like to think that the water has a similar rejuvenating effect on humans as it has on flowers, which grow marvellously well.

Unfortunately those tottering down to the Kursaal of a morning belie the powers, and the breezy comment in the guidebook that the cure can be ideally combined with winter sports under medical supervision does not, somehow, seem a likely one. As a spa, there are certain disadvantages for the infirm. The houses grow tall on the sides of the mountain and the steepness means that you can enter a hotel on its ground floor and leave it at the fifth on the next street up; the difference in height from the valley floor to the highest hotel is 800 feet.

But Bad Gastein has adapted itself as best it can to the needs of its customers and awards walking medals on a points system for the brave ones who try. Fifty points gains the bronze edelweiss, 150 the gold (and you need to do a lot of walking for that). Most visitors in search of health meet their friends for a chat in the Kursaal, soon to become a three-tier congress centre, take coffee over the mid-morning open-air concert, then stroll along one of the promenades, perhaps the Kaiser-Wilhelm walk from the centre of town to the Grüner Baum.

Wherever you are in the resort you can hear the sound of the waterfall that roars noisily through its centre, a spray screen at the bottom to protect walkers on a nearby wooded path. To photograph the water successfully, you have exactly 15 minutes each day, the only time when the sun glints upon it. If it is beginning to sound as though everyone in Bad Gastein must be approaching their centenary, then this is misleading: winter time sees crowds of skiers and international skiing races.

Summer activities can be far more strenuous than strolling and drinking the water and feeding the tame squirrels. On the valley floor is the golf club and riding school with an indoor riding hall for bad weather. Near the railway station and terminal of the Stubnerkogel cablecar is a fancy new swimming complex, the Felsenbad, one indoor pool connected to an outdoor one by a little canal. It has a sauna, restaurant and brightly coloured bulbous plastic armchairs, and Bad Gastein reckons that in winter people will come straight off the ski run into the pool, and to this end they are planning a linking bridge over the road to reach it.

Up the road and heading towards the Tauern tunnel and Carinthia is the unique healing gallery at Böckstein, transformed from a gold mine which had been flourishing in the fourteenth and fifteenth centuries. Hermann Goering, in charge of mining during the second world war, planned to re-establish the industry here, and to everyone's surprise the prisoners-of-war detailed for the job came out of the mine healthier than when they went in, though they found little gold.

A post-war investigation revealed that the humid air contained the same substance, but to a greater degree of concentration, as the thermal waters. There were traces of uranium, too, but well below the radioactive danger point. The situation of the mine is charming, driving up the Nassfeld valley (literally wet field and so called because of all its little cascades) to the mountain of Radhausberg, which means wheelhouse after the wheel used in the gold mining industry.

A little train takes the customers into the mountain at the Stollenkurhaus, where they are tended by doctors in bathing trunks in the old mining galleries. The heat and humidity increase the further in you go, from $37.5°$ Centigrade at the coolest station up to $41.5°$ the hottest. They reckon that ten admissions, an hour at a time, over three or four weeks, completes the cure, and costs around £20. And with 6,000 people from May until October the gold mine is clearly bringing in a different kind of gold.

Plans to make it an all-year-round cure station are difficult, partly because of the dangers of avalanches in the winter. Even if they get over that hurdle and manage to keep the road and valley open then they would need to open up more of the mine. There are still miles of it stretching back to the middle ages, but one's own eerie feeling is that they should not investigate or expand any further, but leave Böckstein as it is, unique and intriguing.

5 Upper Austria

The only proper place to begin in Upper Austria is down a salt mine, for this province lived off the stuff for centuries and contains by far the largest portion of the Salzkammergut (salz for salt, kammer for chamber, gut for area), all dating back to mediaeval donkeys, goats and sheep who revealed the presence of salt to the humans by refusing to move from the grazing ground they found so tasty. It also appeared to do them good.

Salt became known, fairly accurately, as white gold, and could hardly be bettered as a trading commodity. Linz, for instance, the capital, was a Celtic settlement on the plain, neatly situated for passing the white gold to the Adriatic and Baltic and receiving in return amber up the Danube. Hallstatt, the oldest mine in Europe, had a splendid legal bartering charter to insure food in return for its salt. As an aid to communications, the delivering of white gold was invaluable, for the trading ships were the only means of passing on information to somewhere else.

Then people began to wonder if the animals were not right about the properties of salt to keep them healthy, and in Bad Ischl the inhabitants became the first guineapigs for the cure baths. The royal accolade for the healing white gold came from Franz Joseph's mother who, when she did not bear any children, took the waters there. The subsequent royal offspring became known as Salt Princes and Princesses and set the industry developing in quite another way, in spas for the nobility plus this slightly risqué fertility theme, which, incidentally, the natives still believe in today.

Tourism was a natural follow-up to the spas. They are still mining away in all directions, visitors are still heading for brine, sulphur, mud or iodine, depending on their complaint, and the 60

Alpine and lake resorts that make up the Salzkammergut get very crowded with summer visitors.

Going down a mine for the fun of it is not the casual operation it sounds, even at one of the smallest at Bad Ischl, now employing a mere 60 people as opposed to three times as many at Hallstatt. They receive visitors from May to September but themselves work all the year round and have been doing so since 1775. They reckon that there is another century to go before the supply is exhausted, and it is carefully controlled, the output restricted (otherwise the mountain would collapse) and the miners moving down inside, layer by layer.

Visitors dress for the part like the miners, in boiler suits, with string round the ankles and brightly coloured skull caps, then take their places on a little carriage, sitting astride a plank. Rattling into the mountain slightly uphill, with the help of an engine, has 'Orpheus in the Underworld' overtones, and there is no conception of what might be at the other end. What is at the other end is quite a long walk along a narrow corridor, one of the many that has to be enlarged every three years as the mountain contracts, and then down a chute (like in a children's playground) to reach a large lake, prettily lit by fairy lights.

Here is the first of the technical discussions where most of us learn for the first time that the salt is not hacked out of the walls, but cavities are filled with water, the water extracts the salt, the workers pipe off the water, then boil it down to evaporate, leaving the white gold. There are more chutes and more diagrams and we eventually stop feeling foolish in our skull caps clutching our lanterns. We find marvellous red-tinged mineral deposits, then there is a shattering finish back on the little carriage. This time it needs no engine as the route is downhill, and we swoosh out of the mountain like a big dipper at a fun fair, the wind whistling past our ears, the sensation of dark speed quite frightening.

Hallstatt's mine is even more of an eye-opener, for to get anywhere near it you first have to take a cablecar from the town, and here they do not even consider the prospect of closing down in a hundred years, so rich is the supply. Private merchants had the selling rights until the government took over in the last century, and it was while building a new corridor they found a man perfectly preserved, clothes and all, dating from B.C. He probably got lost and froze or starved to death; regrettably, the finders did not think of the historical significance, but only that the poor fellow had lacked a funeral. So they buried him, and Hallstatt never knows when, if ever, they will find another example.

It is a macabre story, but this resort has many more to tell. The lake of the same name is quite the most sinister of the Salzkammergut, hemmed in by high mountains and overlooked by the 9,840-foot Dachstein and its glacier, and these waters are certainly not for swimming. The sun, too, leaves the village early, but do not let the shadows deter you from a visit. The natives have found weapons proving that someone lived here in 400 B.C., and a massive graveyard (1,000 graves) up the hill at the back of the town gave the name Hallstatt to this period of European history. Written records began in the twelfth century and a tower from that time is now a restaurant.

The first place to head for is the church, for several reasons, firstly to watch the mountains turn pink at dusk. The building retains its gothic simplicity, was restored fairly recently and contains an altar with interchangeable side panels. They are called Flügel, after the side wings that open and close, and this example is of gilded wood, made in the fifteenth century.

In the crypt is buried a salt merchant who died in 1658, his will stating that his body was to be taken for an airing round the lake by steamer every 50 years. They only stopped this jaunt in the nineteenth century and when they opened the coffin a decade ago found the clothes (except for shoes) all intact.

In the tiny churchyard are beautiful tombstones, each with its wooden or wrought-iron cross, but so short is space that the deceased rest here for only ten years. Then the skeleton head is hung out to bleach and the name inscribed on the forehead. There are now about 1,200 of them in rows in the charnel house, some with special motifs, for you can leave instructions in your will as to the flowers or other decorations you would like put on your skull. People still do!

With so cramped a town, the people of Hallstatt use every inch of space, covering their homes with flowers—hanging baskets, window boxes, pot plants. The front door is often at roof level, the windows tiny because glass was expensive. The original village was totally wood and almost totally burnt down in the fifteenth century, with the exception of two houses which survived and forever commemorate the blaze by being painted pink.

Most of the others are a mere 200 years old, with wooden upper floors, and a higgledy-piggledy look that makes them seem top-heavy. Or maybe it is just an optical illusion. Hallstatt can produce a crushing, oppressed feeling because of its situation, the dramatic glacier above, its icy lake, the darkness so early in the day, but there is a shivering fascination all the same.

From here, or rather back, because it is the most southern lake, the water gets warmer and the climate sunnier (if you are lucky), and the next one along the road might be in a different country. This is the famed Bad Ischl, visited by Franz Joseph's mother for the fertility cure. Her son continued his mother's patronage, in fact for an unbelievable number of years from his childhood to the first world war, but not, of course, for the same reason!

His summer villa (though we would call it a hunting lodge) was a wedding present to the emperor and empress, and as he was mad about hunting he naturally spent a good deal of time here. He also had a good friend who also spent a greater part of the summer in Bad Ischl—the actress, Katharina Schratt. Poor Katharina, like everyone who had anything to do with the emperor, had to be up at dawn ready to greet him after he had returned from hunting and before going home to breakfast at the Kaiservilla at six a.m.

The exterior of the house—trailing plants, orange trees, a little fountain in the courtyard—is very pleasant, but inside it has been taken over by the trappings and trophies of hunting: how, where, when and what Franz Joseph shot (like 2,000 chamois), gory hunting pictures, and a hideous collection of presents from other royalty. The furnishings and fittings from France and Italy, some shockers from Queen Victoria, an exquisite chest from the Emperor of China, a baroque clock from Napoleon that needs winding once a year, all add to the disharmony.

The fact that the rooms are fairly small completes the clutter, even in the study with its famous three-emperor corner where Edward VII, Wilhelm of Germany and Franz Joseph met. It was the only occasion when the emperor travelled, with Edward, in a motor car; yet he did not despise new fangled ideas, added electricity to the Kaiservilla and put a cigar lighter on his desk. While Franz Joseph was busy with hunting and affairs of state Elizabeth indulged the two major passions in her life—riding and keeping fit.

She had 40 horses at the hunting lodge (portraits of a number of them are scattered through the rooms) and a little cottage up the hill containing her keep-fit equipment. You might imagine that with all these energetic pastimes the royal pair would eat heartily in the evening, but they never did, and like at Schönbrunn in Vienna, an invitation to dine with them was dreaded. It was probably worse here than at Schönbrunn, which at least had kitchens, an item totally lacking at Bad Ischl. The royal meals were cooked elsewhere and reheated on arrival at the Kaiservilla.

The royal patronage not unnaturally ensured the resort's prosperity and development. In the way of all Austrians, the aristocracy copied their emperor by building summer villas around, and the merchants made sure that he had the same amenities he could get in Vienna, including Zauner, Ischl's answer to Vienna's wondrous pastry shop, Demel. The cure began here in 1823 and is flourishing still; the town retains its fashionable, yet old-fashioned quality, and you would be hard put to it to buy at a reasonable price one of the villas used each season by well-to-do city dwellers.

Although Ischl is situated right in the Salzkammergut it is not, of course, on a lake; for water you can drive a few miles to the Wolfgangsee, whose two major resorts are completely different in character from either Hallstatt or Bad Ischl. St Gilgen, officially in the province of Land Salzburg, is up against the popularity of the White Horse Inn at St Wolfgang across the water, so provides a different claim to fame: Mozart's mother and sister lived here.

The resort itself dates from the late nineteenth century and runs both a summer and winter season with its chairlift up the nearby Zwölferhorn. It is also built in pretty clusters, so its atmosphere is less claustrophobic than some other lakeside villages. If you like being with the rest of the world, then you will cross the lake, move back into the province of Upper Austria, fight your way past all the charabancs on the outskirts of St Wolfgang and join the stream of people in the souvenir shops. I was there in June and imagine that in high season there can hardly be standing room along the narrow streets.

Its unbelievable popularity is due to the musical comedy, 'White Horse Inn', written in the hotel of that name here and first performed in Berlin in November 1930. Today the town seems even more musical comedy than the real thing, the Wolfgangsee is certainly the busiest lake with craft of every kind zig-zagging about, and in high season up to 8,000 people crowd in daily. It costs them a good deal, for St Wolfgang can hardly be called one of the cheaper resorts in the Salzkammergut.

With all this modern tourism one is inclined to forget the original St Wolfgang, *circa* 976, who was a hermit on the nearby Falkenstein mountain and a replica of whose cell is in the church; alongside hanging on the walls are the presents brought by pilgrims. It is an ornate baroque church but does have one of the few Flügel—winged altars—like that of Hallstatt, in Austria.

It should be clear by now that each lake has its 'speciality', so on the circuit another stop might be at Attersee, proudly proclaiming its expanse of water is the largest, at 13 miles long, and also the warmest, because the mountains do not crowd in on the resort. The Celts were here once upon a time, built their houses on stilts, whether for safety from wild animals or sheer convenience is not known, and a few of the stilts are still around. In winter Attersee organises a highly dramatic form of ski-joring across the lake, the skiers drawn by motor cyclists with spiked tyres. The nearest most of us will get to this is a look at the photographs in the hotel foyer.

The Salzkammergut is one area of Austria where the road sign showing a leaping deer should be noted even more carefully. I nearly killed a young stag who slipped as he tried to jump back on to the verge, on my way from Attersee to neighbouring Mondsee, along which the scenery changes rapidly from the Drachenwand, a dramatic rock of a mountain, to gentle slopes where is the resort of Mondsee.

It is a lively bustling place, especially if there is a confirmation at the double-towered church, and in the square outside are crowds of little girls dressed in white with coronets and carrying balloons. Inside the church is rather grand, gothic and baroque; and rather gloomy; no wonder, because it is the second largest in the province and because of its size the wedding scene from 'The Sound of Music' was filmed here.

The children run through the market alongside the church and probably do not notice the 1416 farmhouse on the hill above, which is part of the Rauchhaus open-air museum. Nor would the youngsters dare to enter the castle which flanks the other side of the church. It (and the whole lake) has been owned since the end of the nineteenth century by the dukes of Almeida. The current duke lives there, but also allows folklore sessions a couple of times a week, and there is a bar, open to the public, called, naturally, Castello, which is very expensive.

The gothic library is unusual because it has no books, the contents being sent to Vienna when the monastery was closed, and including a collection of illuminated scripts and the oldest bible translation. Dating from 748, this was the oldest abbey in Upper Austria, but its dissolution turned out to be fairly lucky for the town's commerce. Napoleon gave the building to a favourite marshal who transformed it into a castle in 1891 and, while pursuing his two great interests, agriculture and food, discovered the famous Mondsee cheese.

Mondsee continues to sell its cheese to visitors and like other popular Salzkammergut resorts entertains them in midsummer with lakeside firework festivals, which is one excuse to light 250 fires on the fearsome Drachenwand and retell the story behind the curious gaping hole in the mountain's side. It all goes back to a priest's housekeeper who was given to overwork and despite repeated warnings from everybody refused to rest on the sabbath. She was told she would go to hell, disappeared that night, and the hole appeared in the side of the Drachenwand the next day.

Austria's only government fish research station across the lake at Kreuzstein is a modern contrast to the dug-out pine tree canoes the old fishermen used on the lake—and one still does. It is only a decade ago that Mondsee regretfully relinquished its Emmett-style branch railway that connected it with Bad Ischl and Salzburg. Part of the station has become a car park. If you want more fairy stories like the Drachenwand, then drive on to Traunsee, the resort of Gmunden and the seventeenth-century castle of Orth, now a school for foresters, built on a peninsula stretching out into the lake.

This story begins with a powerful count who lived in the castle with his beautiful daughter and left her under strict guard when he went off to war. Nevertheless she met and fell in love with a young knight. Father was furious and dispatched daughter to a nunnery, but the keen suitor was not put off. He built a castle across the lake from the nunnery and swam over every night, guided by a light the young lady left in her window. One stormy night the light went out and he drowned. The young lady committed suicide when she learned of her lover's death and the place on the shore where the two bodies were found is called Antlasort.

The cheerful lakeside town of Gmunden has taken to tourism within the last century. It was a major salt centre under the Babenbergs when the black and white trading ships were the only communication with the farthermost Salzkammergut. This kind of trading went on until 1836, but the railway and steam trains could not help Gmunden, which lost its salt charter a few years later to Ebensee. It had to find another outlet and as it had recently built its famous esplanade more than half a mile long, turned to the obvious choice: spa and health resort, particularly apt as it faces south for warmth and sunshine.

The first thing you should do is take the lift up the Grünberg to view the lake and all that is happening upon it. Naturally the town holds everything possible afloat, like the Corpus Christi processions, fireworks, a lakeland 'shuffle' and a ghostly night tour. This resort's special claim is as the eastern guardian of the Salzkammergut or, more accurately, the Traunstein mountain is the guardian.

It has also, sitting on a hairpin bend on the lake road, a stone lion without a tongue (today's statue is a copy of the original one destroyed by vandals a few years ago). How did he come to be speechless? It is another legend about the man who designed and built the road. He wanted the lion to commemorate his work, though whether he actually did it himself or called in someone else is not clear. But whoever was responsible for the sculpture forgot the animal's tongue and the road-designer was so distressed that he committed suicide by drowning himself in the lake.

It is doubtful whether the poor fellow would find room for a quiet suicide today, so cruelly overcrowded can Gmunden become in high season. The fact that its bathing station has room for 5,000 should indicate that rather more people than that try and crowd into the resort during July and August. But people are essential to the well-being of the Salzkammergut, despite its inconsistent weather, and many visitors never bother to explore further, which is a pity.

Upper Austria may not have the grandeur and splendour of the abbeys and castles of neighbouring Lower Austria, but it has two gems, St Florian and Kremsmunster, both within easy reach of Linz, the provincial capital. St Florian, patron saint of

14 Vienna: Schönbrunn

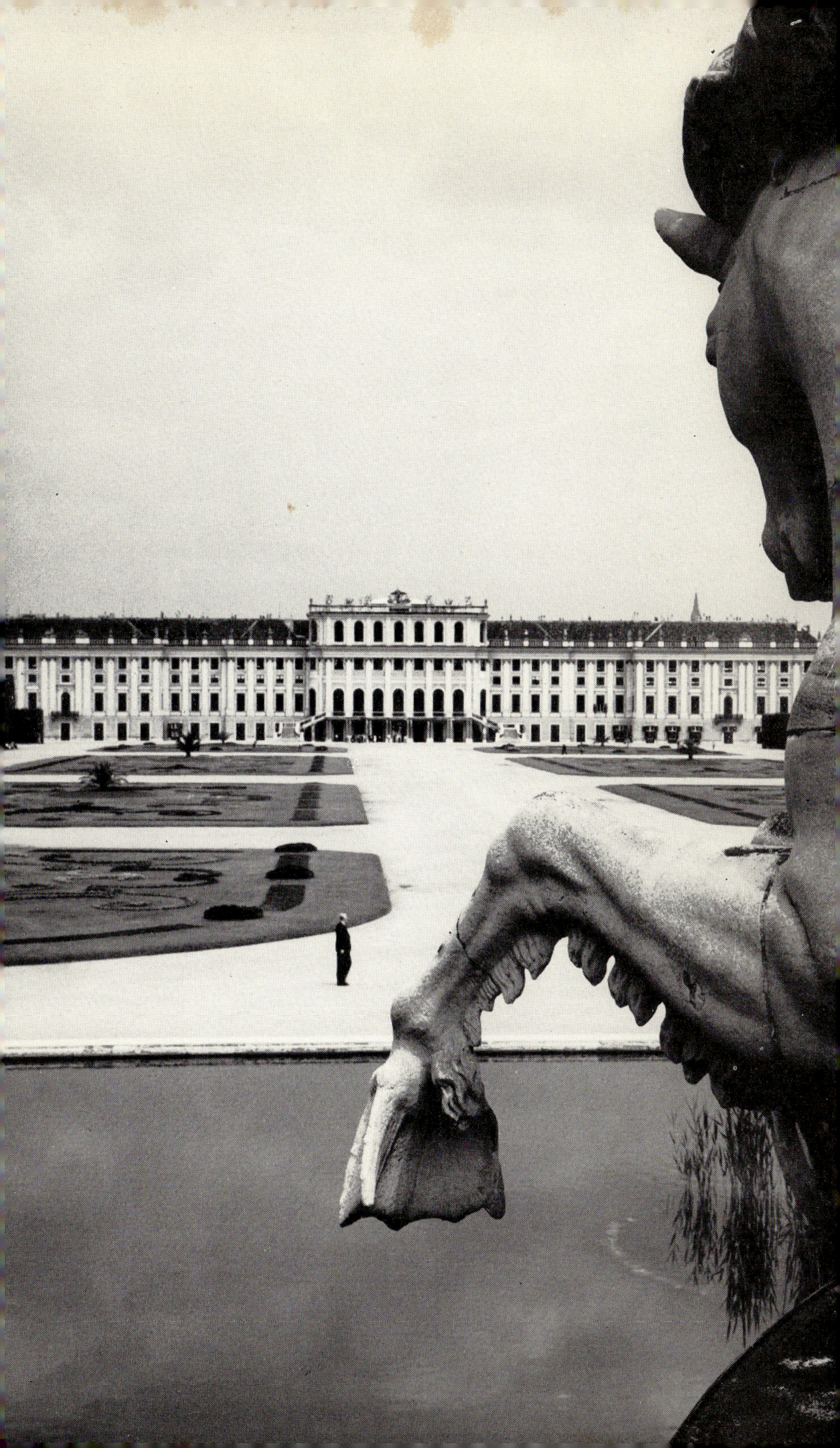

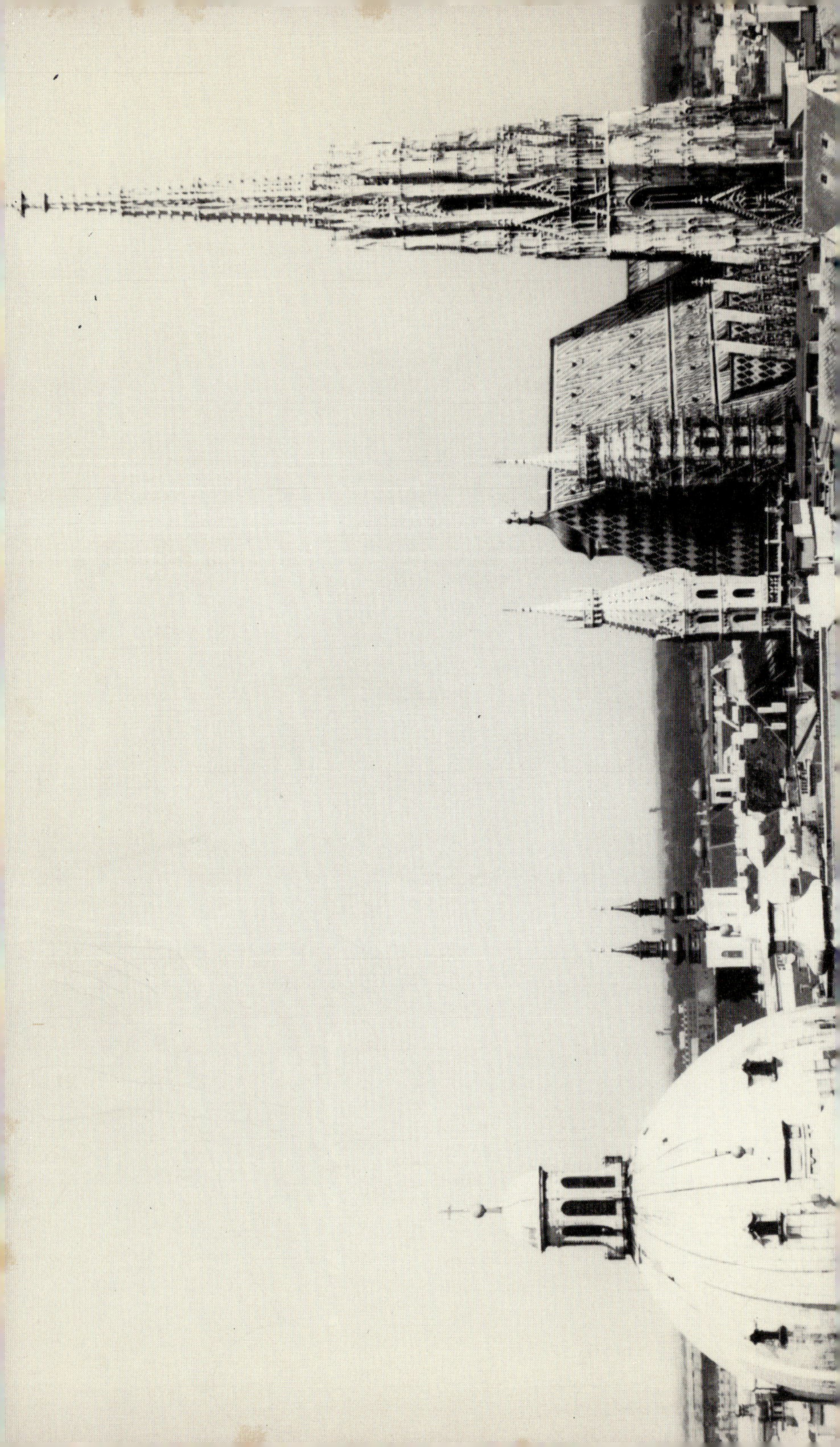

fire, was a Roman officer who became a Christian and was martyred by being thrown into the river Enns with a stone around his neck. They began building the present monastery towards the end of the seventeenth century, and it took something like 65 years to complete.

So it is baroque, of course, by Carlone and Prandtaur, with heavy emphasis, as at Melk in Lower Austria, on the final military victory over the Turks and the final religious victory over protestantism. The Marble Hall alone took five years to build and is a sort of victory bonanza with Charles VI in a golden chariot being drawn not by horses but by defeated Turks; there is a Prince Eugene room, too, though this army commander was never here.

There is also a sense of ingenuity, almost fun, missing in other Austrian monasteries. The dignified library, for instance, with ceiling paintings by Altomonte, has several fancy tricks which would not be out of place as space-savers in today's small modern homes (not that there is any shortage of room at St Florian!). The sides of the writing tables double as hidden bookcases and the chairs fold into the tables; what seems to be just a square table turns into a ladder topped by a pulpit from which a monk read to his companions. The Audience Hall has a real fireplace (unusual in ceramic stove days), and if you stand in the middle of the room and clap your hands there is a curious rattling echo.

Like all monasteries there is an emperor's wing—the stucco staircase and wrought-iron gates are justly famous—but the royal apartments, including Maria-Theresia's in red brocade which was used for one night by Pope Pius VI, lack the finery to be seen elsewhere. St Florian concentrates on its church, crypt and favourite teacher, Anton Bruckner, who was born near here, became first a choirboy, then organist at the monastery and is buried below the organ, the largest in an Austrian church.

Although the composer moved to Linz—a plaque outside St Ignatius church commemorates his 13 years as an organist there —and to Vienna, his spiritual home was always St Florian. But

15   *Vienna: St Stephen's cathedral*

because he was a simple man, the room given over to his possessions is disappointing, containing only Bruckner's piano, brass bedstead, chest of drawers and a few bits and pieces. He never actually lived in it himself.

The church, with Italian decoration, has much marble in pillars and altar figures. When the crypt was being excavated in 1952 walls dating back to Roman times were found, which helped to explain a much earlier discovery in the late thirteenth century of the remains of 6,000 people. They could have been killed in battle, but the bones show no sign of wounds or scars and following the uncovering of Roman walls it is now believed this unfortunate crowd were probably Christian martyrs.

The whole of St Florian is in remarkably good shape because it was renovated for a special exhibition in 1965. On permanent exhibition, though not in the church, are the Sebastian altar paintings from the sixteenth-century Danube school, usually described as realistic, though I would use the word gory, instead!

St Florian was not, in fact, an original design, but was modelled on the other famous abbey, Kremsmunster, which dates back to 777 when it was a fortress against invasions. This building was destroyed by the Magyars, rebuilt first in romanesque style, then gothic, then baroque, and includes the most enchanting fish hatchery I have ever seen. The hatchery is more than 200 feet long, with five tanks fed by 17 springs, so it never freezes, and its style is like an Italian colonnaded courtyard, each linked pond with its own fountain. Fish were bred in this aristocratic setting until the first world war; today's trout are merely for decoration.

Kremsmunster is undoubtedly the Aladdin's cave of Austrian monasteries. Although it is Benedictine, women are allowed on special occasions into the great hall with its 400-year-old chandelier. There are some fine carved wooden ceilings in the abbey but, above all, there are rooms of treasures—gothic and renaissance paintings, elephant bones made into a mid-sixteenth-century chair, 100 snuff boxes covering three centuries, and in an inner sanctuary a bronze wine cup made by Irish monks in 750. The cup was later overlaid with gold and given to the Duke of

Tassilo as a wedding present. Although it is carefully guarded with theft-proof devices, it is by no means just a museum piece. The monks still use it as a wine cup and as a ballot box—which must make it the most precious voting box in the world!

So far there has been hardly a mention of Upper Austria's capital, Linz, but its commercial weight alone justifies a short stop. On the way there from Kremsmunster there are a couple of worthwhile diversions, first to Bad Hall to mingle in a splendid tree-lined park with those taking the cure and find out how and why this spa is famous for eye treatment.

The story goes back to the eighteenth century when a large proportion of the population in the area, though not in Bad Hall itself, were attacked by a mysterious throat disease. Bad Hall inhabitants escaped because they made bread with their 'magic' water. It was in 1824 when they put a name—iodine—to the special property of the springs and began developing the cure.

The second diversion is to Steyr, on the river of that name where it meets the Enns, and a very under-rated place often missed out because people have read somewhere that it has the biggest iron and steel works in Austria and imagine nothing but heavy industry exists. But the plant, bombed during the war, is quite separate from the old town, an elegant quarter built on Steyr's wealthy past.

The town grew up on iron and there is a 1287 document setting out the right to transport ore down the Enns from the iron ore mountain near Eisernerz with a neat clause to protect Steyr's inhabitants. They were given the first option to buy, and, only when they had obtained all they needed over a period of three days could the iron ore merchants sell the product elsewhere. The boats carrying the ore drifted without any power down the fast-flowing Enns and took wheat back in return (there is an old corn warehouse on the river bank still in good condition), this cargo being pulled by horses from the towpath.

Steyr was one of the few places not under a feudal wing and thus able to control its own destiny, electing its first mayor in 1500. But its history was not entirely prosperous. Ninety per cent of the population were protestants and forced to flee during the Counter-Reformation. They wisely chose places in exile where they could still trade in iron while awaiting a suitable moment to return.

After the subsequent depression in the early nineteenth century, one man in particular gave the lead to put Steyr back on its feet. Joseph Werndl, a much-travelled local businessman, had returned from an American tour of gun factories and decided to start manufacturing weapons in his home town. They are still making them, for sport only, and so famous has the factory become that the tables have been turned, and now it is Americans on European tours who make a point of stopping at Steyr to buy their sporting guns.

The old town has one interesting architectural facet if you look closely at some of the pleasant gothic and renaissance houses. All the shutters on the top floor seem to be permanently drawn, because the top floor is a sham. Merchants who ran out of money could not bear 'losing face' by making their homes a mere three, instead of four storeys, so they pretended to have four, but built an internal roof one floor below and left the top storey as a façade.

Steyr has one famous and charming modern function: its post office replies to thousands of children who write to Baby Jesus (Christkind). The letters are automatically delivered to Steyr because there is a pilgrimage church called Christkind just outside the town.

Arriving, finally, at Linz, the overwhelming impression is of its industrial strength. There is a castle, which has seen duty as a hospital and prison, and is now a museum, but it is architecturally uninteresting and the only real lure is to visit it on a clear day for the view over the town. The iron and steel plant pioneered a new method of smelting iron into steel, cutting the process time from hours into minutes, and it is a system used all over the world under licence from Linz. More than 20,000 people are employed here and produce getting on for a couple of million tons of steel each year, supplementing the local iron ore with that from Sweden, South America and Russia.

All of this would not have been possible without the Danube, the life-line to the commercial port. Although you can smell the steel and fertiliser industry from far away if the wind is blowing in the right direction, Linz makes some offerings to tourists, notably its five favourite sons. They are a local mayor, an architect, Anton Bruckner, Kepler the astronomer (who lived here for a number of years) and Frederick III, the only emperor to choose it as his temporary home, in the late fifteenth century (though Archduke Ferdinand and Queen Anna of Hungary were married at the castle in the early sixteenth century).

Regretfully, Linz cannot count Beethoven, though they point out that he dropped in often to see his brother, who was a chemist. Mozart also stopped off and composed a symphony at breakneck speed for a concert in the Landestheater. This C major one is naturally known as the Linz symphony. The town does have one unique church, St Martins, which may well be the oldest building in Austria, with Roman foundations below the present building. You need to walk around the outside to disentangle the various periods, for inside it has been restored to as near as possible its character of 700.

During the renovation a beautiful fresco was uncovered which had been walled up to save it from destruction because of its 'heretic' line; an honest violinist, Lucca, playing at the feet of Christ and receiving from him his golden shoe. The theme sounds innocent enough but in those days it was a forbidden image and anyone that possessed it in whatever form discreetly hid the evidence. The luck of St Martins is that the Lucca fresco was so well preserved by its disappearing act.

6 Lower Austria

At one stage during its history the provincial government of Lower Austria actually put a ban on the building of castles and fortifications because they were becoming too numerous! At a very rough count today the region boasts 800 or so of various kinds, the most important of which are luckily situated along the banks of the Danube so that the tourist can take them in with a sweeping glance. The motorist driving the Valley of the Wachau (Wach to check or survey, au meaning area) is subjected to a concentrated history lesson, some of Austria's most magnificent buildings, an intriguing link with Britain in Richard the Lion Heart and some shiver-me-timbers piratical tales of old.

The Danube controlled the commerce and wealth for centuries when it was the only communications artery, and to control the Danube the many fortresses sprang up, though not always with a legal or upright end in view. One splendid character with a towering top-of-the-cliffs castle was given to showing guests his beautiful rose garden and calmly toppling over the rocky edge into the waters below those he disliked. Nor was the river itself always the broad, calm sweep of today, and sailors who had managed tricky currents and nastily placed rocks could still be pounced upon by cunning marauders who swept down from the hills, having trapped the merchant fleets with chains strung across the river.

The lovely 16-year-old Elizabeth travelled down the Danube by ship from Linz to Vienna for her marriage to Emperor Franz Joseph, and her journey certainly took a lot longer than today's steamer services which cover the distance from the German frontier town of Passau to the capital in 12 hours, but take more than twice as long (those currents again) to do the return trip.

Few holidaymakers could resist doing at least a part of the Wachau by boat, but really to learn about the area and the province—the only one without a capital city because until the end of the first world war it was joined to Vienna—you need to meander the banks by car.

Ybbs, at the western end, makes a good starting point, firstly because it is the beginning of the Wachau, secondly because it has the only bridge over the Danube for a long time, and thirdly because its twin town across the river, Persenbeug, is where Charles, Austria's last emperor, was born. A rather delightful though somewhat shabby ducal palace guarding the river is still occupied by a duke, but both townships tend to nestle modestly on the banks content to play second fiddle to the Danube, which is the master here.

Surprisingly, even this river looks insignificant further upstream, but then it faces enormous competition. It is as well to stay on the Ybbs side for the moment, to be ready for Lower Austria's greatest masterpiece, the abbey of Melk, which is only 12 miles away. Melk the magnificent was the first home of the Babenbergs, with Leopold I establishing Canons, Leopold II summoning the Benedictines and Leopold III handing the whole place over to the monks.

Says the little guidebook: 'Times of prosperity alternated with days of calamity caused by wars, misfortunes and the influence of hostile agents.' It is a neat summing-up of an almost catastrophic history. Melk's original format in romanesque style was destroyed by fire in the thirteenth century; the Benedictine order went into a depression during the reformation and hardly had it recovered when in 1683 another fire destroyed the church tower and the invading Turks plundered the abbey's property.

So Berthold Dietmayr began all over again in the early eighteenth century, only to see one side, the towers and bells go up in flames in 1738. The abbey struggled on, but only just, for by this time Emperor Joseph II was busy closing down all contemplative orders. Nor did the French wars help. Napoleon stayed at Melk for a couple of weeks, ordered the monastery to be fortified and had the cannon pointing menacingly out over the river. A small garden named after him remains a picturesque reminder of not so picturesque days.

Finally, after World War II, when the latest damage was being repaired, yet another fire broke out and you can see the repainted figures in the dome of the church looking a little darker than the rest. With this sort of background it is even more surprising that Melk manages to look so lovely and so harmonious, in pure baroque style emphasising the reaffirmation of catholicism, the final defeat of the Turks and, at last, after the dreary Thirty Years War, something to lighten everybody's hearts—except that if you lived in the town below you must have felt like a dwarf in a doll's house!

Of the seven courtyards one survives from the mid-fourteenth century; the remainder, except for the walls, were rebuilt after the Turkish wars. The rounded front is interesting architecturally, though you need to be flying past in a helicopter to realise how cleverly the wings have been 'fitted' to the natural line of the rock. What seems to be a little entrance set in this front is not one at all, but a special opening for passing sailors to enable them to see the lighted candles in the church. The river has since changed its course so radically that only an old arm of it is actually outside the abbey, and now far below the secret opening.

Melk's royal wing is, as expected, lavish, with an elegant staircase, peace and war statues set in wall niches and a stucco ceiling. Corridors are more than lengthy, the first floor one stretching for 643 feet with endless portraits of the Babenbergs and Habsburgs, a sobering thought for mediaeval schoolboys who studied here. There has been a school since the monastery's foundation, with a Book of Honour and a Book of Shame in which was entered the name of the good or bad youngster; today there are 250 pupils preparing for all professions as well as the priesthood.

Three major items at Melk clamour for attention: the Mirror Hall in one wing; the library in the other, where most of the

80,000 volumes have been specially rebound to blend with the inlaid gold and brown walls; and the golden gilded church which has operatic overtones with lots of theatre boxes and dramatic statues on the high altar, like actors on a stage.

There are innumerable and irresistible chances to look back on Melk as you head for the short car ferry to cross the Danube and pause this side to look at the flood marks on the riverside house by the landing stage. The river reached the top of the ground floor window in 1954, a good improvement on 1501 when it overflowed to the second floor! Today's Danube is quiet enough to float hundreds of eggshells filled with lighted candle-wax on midsummer's night.

Having crossed, you will find that the road on the left bank stays close to the water for the first dramatic view across to the ruin of Aggstein Castle, originally thirteenth-century, destroyed two or three times by the Swedes and once the property of the Kuenringers, sort of regional 'managers' for the Babenbergs. It was one of these courtiers who disposed of his guests from the rose garden.

Spitz is one of several little villages along the way, its centre luckily off the main road, so that it has been able to preserve its narrow streets. Straw wheels hang outside the wine shops to indicate they are in business, probably much as they did in the fifteenth century, from when the gothic church dates. Its only baroque touch is the altar and statues of the 12 apostles set in niches at the back of the nave below the organ, and, like quite a few similar ones, there is a large area behind the altar which was originally occupied by the hidden choir in pre-organ times.

Outside the village is a small rounded hill covered with vines and aptly titled the 1,000-barrel hill. Each barrel contains 56 litres of wine and a thousand barrels is what they reckon to reap from this vineyard in a good year. The oldest church of the Wachau—it was the starting point for the first missionaries—is a mile or two away at St Michael's, well fortified, as they all are, with its own water to defeat enemy plots to poison the general supply.

Only a couple of years ago it was given a new twentieth-century title: that of pilgrimage church for motorists. St Michael's has one rather startling aspect: running across its roof is a line of stone animals and there are two theories for their presence: either in the old days there was so much snow that the real creatures at one stage sheltered in the church or, more likely, simply symbolising hunting.

Next along the road is the village that gave its name to the valley, except that instead of being called Wachau it has been renamed Weissenkirchen. The Wachau museum, in the style of an old farmhouse with splendid courtyard and first-floor galleries, dates from the fifteenth century. Next door to it is the church, with steep steps under a wooden canopy leading to its high entrance and inside, in June, the intoxicating scent of lilies of the valley lining the altar. It has been restored and has one daring example of sculpture, daring, that is, for the sixteenth century. Earlier statues of the Virgin Mary in gilded wood showed very modest drapes, but this one, from 1520, actually indicates the presence of knees beneath the skirt!

Dürnstein has been 'cashing' in on Richard the Lion Heart ever since he was a captive in their castle. There are several versions of the story, the most popular being that Babenberg Leopold IV had conquered a Moslem fortification in the twelfth century and was so furious when he heard that Richard had retaken it and replaced the flag with the English one that he pursued the British king back to Vienna. Richard sent his servant out to buy food with foreign coins, the servant betrayed him and off Richard was sent to Dürnstein.

The fairy-tale ending tells of his trusty troubadour Blondel, who sang his way along the Danube until he found the castle in which Richard was a prisoner (the British king recognising the sound of the troubadour's voice, of course). Blondel then hotfooted it back to England to collect the enormous ransom which gained Richard's freedom and enabled the Austrians to build a couple of cities on the proceeds.

One of the Dürnstein castles is now a fancy restaurant, and

one of the monasteries has been transformed into a hotel called, naturally, Richard the Lion Heart. The Augustine church, authentic baroque, has a fine carved-stone entrance and looks out on the courtyard, with big willow tree and tiny fountain, in which are presentations of Son et Lumière and open-air concerts.

In the gothic town hall is the precious document by which Frederick III, the Habsburg emperor, granted Dürnstein the right to be a city in 1476. Like many Austrian towns it fell into a depression, and was put back on its feet by the eighteenth-century provost, Hieronymus Vebelbacher. He cleverly developed the vineyards to produce the money to rebuild the monastery, and also to enlarge the wine cellars like the Keller Schlössl just outside the city, which is now a storeroom for the Co-operative Winegrowers' Society whose 1,000 members all operate in the area between Melk and Krems.

The Society emphasise the quality of their product and also the fact that their operating costs are three times as high as in other areas because most of the vineyards are on steeply sloping terraces. To ensure the validity and reputation of the wine they designed their own bottle in 1960, the Dürnstein-Flasche, so that people could tell the real thing from any fakes. Vebelbacher's private cellar, which conveniently led straight up to his castle home, is part of today's wine-making complex, and attending a tasting in the damp, dark, cold place can be an exhilarating experience with a group of enthusiastic teenagers studying to be wine-growers.

Richard the Lion Heart appears on innumerable labels; so does a rather amusing cat disguised as a butler. This particular wine is called Dürnsteiner Katzensprung (Cat's Leap) with two meanings: the leap was a short distance, translatable in wine terms as drop in and have one; and the cat's kind face is supposed to mean that you will not have a hangover the next morning. It was, incidentally, the wine served at the signing of the Austrian State Treaty in May 1955, so maybe the signatories to that treaty could have confirmed the lack of a thick head!

If Dürnstein was the major fortress city, then Krems was the aristocratic and business centre, though it governed itself and minted its own coins because it, too, was able to defend itself against invaders. Many of the elegant ornate houses from the fifteenth to seventeenth centuries which still survive would have been owned by rich merchants and tradesmen, and Krems is very keen on restoring its houses while adding modern amenities to the interiors.

The mayor, for instance, lives in pure gothic surroundings to which have been subtly added modern lamps. When the city was repairing World War II damage it discovered the most lovely gothic arcades which had been bricked up in a little castle once occupied by a mediaeval judge. Krems has more than its share of churches, of which two are especially worth visiting. The parish church, renewed quite recently, was built by an Italian in the seventeenth century and is fine early baroque with ceiling paintings by Kremser-Schmidt, so called because he was a local man and needed to be distinguished from others of the same name. The choir stalls have golden motifs above and golden reliefs in the backs of the seats.

The Piaristenkirchen, not quite so fine, has a sixteenth-century nave and baroque altars. In the city centre is a fountain and statue whose purpose is perpetuated in modern Austrian life. It shows Simandl Brunnen, a weak fellow, down on his knees asking his wife for the keys to their house. A hen-pecked husband has ever since been caustically referred to as a Simandl.

From Krems there is another bridge across the Danube and then a drive through steeply-rising woods, the trees meeting overhead to form a green tunnel, to reach Göttweig, the monastery that seems to sit on top of the world. It was founded in 1072 by St Altmann, the Bishop of Passau, who lies in the crypt in a filigree coffin, and like other abbeys, Göttweig burnt to nothing, first in 1580 and then in 1718. Hildebrandt designed the new building, but the Napoleonic wars intervened, money ran short and only the north and east wings and the front were ever completed from his extensive plans.

Though there is the same basic lavishness as at Melk, this monastery is in nothing like such fine order, except for its impressive staircase by Hildebrandt, in white and gold, with statues depicting the four seasons, famous artists and musicians, and Paul Troger's ceiling painting to set off the splendour. Of the emperor's apartments, none are particularly interesting bar one room which uses leather for wallpaper and has leather pictures of animals inset into the walls. The gothic church, which survived the fires, has walls of pastel pink and blue. Today this Benedictine monastery is responsible for 30 parishes in which most of the priests live, leaving only about a dozen in residence in enormous Göttweig.

The Danube flows almost centrally through Lower Austria from west to east, making two neat halves of the province. These further subdivide, geographically, scenically and economically, into quarters. The top left-hand segment is of the wood, or Waldviertel, with a rough climate capable of producing only potatoes and a kind of corn. It has one speciality, an area named Band'lkramerland'l, meaning merchantband land, the band being a decorative one for cloth which the natives wove from flax in winter and then sold, wandering minstrel-style, around the country during the summer. This was always a poor part of the province and the effects of depopulation can be seen in sad derelict buildings.

The bottom left-hand segment is of the apple, grown on the foothills of the Alps which lead into the Vienna woods. It is much richer, with its sweet orchards and fine farmhouses built on a square round a courtyard like the Wachau museum. The top right-hand quarter, which spills south a little, is of the wine, Weinviertel, a sandstone region with wine cellars built below the earth. It is the number one vineyard region in Austria, and 90 per cent of the product is white wine.

The bottom right-hand segment, Wienebecken, means Vienna plain, and here is the industrial region, with some corn, some oil wells and lots of ruined castles. Although it sounds the least attractive it is the area best known to tourists after the Wachau, because of its easy accessibility from Vienna and because of the Wienerwald, the woods most beautiful in the early morning when deer and rabbits are scampering about.

Sitting on the edge of the woods south of Vienna is Baden, with two sinister ruined castles guarding its entrance. Rauheneck and Rauhenstein were lived in by fifteenth-century marauders who nipped smartly down to the road to rob passing merchants. The little river that runs through the spa is called Schwechat (bad smell) from the sulphur springs which tarnish gold and silver and certainly make the town a pungent place on some days. The value of the water was fully realised by the early nineteenth century, Baden's heyday, after it had survived a terrible beating by the Turks in 1683, the bubonic plague in 1713 and a disastrous fire in 1812.

Maria-Theresia began the aristocratic gold rush here and Emperor Franz Joseph came for his rheumatism. So there is the usual collection of old-fashioned palaces and villas built by noblemen following the royal lead. Beethoven, living above a bakery in a little yellow house, composed his Ninth 'Choral' Symphony during one of the 15 summers he spent in Baden, and also gave the takings from one of his concerts to help rebuild the town after the fire.

Most of the hotels date from the turn of the century, and quite a few of the customers look as though they have been coming here since then (though there are some mini-clad young mothers wheeling prams in the grounds of the open-air thermal swimming pools). As a spa, Baden has lost its exclusivity and never really recovered from ten years of Russian occupation after the second world war. When the troops moved out, few hoteliers had money enough to renovate and restore to twentieth-century comfort and style.

Running through the Wienerwald from a point nine miles outside Vienna and south into Styria and Mariazell is the route early pilgrims took, more than 90 miles of it. Part of the journey is called the kleine Barokstrasse, because of the many churches and abbeys to be seen along the way. The long walk starts on the plain at Maria Lanzendorf, going through Mödling to the first famous stop at Heiligenkreuz. Holy Cross Abbey was founded in 1133 by a Babenberg emperor who needed the Cistercian monks from Burgundy, not only because they were good farmers but because they could do his writing for him.

The order were very strict, gathered for prayers seven times a day, ate twice a day, slept on the floor in unheated dormitories and were excellent shoemakers, which was odd because they themselves went barefoot. So many died or left because of the spartan life that the abbey softened the regime by adding cells, and in its prosperous days there were 300 monks at Heiligenkreuz as against 25 today. The pilgrim's fountain in the courtyard is overshadowed by a 100-year-old plane tree. In part of the cloister is the foot-washing corridor, so called because the abbot washed the feet of a dozen old men here once a year.

The abbey is romanesque and in the church is the work of the painter Altomonte, who lived with the monks. The Italian sculptor Giuliani also lived here and dedicated his work of two years —choir stalls of oak and linden showing in relief the life of Christ—to the order. Although the church was finished in the late twelfth century the transept and altar were added later and used as the model for St Stephen's cathedral in Vienna. It is here the Babenberg rulers are buried.

Modern 'pilgrims' usually make a detour or two in the area before continuing the route, perhaps taking a look at the castle of Hinterbrühl, one of the many that became roofless in Joseph II's day. He not only closed monasteries but imposed a tax on roof acreage, so if you were not using the place you stripped off the roof to avoid paying the tax. There are many still in this sad condition, though Hinterbrühl has been renovated and turned into a boy scouts' home.

Nearby is the largest subterranean lake in Europe, Seegrotte, interesting enough as it is, but more than usually so because the photographs outside show its wartime purpose as a plane assembly factory after the Germans had drained off the water. The other side of Heiligenkreuz produces a 'must' on visitors' lists, but it is rather disappointing despite its beautiful pastoral setting. You cannot go in, because Mayerling, the hunting lodge where Crown Prince Rudolf committed suicide, is a Carmelite nunnery, the chapel built on the site of the bedroom where Rudolf and 18-year-old Baroness Vetsera shot themselves on 31 January 1889.

All sorts of theories have been expounded on the reasons for the tragedy; one likely idea is that Rudolf, then 31 years of age and married to a Belgian princess with a five-year-old daughter, was incensed and unhinged by his father's rigid views on Hungary—the two had for a long time quarrelled over the empire's policies. Franz Joseph ordered Mayerling to be destroyed after the shooting, and only the walls and the tea pavilion remain.

Back on the Kleine Barokstrasse the road passes through Hafnerberg to Kleine Mariazell, now a little dilapidated and not original because the church was destroyed by the Turks in 1532, and on to Lilienfeld, one of the biggest abbeys in Lower Austria. Although it is not so impressive as Heiligenkreuz it was once very rich, for the abbey owned the surrounding forest and sold the wood for a lucrative profit. It was rebuilt after a fire in 1810 and the church is a mixture of baroque and renaissance, with four paintings by Altomonte.

From Lilienfeld the road runs straight to Turnitz, on the way into neighbouring Styria, but motorists are much more likely to back-track and reach this province by a better-known route. It is the same road the Viennese use to reach their 'home-grown' winter playground. But it should not be a fast journey at wine festival time, for there are too many distractions along the way. All along the outlying villages of the capital are the visible signs of the wine industry, whose annual output is more than a million litres. A Viennese daily paper usefully prints a whole page of that day's Heurige, but they are easy enough to find without advice.

At Perchtoldsdorf, for instance, the wide main street seems hung with pine branches, but it is worth stopping here for another reason, to see Austria's oldest romanesque church, which

16 Vienna: Chinese room in Schönbrunn

17 Vienna: the Karlskirche

doubled as a fortress in wartime when outlying farmers and town inhabitants took up their positions in the tower to bombard invaders through the slits. The journey south, through one of Austria's most industrialised zones, is not particularly interesting until you reach Wiener-Neustadt, about 30 miles from Vienna, which rightly looks modern because almost the whole town was destroyed in the second world war.

But the famous military academy has been cleverly restored to what it was. It began life as a castle under the Babenbergs, and Habsburg Maximilian I is buried beneath the altar steps of the simple St George's chapel, one pillar and stained glass windows original and the only ostentation an outside panel showing all the coats of arms of the Babenbergs. The castle lost its importance until in 1752 Maria-Theresia founded the academy. Unfortunately there was an earthquake in 1768 which so damaged the building that three of its towers had to be pulled down. Today the academy is surrounded by a pleasant park and 300 cadets are there at any one time on a three-year course.

From Wiener-Neustadt runs the longest stretch of straight road in Austria, nine miles to Neunkirchen, where the scenery changes from the flat plain with corn fields to the beginning of the hills and forests up to Maria Schutz, with a baroque church, and far more important to the Viennese, a cablecar to the Sonnwendstein mountain, one of their skiing areas only 1½ hours' drive from the city.

Looking across the valley from here is the first railway in the world built over a mountain pass. It runs from Gloggnitz up through Semmering and down to Mürzzuschlag, a distance of 25 miles, and though the statistics may not sound all that impressive today, it must have been a nerve-racking moment for the builder, Karl Ritter von Ghega, when Emperor Franz Joseph on 12 April 1854, took the train through 15 tunnels and over 16 bridges rising 1,400 feet on the Lower Austrian side and 650 feet on the Styrian side.

The Semmering pass divides the two provinces and like the Brenner in the west of the country, it is the vital north to south highway. The resort of Semmering is reckoned to be very health-giving and combines a summer and winter season. If you prefer to reach it the hard way, the old road up the hill from Schottwien is still there, and a bumpy journey it must have been in horse-and-carriage days.

If you want to remain in Lower Austria and not cross the border, then a different route back is between the two high alps, called the home mountains of Vienna because, like Sonnwendstein, they are so near the capital. Rax-Alpe and Schneeberg both just top 6,000 feet, one has a cablecar and the other a cog railway. The river between the two, in the valley of Höllental, is the Schwarza and it is a great area for lumbering.

Years ago a Lutheran woodchopper who became known as the King of the Rax had a fanciful scheme to use the Schwarza and a series of canals to transport the wood right into Vienna. He came to grief not so much because his plan for regulating the waters was a rotten one, but because the crown was against him and, even worse, the church. You could not have devised two more powerful enemies.

The narrow steep-sided Höllental eventually opens out into gentle farming territory and the road takes you from Rohr to Gutenstein and a worthy detour to the church of Mariahilfberg, a delicious quiet hill setting with several restaurants and souvenir stalls nearby. It is the scenery rather than the baroque church and monastery that is the charm, especially on a day when the altar boys from a wide area are making a pilgrimage and consuming enormous quantities of ice cream before carrying their vestments up the hill to the church.

7 Vienna

Way back in the first century A.D. when Vienna was Vindobona, the Romans had difficulty in supplying the regulation wine ration to each soldier of two glasses per day. Bringing gallons of the stuff from Italy was both expensive and troublesome, so the occupiers went one better and sent for the vines to grow their own, a successful experiment which centuries later provides the district around the city with the largest wine-growing area in the country.

Although Vindobona could take 6,000 men and was enclosed by a thick wall, it was a mere village compared to Carnuntum, 20 miles downstream on the Danube, which the Romans made the capital of their province of Pannonia. But Vindobona it was that successfully fought off attacks by the Huns and Bavarians, and during the Babenberg rule its name gradually evolved into Wenia, probably a small tributary of the Danube, then into Wienne, and finally Wien.

The thirteenth century saw its establishment as a trading post for oriental treasures, the fourteenth saw a series of disasters that might have erased a lesser mediaeval city: first fire, then destruction of the harvest by locusts, then floods and an earthquake, and finally cholera to dispose of those who had survived the previous catastrophes.

Throughout its history Vienna has had to fight against a multiracial collection of enemies, of whom three stand out above the others: the Swedes, who were responsible for the Thirty Years War; the French, who nearly 200 years later twice occupied the capital; and above all, the Turks, whose second siege in 1683 might have brought down not just the city, but the whole empire.

The enemy had swollen to nearly a quarter of a million with

Magyar and Tartar tribesmen by the time it reached the outskirts of Vienna, from whence had fled the emperor, Leopold I, in search of relieving armies, accompanied by most of his court plus a large proportion of the inhabitants. Left inside the city were a total of 16,000 people, but of these only a few were regular troops, the remainder merchants and students.

The Turks sent in an ultimatum: 'Accept Islam and live in peace under the sultan. Or deliver the fortress and live in peace under the sultan as Christians. But if you resist, death and spoilation and slavery shall be the fate of all.' The garrison commander's reply to this was to wall up the city gates and prepare to defend, but by the time the decisive battle was fought a couple of months later the clause about death in the ultimatum was beginning to come true. Count Starhemberg, chief of Vienna's defence corps, was losing more of his precious army through dysentery, other diseases and starvation than were being killed while fighting.

Eventually Emperor Leopold mustered support from Poland, Saxony, Franconia and Bavaria to add to his own army, and they took positions outside Vienna on the Kahlenberg and Leopoldsberg, but it really cannot be said that their military skill swayed the balance. The various commanders of different nationalities were busy quarrelling about the best way to attack up to the first gunfire and the battle must have looked a confusing affair to poor Starhemberg watching from St Stephen's tower.

The Austrian victory was also due to the mistakes made by the Turks, who had not thought of occupying the heights of the Vienna woods and, anyway, did not believe the poor garrison in the city capable of launching another attack. The battle lasted less than a day, the Turks were successfully rebuffed and later driven back into the Balkans in a campaign that made a hero of Prince Eugene of Savoy. The unfortunate man who had led the second siege against Vienna was strangled by order of his ungrateful sultan. The victorious armies went on quarrelling, now about the style and order of precedence for the celebrations!

Just as Vienna had gained something of lasting value from the Roman occupation, so did she from the Turkish battles, for the invaders conveniently dropped a few bags of coffee beans which a Polish fellow appropriated for his first coffee house, 'At the sign of the Blue Bottle'. Today's social and business scene is still the coffee house, with round marble tables and red plush seats, though sadly it is being replaced by the stand-up chrome-plated café where the coffee is cheaper and you are not supposed to sit with one cup all afternoon, the waiter bringing a fresh glass of water every half an hour or so.

Coffee is almost a national disease in Vienna and it is certainly the excuse to stop whatever project in hand in favour of something more leisurely. The girl at the tourist board, for instance, having difficulty in finding me a guide because the music festival is on, makes innumerable telephone calls, then smiles engagingly and says: 'Well, I invite you for a cup of coffee, then we try again.'

No-one knows quite how many varieties there are, and to this liquid refreshment the Viennese invariably add a little snack. Those who have given up their waistlines have a five-meals-a-day routine: breakfast, a fork breakfast of cold meats mid-morning, a substantial lunch, coffee and cakes in the afternoon and a light supper of omelettes and sweet dumplings. All the inhabitants took sides in a famous court case which lasted seven years and hinged on a thin layer of apricot jam and whether Sacher Hotel or Demel's cake shop, both equally renowned, were entitled to call their version the original Sacher Torte.

But creamy cakes and coffee are just one of the ways in which the Viennese sustains himself; in between the meals and snacks he'll probably call in at a street Würstelstand—not just any old sausage, but frankfurter or debreziner, krainer, burenwurst, each served on a cardboard plate with mustard and a kaisersemmel roll. Franz Joseph, who always feared being poisoned, used to send his doctor out for two pairs of frankfurters, one for the emperor, the other for the doctor.

It was during this emperor's reign that Vienna's old town walls and fortifications were pulled down to be replaced by the famous boulevard, the Ringstrasse, which is a good moment to stop talking of the past and take our first stroll in the city. The rest of the history will present itself along the way. . . .

The Ringstrasse curves protectively around inner Vienna like a great horseshoe, the open ends resting on the banks of the Danube canal, the studs positioning some of the most important buildings in the capital, nearly all put up during the last half of the nineteenth century in the most bewildering collection of architectural styles. One reason for the variety is that there was a series of contests to design the buildings and the winners took flights of fancy with their favourite period of history. The other reason is simply the Austrian character, which likes to ape and mimic, to reproduce and adapt for itself what others have first thought of.

The street has five major sections, is 185 feet wide, and includes three major museums, four parks and endless amusement. The best, indeed the only, way to appreciate it, is to begin at one end and finish at the other, a sightseer's paradise and no chance of getting lost! Start walking then, from the canal up Stubenring, pausing for a brief look at Field Marshal Radetzky on horseback. He was Franz Joseph's favourite commander-in-chief and, ironically, is pointing dramatically at a bank; ironically, because the poor soldier had to sell his medals to make ends meet and even then died badly in debt.

Near here and flanking Parkring is the first of the parks, Stadtpark, with Johann Strauss, in marble, playing the violin. The Ring then wheels from Schubertring into Kärtner Ring into Opernring with the reconstructed Opera House, to which we shall return later, in a solo position. From the Opera House onwards the choice is to alternate between sightseeing and sitting.

Two of Vienna's prettiest parks (and there are 898 all told in the city!) are in this section: the Volksgarten, where the sparrows are so tame and confident of a welcome they will perch on your finger, and the roses are beautiful; and Burggarten, with more trees, less flowers and statues of two favourites,

Mozart and Franz Joseph. Actually you need not even stagger as far as the parks, for all round the Ring stand the trees, long rows, shoulder to shoulder, forming a continuous umbrella under which the natives and visitors sit. You would do well to join them for a while, especially if you are in a museum mood and are about to embark on a tour of the masterpieces.

The Natural History Museum on Burgring has one particular gem inside: the tiny Venus von Willendorf dating back to remote times and found in 1908 in the valley of the Danube. She is made of chalkstone and is a fertility goddess about four inches high. Sitting imposingly between this museum and the next one, of Fine Arts, is Maria-Theresia, called by her devoted admirers 'the best lady's monument in the world'. The empress is looking majestic and is surrounded by her helpers—military, medical, musical and legal.

It was Franz Joseph who built the Kunsthistorisches Museum, bringing marble from all over the world to do it. The statue halfway up the central stairs was commissioned by Napoleon to show him, in classical style, killing the centaur, supposedly the evil spirits of the French revolution. Unfortunately, by the time the sculptor Canova got around to completing it and asking for the bill, history had changed somewhat. Napoleon was anything but victorious in Austrian terms, so they neatly changed its theme, though not its shape, and called it the Holy Alliance killing the spirit of Napoleon.

The staircase is glorious and above it is a painted ceiling, mostly restored, but one corner showing the original distinctive luminosity of the paint. The same quality is to be seen in the imperial portraits and those of the aristocracy, who paid the artists highly for their work, because to mix colours so cleverly was expensive, and they would not begin painting unless they were assured of the money.

The picture galleries trace a galaxy of different painting schools, among them Dutch, Italian and Spanish. The sharp-eyed will see how the same lady changes according to who has painted her: the northern European school probably shows the truth, a rather plain woman, while the Italians, on the other hand, make her very pretty.

There are rooms of Rubens, with his early cruder work, small originals and big copies made by pupils, and Breughel's work, too, including his early political accusations against the Spanish. It is, like all great museums, one to take in small bites, to return to, choosing a different subject and mood on each visit and not missing, whatever else, Cellini's golden salt cellar with two exquisite figures, he with trident, she on an elephant, both travelling through the sea.

If you can face more museums there is a cluster of them on the opposite side of the road. But perhaps you will prefer to stroll some more and change the period of history completely when you reach Parliament, designed by a Danish architect who was previously in Athens and clearly much affected by the experience. The sculptures are Grecian and Roman philosophers, the Goddess of Wisdom (with fountain) is flanked by sword and book, executive and legislative power.

By this time you are in Dr Karl-Renner Ring, leading into Dr Karl-Leuger Ring, the fourth of the parks, Rathauspark, and standing alongside it, another contest winner, the neo-gothic Rathaus, this by a German architect with a 300-foot tower, on top of which is an iron figure standing guard over the city. The Burgtheater opposite almost manages to look insignificant by comparison.

The university, renaissance-style, is nearly the last major building on the Ring. It was built for 5,000 students and in 1965 celebrated its six-hundredth anniversary as the oldest university in a German-speaking country. 18,000 students attend now. The boulevard curves round again into Schottenring for the final leg back to the Danube canal and has the Stock Exchange as its contribution to the sights.

This multi-styled feast will probably be quite enough for the first day, especially if you have obtained a ticket for one of the many musical events that evening. You will have already noticed that any building of historical interest has a red and white flag fluttering outside, the better to be spotted, and you may now be reaching the conclusion that every second flag seems to produce another link in the vast musical chain.

The Viennese have such a concentrated musical heritage that it would be easy for a cynic to dismiss their enthusiasm as a lucrative gimmick, but all the musical monuments are genuine and the native absorption in these things is a natural one, perpetrated basically for his own pleasure, but in which the visitor is invited to join if he so wishes.

There is no doubt that the much earlier patronage and interest displayed by some of the emperors helped to set the later scene. Ferdinand III, Leopold I, Joseph I and Charles VI were not only music-lovers, but no mean performers and composers as well. Leopold's musical compositions (102 dances and nearly 100 pieces of church music, including a requiem for his wife) are still played on the radio, and it is said that he died happy listening to the imperial orchestra playing his favourite pieces in an adjoining room.

Charles was a violinist and conductor. Joseph II devoted an hour after dinner to music and held concerts three times a week in which he played piano or cello. Franz I played first violin in a string quartet. Once the Imperial court had given the lead, the aristocracy naturally followed in lending support and encouragement, and though Vienna's classical period would not have been possible without this sponsorship, some of the mighty masters of composition were hardly popular in their lifetimes.

Haydn was financially stranded after his voice broke and he could no longer sing in the choir of St Stephen's cathedral. His temporary answer to the problem was to go out in the evenings with friends, playing impromptu open-air concerts, until in 1760 Prince Esterhazy took him on as court music director with the proviso that he was to be regarded and treated as one of the domestic staff.

Unlike Mozart, who chaffed and rebelled under this kind of 'servantry', Haydn did not mind at all, wrote prolifically while he was serving the prince and commented: 'My employer was very satisfied with my work; I was commended, and with an orchestra at my disposal I could make experiments and observe which of them represented improvements and which not. I could make corrections and additions, cuts and innovations. I was cut off from the outside world and there was no one to put me off or irritate me. I was forced to be original.'

The composer's early life had been a simple one, as the son of a wheelwright and the cook who worked for the Counts of Harrach. They lived in the little village of Rohrau at the extreme eastern end of Austria. Haydn's reference to being 'cut off' was that, as Esterhazy's musical director, he lived in Eisenstadt, now the capital of Burgenland, then part of Hungary.

By comparison Mozart was a revolutionary, though most people count Vienna's rich musical harvest from the day in 1781 when he came to live there. In fact only the Abduction from the Seraglio was often performed during his lifetime; most of the other works given an airing were followed by such rotten reviews that publishers refused to print them.

Despite his father's comment that there was not a single house of quality in Vienna where his son and daughter had not performed alongside the most famous virtuosi of the day, they were all private concerts. Despite Mozart's opening debut at Schönbrunn before the imperial household at the age of six, no composer could, on his own, make ends meet.

During a rare prosperous period, he lived in a house at the back of the cathedral, now called Figarohaus, after the opera he composed there. It is said that he took the place because he liked the stuccoed bedroom, supposed to be a sampler room for the stucco craftsman who was the previous tenant. Occasional prosperity or not, Mozart's end was a sad one, buried in a common grave in St Mark's cemetery in Vienna. Today his memory stays far more alive in Salzburg, which he deliberately left, than in the capital.

Beethoven had already planned to come to Austria from Bonn at the time of Mozart's death. He was attracted by the surrounding hills (beauties of nature were much in vogue in those days), and during his walks on the outskirts of the city gained the inspiration for his Pastoral Symphony. As a householder he was a particularly restless fellow, for there are no less than 62 different apartments which he occupied at one stage or another.

His monument has nine angels symbolising his nine symphonies, three of which had their first performances in the Theater an der Wien, to become the centre for the golden age of operetta which lasted from 1874 (Strauss's *Die Fledermaus*) to 1905 (Lehar's *Merry Widow*). But of the vast number produced only about a dozen survived and operetta never managed a comeback after the dissolution of the empire. *Die Fledermaus* is still the traditional performance at the Opera House on New Year's Eve.

The Theater an der Wien was the first to reopen after the second world war as a temporary home for the Opera House and was used for ten years as this before being closed for reconstruction. The first performance on its reopening in May 1962, was Mozart's *The Magic Flute*, a fitting choice because the opera's librettist, Emanuel Schikaneder, had been this theatre's first director.

By the time Schubert arrived on the scene the influence of the court and aristocracy on the musical world had waned. He was, to all intents and purposes, supported by a group of friends and the families with whom they were connected. They were not rich romantics, but professional people who devoted their time and money to helping Schubert. This most Viennese of composers would have starved without them.

The second half of the nineteenth century saw the beginning of what were regarded as the 'moderns', like Brahms and Bruckner, no one knowing that still later would come Mahler and Schönberg. The Austrian passion for baroque in all forms, extending into music, had now a tremendous boost with what the natives call the 'Strauss dynasty', meaning J. Strauss senior, director of music to court balls, and his two sons, Johann, the most well-known, who succeeded his father, and Joseph.

The waltz king was tuned right into the Viennese taste for

pomp, festivities and pageantry. They are, it is said, 'always ready to abandon themselves to sensory impressions, to the flowering of the fleeting moment, to fantasy and a kaleidoscope of colour'. Vienna is the only capital in the world where balls are the social activity during the winter, the programme as full of etiquette and elegant as it was in Johann's heyday.

Their Fasching lasts from New Year's Eve to the beginning of Lent, about seven weeks and 300 balls later, of which the Opera House Ball, started in 1935 and revived in 1956, tops the calendar. It is the only time of the year when people of all classes mix, and anyone can buy a ticket for the Opera Ball. To be selected for the opening dance depends more on proficiency in the intricate counter-clockwise waltz than on family connections.

The Romans began the forerunner to Fasching with their winter Saturnalia in honour of Saturn, when all distinctions of rank were abolished; the Viennese keep it up, but with none of the crudity of the German variety. Theirs is white-gloved and formal, and the law student who is my guide one day excuses himself early in order to prepare for an all-night ball. Of course he will be working the following day, he says, even though he will not have time for sleep.

When it comes to the Opera House, opened a century ago and referred to by every native with a possessive pronoun, nationalism is at its most fanatical. The visitor may regard what the critics said about last night's event there as a trivial matter; not so the population, who will all give voice on the subject. The original building had been commissioned by Franz Joseph, but neither of the two architects, Eduard van der Nüll and August Siccard von Siccardsburg, survived to the opening in 1869, six years after the foundation stone had been laid. One committed suicide, the other died of a heart attack.

The catastrophic blow to its history happened only three weeks before the end of the second world war. It was hit by bombs and the ensuing fire destroyed stage and auditorium. The restoration and rebuilding were more important to the Viennese than new homes, hospitals or schools. Luckily the staircase and foyer were unharmed, and in the reconstruction were added six modern galleries where music-lovers stroll during the interval. Gustav Mahler lasted ten years and Herbert von Karajan seven years in the post of director.

During Festival time, an annual musical banquet that has been going on since 1951, most of the opera-goers will be anything but locals and will have paid a high price for what may be more of an emotional than a great musical experience. The Viennese would hate to believe that their standard is not still the best in the world, for they are incurably sentimental about their music.

The traditional Sunday morning concerts of the Vienna Philharmonic in the gilt-plastered Musikverein, reckoned to be so sensitive acoustically, that the walls vibrate, are nostalgic affairs, for tickets are by subscription only and when a subscriber dies his allocation reverts to the orchestra's management. The audience who meet here eight or ten times a year and have no need of the public rehearsal the preceding afternoon are mostly old-style inhabitants of the city who remember bygone days. They see nothing outmoded in the fact that the 100-odd members of the orchestra are still treated with the same courtesy that elsewhere would be reserved for only the highest VIPs.

For the subscribers, there is a competing event at the same time, another traditional musical item: mass in the Hofburg Chapel, with instrumentalists, tenors and basses from the Vienna Opera and sopranos and altos of the Vienna Boys' Choir which has been singing here since the chapel was built in the late fifteenth century. Nothing very much has changed in the choir's performance or the music since then, except that the boys have become world renowned.

But over the centuries the chapel has been so overrun by the other rambling buildings of the Hofburg that now only a small section of it is externally visible, jutting out from the courtyard walls. Fit the other pieces of this giant jigsaw puzzle together and you will have learned almost the entire history of Austria as well as amused yourself should it rain for a week!

The palace was begun by the Babenbergs in the thirteenth

century, and not finished until 1911, though the three architects who designed the last addition forgot the plumbing, so Ferdinand never lived here and it now houses musical instruments, antiquities and an armoury. In the intervening centuries almost every Habsburg added his own speciality, starting with Rudolf I's Swiss wing. Prince Maximilian in the sixteenth century had a special palace built outside the walls because he was, like the majority of the city's inhabitants, a protestant. The imperial family were, however, Roman Catholics, and that was the required religion for living within the palace precincts.

Not long after the prince finished his handsome home the reigning emperor died, and perforce he had to become a catholic to take over. The house he never occupied, in Josefplatz, was changed to stables. Only recently was discovered the interest Rudolf II must have had in astronomy, for beneath the top layer of a clock tower were revealed a sun dial and moon dial which this emperor had ordered.

Maria-Theresia opened the imperial apothecary (now the riding school) in 1746, a forerunner to the welfare state, where palace servants had a free medical service and nearly 1,000 of them called in during the opening year. It was she who first introduced vaccination against smallpox, having had the disease herself. She sent for an English doctor, instructed him to try out the serum on her favourite grandson and, when it succeeded, gave it to the 30 orphans she was bringing up.

She ruled her children with the same kind but firm hand as she ruled her empire. Only one of the girls was permitted to choose her own bridegroom, Marie-Christine; otherwise they married as mother dictated, to ensure the dynasty and its continuing prosperity. The girls were expected to join their mother in democratic sewing sessions every week, and there was an ulterior motive here: not simply to improve their needlework but to enable the empress to keep in touch with the gossip through the servants who also took part.

Despite her father's efforts to ensure her succession (like 'bribing' the satellite countries not to make trouble), Maria-

Theresia was not at first, absolutely safe on her various thrones. Austria called her archduchess, Bohemia a queen, Hungary, contrariwise, a king. When she was married to Franz Stefan of Lorraine she was empress by right and ruled with benevolence and progressiveness.

There was never, anyway, a coronation for the ruler of Austria, though he was crowned emperor of the Holy Roman Empire and king of Hungary and Bohemia. The Holy Roman Emperors were elected by proving their right, and there was only one way in which to do this: by possessing the insignia and regalia. One hapless emperor fighting in Budapest thought he was going to be taken prisoner with the crown jewels and to save the dynasty had them smuggled out in a fish cart, knowing that this, with its fresh cargo, would have to travel as speedily as possible. The jewels arrived safely at the free imperial city of Nuremberg, where they were kept until in Napoleon's time they were brought to Vienna.

The public never see the cellars beneath the Hofburg where prisoners and wild animals were kept, because they are now basically a giant boiler house to keep the complex heating system going. After a first bewildering stroll through the courtyards the visitor has to decide which of the many aspects of the palace shall first engage his attention, and it is impossible to cover them all in a day.

Logically, the imperial apartments should be the opening visit. They are on the same style as at Schönbrunn but with not such good taste, except for the tapestries, and the most interesting rooms are those which shed light on the lives of Franz Joseph and Elizabeth. He ruled conscientiously, just like a good soldier should, so the list of one day's audiences is almost entirely grateful citizens coming to thank him for decorations.

His study has warm brocade walls and snapshots of the children; his bedroom is expectedly spartan, with the iron bedstead on which he always slept. Above it is a picture of his military teacher who was killed by the Hungarians. For the emperor it was a constant reminder of the tragedy, because he never forgave his enemies, and some people say this killing was the start of the subsequent collapse of the entente between the two countries. On the other hand, he was constantly faithful to friends like Field Marshal Radetzky, who remained commander-in-chief of the army until a ripe old age simply because he was a close confidant.

Franz Joseph is called, a little unkindly, the emperor who went on for ever, having taken over from his uncle Ferdinand in 1848 and ruled for 68 years. But operettas still performed always put him over as a benevolent old man, and Austrians refer to him as the Old Gentleman. Hardly anyone thinks back to recollect how much of his personal life was tragedy. His two sisters-in-law were killed in fires, his younger brother was the disastrous king of Mexico, another sister-in-law went mad, one heir was assassinated, he saw the crumbling of the empire and, worst of all, he lost the ones he loved.

When, in January 1889, the emperor was told that his only son had shot Baroness Marie Vetsera, the 18-year-old daughter of a wealthy and ambitious Viennese family, and then himself in the hunting lodge at Mayerling, Franz Joseph at first acceded to the police chief's efforts to conceal the tragedy. Marie's body had been smuggled away and it had been announced that Rudolf had had a heart attack. But then the Old Gentleman changed his mind and told the Austrians the truth—that Rudolf had shot the girl and then himself 'while of unsound mind'. The court observed three months' mourning, one of deepest, one of deep, one of minor.

Nine years later there was another family tragedy when Empress Elizabeth was stabbed by an anarchist near Geneva. She is still a romantic legend and most Austrians refuse to be disloyal to her memory. In fact Franz Joseph had been engaged to her older sister, but fell in love with Elizabeth as soon as they met and switched fiancées. As a young bride, newly arrived in Vienna in 1854, she won the people's hearts with her beauty and her sweetness. She was excused for her shyness and the fact that she always kept her face hidden by a fan on rare public appear-

18 *Vienna: the Spanish riding school*

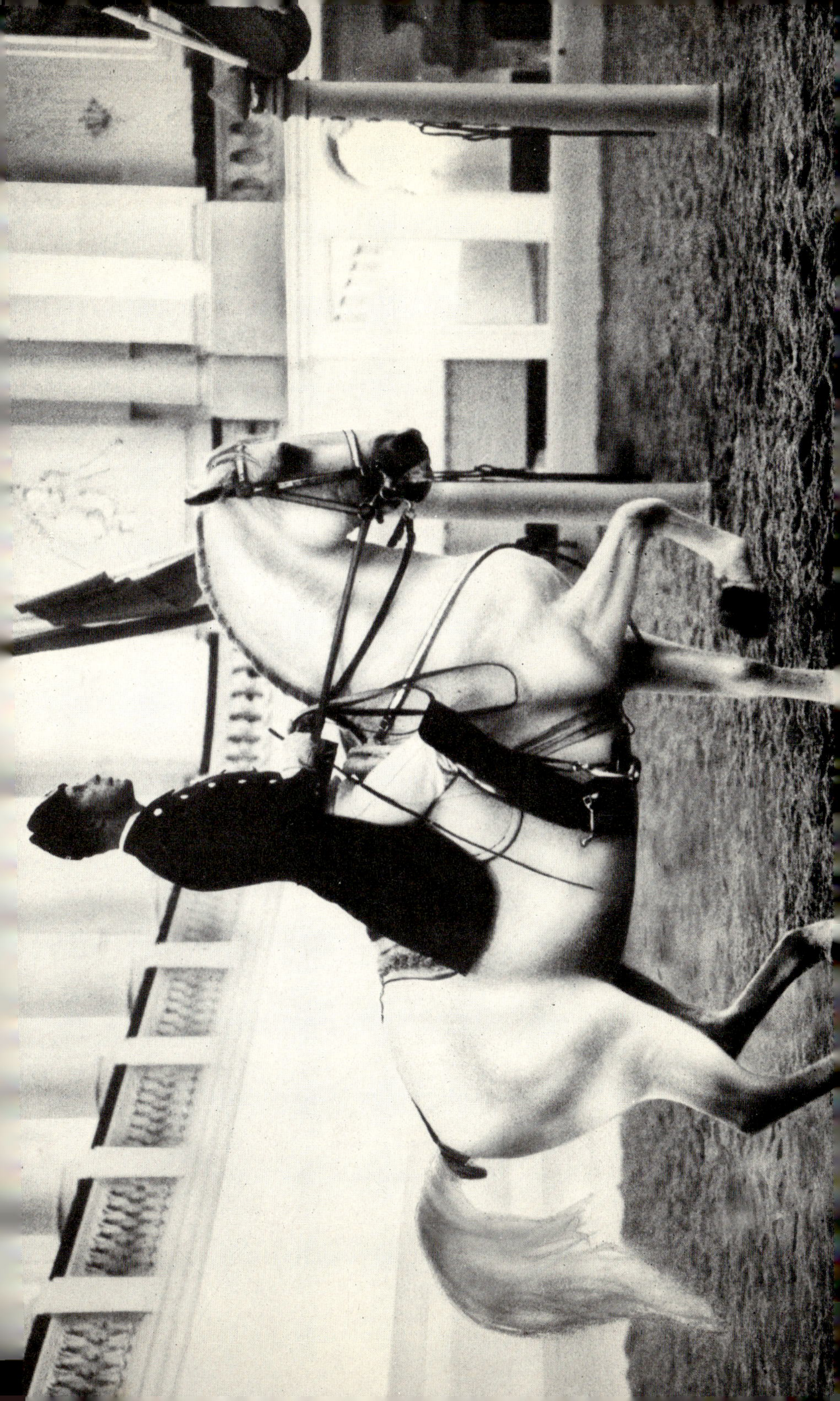

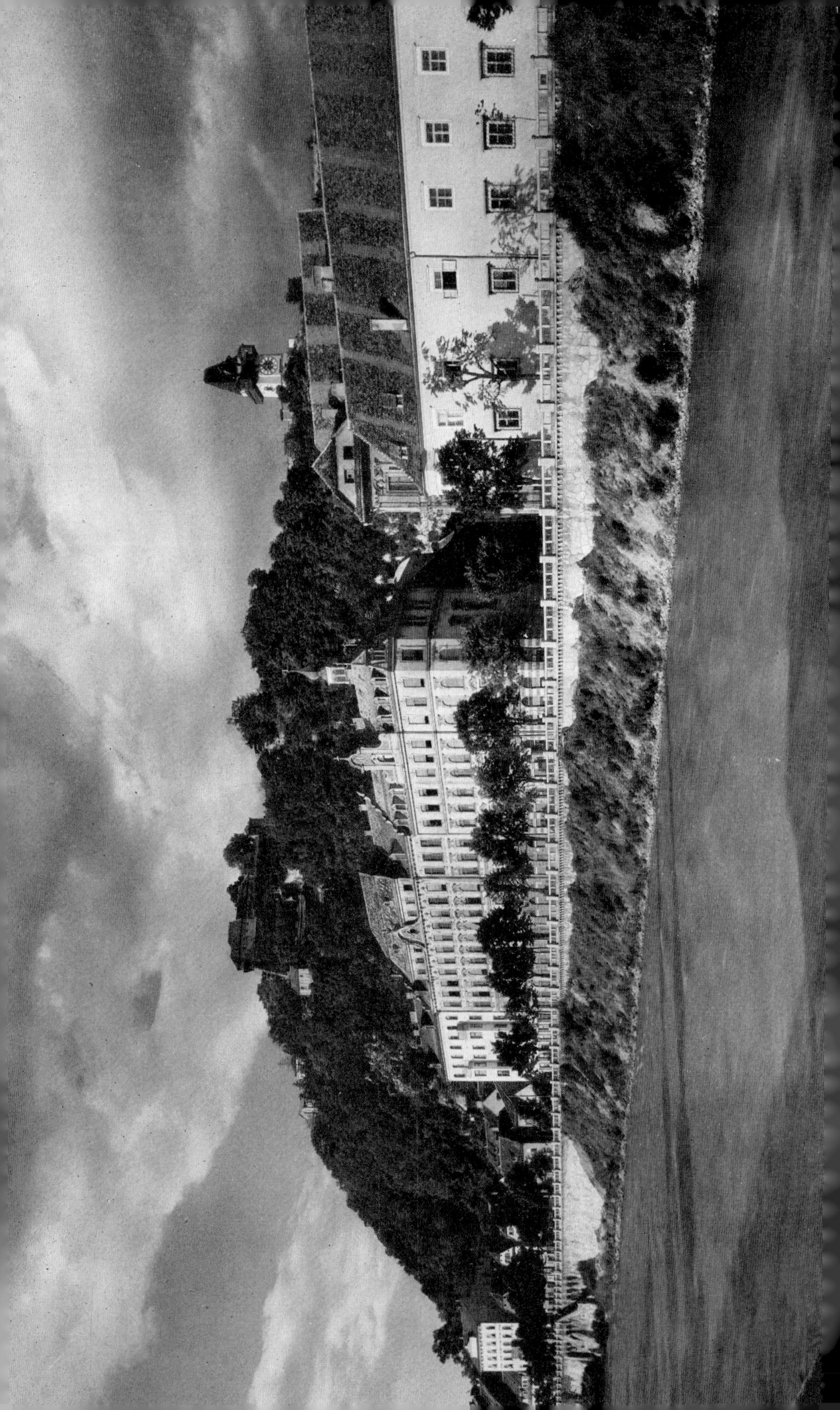

ances, but later never forgiven for her apparent indifference to the emperor and her transparent love of being somewhere other than by his side (like fox-hunting in Ireland)!

It was Elizabeth who arranged that her husband and Katharina Schratt, the actress, should meet, though the two women were alleged to have been good friends, too. The Viennese love to tell how Franz Joseph would leave Schönbrunn early in the morning to breakfast with Katharina in her villa nearby and, incidentally, painted in the same imperial yellow as the palace, and she had a reputation for baking better pastry than the royal household chefs.

Compared to Maria-Theresia, Elizabeth did precious little for her people and she was, too, extremely vain. Her apartments at Schönbrunn, for instance, have exercise bars for keeping fit and three ladies-in-waiting in relays had to run with the empress ten miles a day, the minimum distance that would do for retaining her youth and beauty.

Being invited to dine with the pair of them, either in the Hofburg or at Schönbrunn, was a terrible ordeal. The imperial table is a splendid sight, set for 24, one servant to every two guests. The only trouble was trying to get anything to eat, for protocol meant that the emperor and empress were naturally served first, and as soon as they had finished a course all the plates around the table were removed.

As Franz Joseph, with a soldier's outlook, always ate lightly, and as Elizabeth was always on a diet, they had tiny portions and finished them before those at the end of the table had even been served! Wise guests went out to dinner first, before coming on to the royal banquet.

The Schatzkammer part of the Hofburg is as interesting for the stories behind the glistening contents as for the jewels themselves. Because the regalia was in safe keeping at Nuremberg, the emperors could use it only for the coronation itself, and for the remainder of the ceremonial occasions they had to have their own sets made. Most of the ones dating from the late middle ages and the renaissance were later melted down.

19 *Graz: the river front and castle*

But while the private regalia was designed to show off the rank and position of the ruler, the baptismal robes were extra beautiful, for they marked the special position of the child at its first public appearance, and a small chain of the order of the Golden Fleece was always laid in the cradle. Philip the Good in 1429 founded this order, one of the few great chivalrous orders to remain, and you will see the ram hanging on a chain with his red velvet and golden robes.

The christening robes, consequently, were almost as important as the jewels, for they proved the child was born in wedlock. Maria-Theresia, who was a very handy seamstress, made a set, including a gold and silver shawl. A sixteenth-century christening platter and jug may have started its golden life at banquets as a washing set for the hands, but became obsolete when forks came in. They thought the ensemble would do for imperial christenings, but the first fellow to pick up the jug almost collapsed under its weight of 50 pounds, so a lightweight replica had to replace it.

Marie-Louise, so unhappily married to Napoleon, needed to ensure the succession of her baby son, so when she returned to Austria she brought with her the child's cradle which had been made in the shape of a throne with suitable royal embellishments. Her son, Napoleon Franz Karl, born in 1811, received the title of King of Rome at birth. He used only his second two christian names after his father's downfall, became Duke of Reichstadt in Bohemia at the age of seven and died of a lung disease when he was only 21.

The history of the Habsburg acquisitions, as well as some of their eccentricities, is all here, if you look closely. The Burgundians were the most elegant and sophisticated court in Europe. Maximilian I was married to Mary of Burgundy for only five years when she died in a fall from her horse. Among the mementoes of this period is her picture, showing her beauty; the Burgundy brooch showing a pair of lovers in a rose garden; and the crystal cup from which a toast drunk was as binding as a state treaty. These rulers needed no coronations—the successor simply took over the fine robes.

The display cases Maria-Theresia ordered in 1747 to show off the treasures to the best advantage are still here, and they gained a good deal by her marriage. Her husband brought with him precious stones and diamonds, the most famous being the giant Florentine diamond, and while he increased his wealth his empress turned constantly to her lady-in-waiting for the royal purse to distribute money to the poor.

Some of the rulers were remembered for things other than jewels or benevolence. Rudolf II earned the title of the emperor of good taste because he was an art collector, and you can spot his selections a mile off in the art galleries, for the pictures always contain ladies, usually nude; true to character, there is a tiny nude on the lapel of his bust in the Schatzkammer. He also established the Imperial Court Workshop in Prague, who made the crown, sceptre and imperial orb.

Charles VI was very fond of birds, but you were not supposed to have anything of this sort in robes, so a parakeet was cunningly disguised in his with a flower for its head. This emperor became so distressed when one of his birds fell ill, that he called the royal doctor, who prescribed red wine with honey. Years later they went through the royal household accounts and discovered that 40 bottles of red wine had been ordered—and disappeared—daily, one for the sick bird and 39 for the servants.

Despite the accidents of history, some renowned items neither disappeared nor were melted down. The coronation crown, for instance, shines out. Its shape embodies the laurel leaf from Holy Roman Empire days and a helmet signifies the head of the army. It was made around 950 and may contain stones from Charlemagne's crown. His bible is certainly here, its parchments dating back to 750.

The sword of state also used at the coronation is a magnificent weapon, said to have been actually used in the battle of Lechfeld in 950 when the Magyars were fighting Otto the Great, who held it up to order a troop movement and subsequently won the battle.

Apart from all the glitter, the Schatzkammer has one other delight: some quite beautiful needle tapestry-pictures made in the fifteenth century and showing on vestments the stories of the bible. They are incredibly fine, in gold and silver, even down to the expressions on the faces. The three priests who wore the copes would stand next to each other so that the story could unfold.

These items are but a selection of what caught my whimsical eye. The treasure chamber has, in fact, been sadly depleted by events. The sons of Ferdinand in 1564 made an agreement to ensure that the priceless agate bowl and the unicorn should remain Habsburg property; that they should never be sold, pledged or taken out of the country. And so it was.

But after the first world war the Grand Chamberlain of that time took the imperial jewellery abroad for safe keeping. The diamond crown used by Empress Elizabeth at the Hungarian coronation in 1867 and the famous Florentine diamond were among the treasures lost. And with the dissolution of the Habsburg empire came requests from Italy for their insignia and from Hungary for theirs. In 1939 Hitler ordered that the contents of the treasure chamber be taken back to Nuremberg. They were returned to Vienna in 1946 and the Schatzkammer reopened to the public in 1954.

The ecclesiastical treasure, in the same building, is rather disappointing; twice the emperor demanded it to raise cash and Napoleon melted down suitable pieces to mint coins. So there is very little glitter, but lots of crystal and porcelain and one poignant robe: of silver lamé with rich gold and silk embroidery. It was a gift from Pope Pius VI to Joseph II on the only papal visit to Austria in 1782.

A modern version of tapestry is still going on in one part of the Hofburg where experts are restoring Gobelin carpets and tapestries. To reach it, ask directions to the Kaisertor and ring the bell inside marked 'Gobelin Manufaktur'. They will take you in, past pre- and post-war diplomas and grand-prixs hanging in the foyer to the work rooms where some carpets are being darned and others painstakingly rebuilt. Modern ones in abstract designs are part of today's work, and around the rooms are the cabinets with hundreds of woollen reels in hundreds of shades, like so many colours in a giant paintbox.

This imperial complex has one other sight, and a quite unique one, the Spanish riding school. The horses came to Austria about 1562 and in 1580 Archduke Charles built a stable at Lipizza, near Trieste. After the first world war some of the stud returned there, after it had become part of Italy, and the rest found a new home at Piber, near Graz. During the second world war the mares were moved to Czechoslovakia for safe keeping and nearly whisked away by the Russians, were it not for a timely intervention by the American General Patton.

There are 60 stallions in all and only two of the present stable can perform the most difficult items, called Capriole and Courbette. The young horses, who turn white between four and eight years old, are taught by the old riders, the young riders by the expert horses. Every morning there is a training session, probably the most popular tourist attraction in Vienna, and spectators line the upper and lower galleries to watch this meticulous ballet beneath the chandeliers.

One charm is the silence, because you cannot hear the horses' hooves on the sand; the other is the pas de deux delicacy and the faraway dedicated look of the riders in their brown silk jackets, cream jodhpurs and Napoleon-style cockatoo hats. There is one earthy touch: the man with the small brush and pan to remove the manure; and one human touch: the 'valets' in faded blue who lead the horses away at the end of the session and give them a rewarding morsel for performing so well.

The Hofburg is certainly the largest and most important palace in Vienna, but it is by no means alone! The city's earlier investment in them means there are literally hundreds, almost one on every corner, to tempt the visitor on his city walks. Two of them especially, Upper Belvedere and Schönbrunn (to which we shall return later), must appear on any itinerary. Upper Belvedere now seems almost centrally situated, yet it was the summer hideaway built by Hildebrandt for Prince Eugene of

Savoy, who fled from his home country because he was too short to join the French army.

With an arrangement which allowed him one quarter of all the booty from the wars he obviously became very rich, and this palace is a perfect example of what a Field Marshal of 17 years standing might choose. The gate reflects his pride in being a knight of the Golden Fleece, for the lions are holding his coat of arms and two angels are holding the chain of the fleece. Belvedere's roof is like a series of tent shapes, such as you would find in a military camp, and on top of each are swords supplemented by military statues around the parapet.

There was nearly a nasty error in design when it was found that the palace appeared to sink, though only visually, slightly into the ground, but an ornamental lake in front 'lifts' the building by its reflections. Eugene was sometimes called the Secret Emperor, and the Viennese point to his 'crown' in the gardens, a neat bush trimmed into that shape. A small lodge in the forecourt is where Anton Bruckner died, having been given the one-storey house when he became too infirm to climb the stairs to his previous flat.

The interior of Upper Belvedere is now a permanent exhibition of Austrian paintings, but they are not the main lure to the visitor, who walks to the back, past children playing hopscotch and football, to discover the Belvedere (fine view) of the name, looking down across the French formal gardens to Lower Belvedere, also a museum, and out and over Vienna.

What you now realise with a shock is that you have seen a great deal of the capital without even going inside a church, for the Belvedere panorama is scattered with spires and domes. They are a study in themselves and I do not propose to go into much detail, but only to point out a few features that remain crystal-clear in my own mind. Their fascination is that each has a distinguishing mark, so to speak, and long afterwards you will remember: 'Oh yes, that was the one with. . . .'

Votiv church, on Rooseveltplatz, was dedicated by the Emperor of Mexico to his brother Franz Joseph, and guidebooks talk of how it resembles Westminster Abbey and has a rose window like Notre Dame. What you will remember is its nighttime garb, when the twin steeples lighted from within look like delicate lace embroidery patterns.

Karlskirche, on the other side of the city, is much more solid, by Fischer von Erlach, but unlike most baroque churches its dome is oval instead of round. It is named after St Charles, saint for warding off the plague, and put up in gratitude for the quick passing of an epidemic. You will remember its thin twin towers topped with bells and clocks to show how time flies, Charles VI's coat of arms above the main door and a macabre frieze to remind you how many unfortunates passed away.

St Rupert's, built over Roman walls and dating from the eighth century, looks, with its ivy-covered exterior, exactly like a village church. Until recently, it proudly held the title of the oldest one in Vienna, but now they believe St Peter's may have been founded even earlier, though its present building is baroque, by Hildebrandt. The Schottenkirche, just off the street of the same name, was christened the Scots church after the monks who came to Austria, except that they were not Scots at all, but Irish!

The Church am Hof is unique, not for style, but as the one from which Pope Pius VI addressed the public, with the difficult job of trying to persuade Joseph II not to close down the contemplative monasteries. A few minutes from here is the Deutschordenkirche with an irresistible setting in a courtyard of ivy-covered houses and, if you are lucky, you might find a small orchestra rehearsing here for its open-air matinee.

Every Viennese has a favourite church, his own among the many; the visitor can 'adopt', however temporarily, all of them. I have left until last the one that means most of all to everyone: the cathedral. My two guides in Vienna who accompanied me on alternate days preceded the sightseeing with a short history lesson. Although they knew each other slightly, in the way of colleagues, there was persistent subtle rivalry between them to pull off the 'coups' of Vienna.

When one discovered that I had been taken to St Stephen's the day before she gave an angry snort, quizzed me like a teacher on the more obscure facts (which, of course, I did not know), then said: 'Come, we return. I must tell you that only a few guides in this city really know Stefansdom, and I am one of them. Besides, I love it.' (This last with a beguiling smile.)

So back we went to try and understand why this cathedral is so important to the Viennese. One can see its place in history, because almost everything that happened from about 1500 was somehow connected with it. One can see the pride of the natives in their church. But it is still surprising to learn that, like the Opera House, it was above housing as a priority repair after the second world war. Contributions were largely in cash, but a young American soldier presented his modern painting, which hangs inside.

St Stephen's antecedents go back to the twelfth century when Vienna wanted a bishop, but knew she stood no chance of 'luring' one unless she could offer him a cathedral. So she began to build one and over its entrance are the masterbuilder and his mate keeping out the evil spirits. The Turkish siege we have already discussed, and their defeat is forever commemorated by one of their cannon balls, found embedded in the wall, upon which the Austrians carved a Turkish face.

They also melted down all the enemy cannons to make the famous bell, Pummerin, used for the last time at the funeral of Franz Joseph and not tolled now because of the danger of its collapsing. A bomb in the second world war dislodged Pummerin, which smashed an altar on its descent. The thrifty Viennese gathered up the bits of the big bell and sent them to Linz to be recast. Other war damage to Stefansdom was considerable, for the roof had fallen in and most of the walls and stained glass were destroyed.

But in a way some good came out of it, for in the rebuilding they discovered that the canopy above the pulpit did not fit there at all, but was the cover of the font in St Catherine's chapel. This pulpit is late gothic, with prophets of the old testament around its base and new testament apostles halfway up. Up the staircase climb frogs representing fire and evil and salamanders to combat these forces; but just in case any escapes there is a barking dog at the top to catch it.

Madonnas are often associated with miracles, but there can hardly be a more charming story than that of the Hausmutter in one of St Stephen's chapels. A young Styrian girl became a nun in Vienna and was put in charge of the convent porch, helping the poor. She fell in love with a nobleman, but before eloping took the porch key and laid it at the feet of the madonna in the cathedral chapel.

Sadly, her lover was killed and the young nun returned to plead, repentantly, with the abbess, for her old job back. The abbess claimed not to know what the young woman was talking about. The porch, she said, had been well looked after and she did not believe the nun had ever eloped. In the cathedral, the nun knelt down to pray to the madonna, who leaned over and returned the key.

St Stephen's cathedral houses several well-known tombs, that of Mozart, though not his body, that of Prince Eugene and of Frederick III, which is said to be among the most beautiful in Europe, in marble, by a Dutchman, showing the good works of the emperor and the man himself sculpted across the top. Like all the Habsburgs except two, the body of Frederick III lies in the imperial vaults in the Capuchin church not far from the cathedral.

There was a rigid protocol for the burial. When the funeral train reached the vault the coffin was opened, and the father guardian of the convent asked by the Grand Chamberlain if he recognised the dead person. After an affirmative reply, the coffin was locked with two keys—one given to the father guardian and the other kept in the treasure chamber, where the chest now contains 139, the earliest death being that of Duke Otto the Gay in 1339.

Most of the coffins inset into the walls of the vault are very simple, but there is a spectacular exception, that of Maria-

Theresia and Franz Stefan, who are sculpted at their resurrection across the top of the tomb. As well as having her own coffin prepared, this empress broke all the royal rules by insisting that her governess, Countess Fuchs-Mollard, whom she called her second mother, should be buried here, too. No one else ever managed that honour and the countess remains the only non-royal in the vaults.

Her tomb is a good deal more ornate than her employer's son, Joseph II, who tried to carry Maria-Theresia's liberal and benefactory ways a good deal further but still insisted before he died that he had achieved nothing because he was acting in advance of his time. Nevertheless, the reforms he began—abolishing torture and freeing slaves among them—did come to pass much later. His memory in the vaults is a simple one because he had decreed there would be no more funds for expensive imperial tombs.

After St Stephen's cathedral, there is one other building ranking high in Viennese hearts: the palace of Schönbrunn. In a similar way to that in which they drop in, informally, to their cathedral, families drop in, for an afternoon, at what they regard as Europe's most beautiful palace. They do not see it as an awesome historical monument, but as part of the Viennese way of life, which indeed it is.

State banquets and receptions are still held in its elegant rooms, young drama students perform in what used to be royalty's private theatre, and the ordinary folk take their coffee on the same terrace where Maria-Theresia used to breakfast. They do it without any selfconscious 'reincarnation' of past glories, but with an easy transposition of their heritage into modern terms.

Today's building has grown out of a manor house that Emperor Maximilian II bought in 1569 in the middle of what was then a magnificent sporting area conveniently near the centre of Vienna and the court. It is said that the seventeenth-century Emperor Matthias was the one who found a spring in the grounds after which Schönbrunn (beautiful fountain) was named. This favourite Habsburg hunting lodge was destroyed by the Turks in the 1683 siege, and a dozen or more years passed before Leopold I commissioned Fischer von Erlach to design a summer residence to take its place.

Erlach never did anything by halves and first turned in a grandiose scheme for an enormous series of buildings along the top of the hill where the Gloriette now stands, with terraced gardens rolling downwards. The plans never got further than the paper stage, because even by Habsburg standards they would have been terribly expensive. The architect's next effort was accepted, and at the end of the seventeenth century the first Schönbrunn took shape as a two-storeyed building with Italian flat roofs. The inside, however, was never completed, and as Leopold's sons took no interest in the palace it lay dormant for 40 years until Maria-Theresia adopted a new style for it.

Her architect changed the flat approaches into flights of steps, the roofs into sloping ones, and increased the number of rooms by inserting an extra floor. In 1746 the Empress took up residence in her imperial country-home and Schönbrunn was launched on its glittering career, its style remaining the same for more than 200 years. Maria-Theresia herself sang arias in the theatre, Mozart played here for the first time at the age of six in the Mirror Hall and is supposed to have clambered on to the emperor's lap afterwards.

Some of its memories, however, are not so artistic or so pleasant. Napoleon occupied the palace in 1805 and again in 1809, using the Chinese lacquer room as his study, signing the peace treaty here and topping the two obelisks on the gate with golden eagles as a victory sign. After his downfall it was, ironically, the setting for the Congress of Vienna. It was the birthplace and deathbed of Franz Joseph, and Napoleon's son died here. The last Habsburg emperor, Charles, signed his abdication on 11 November 1918 at Schönbrunn, ending its life as a privately owned house.

During the second world war most of the treasures were stored in the salt mines, and afterwards the palace became the headquarters of the British occupation forces. Today the first floor still houses the state apartments, but the rest has been turned into 250 flats in which live government staff, presumably the rooms much modernised, for the original palace boasted 139 kitchens and not a single bathroom!

The layout of the apartments was ruled by court ceremonial, giving every member of the imperial family entitled to hold court five rooms; an ante-chamber, audience chamber, drawing room for special guests, living room and bedroom. A married couple usually got twice the allocation with two bedrooms in the middle of the apartment and separate entrances. How the Habsburgs chose their quarters reflects their personalities. Joseph II and Franz Joseph lived in a cool, dark suite on the north side; Maria-Theresia had the south-east corner which catches the morning sun.

Schönbrunn is the only museum in Vienna to make a profit, and in 1964 there were 600,000 visitors, some of whom came in the evening when the Bohemian cut-glass crystal chandeliers are lit. In pre-electricity days it needed 20 servants just to light the candles. The chandelier in Franz Joseph's audience room is an exception to the delicate glass, for it is carved wood gilded to harmonise with the walnut walls and wood inlaid floor, to which somewhere in the palace you will find a 'twin', the light and dark wood patterns reversed.

This emperor's apartments are austere, the bedroom with a prayer stool, and a bowl and jug in place of a bathroom. His empress's drawing room, on the other hand, is delicate and feminine, with pastel paintings of Maria-Theresia's 16 children, 11 girls and five boys, ten of whom survived to adulthood and whose efforts at embroidery can be seen in their mother's breakfast room.

What you never see is the labyrinth of servants' corridors behind all the imposing apartments, to enable the staff to stoke the endless ceramic stoves without clattering among the royal inhabitants. And there is a very nifty device in Maria-Theresia's Chinese cabinet room to prevent the servants overhearing confidential meetings with ministers. A circular section of the floor can be lowered to one of the kitchens and then hauled up so that the cabinet could continue their deliberations uninterruptedly over lunch.

This, by the way, is one of several Chinese rooms. There is also the one used by Napoleon and the most precious of all called the Millions Room, presumably a reflection on its cost, with Chinese rosewood panelling and Indian miniatures, some of them more than 1,000 years old, set into the walls. By far the most charming overall aspect of Schönbrunn's state apartments is the preservation of its eighteenth-century rococo style, white and gold leaf panels, stuccoed ceilings, and those stoves and chandeliers.

While the palace itself is memorable enough, its surroundings and ancillary entertainments are even more so, because they have been designed to complement and enhance the whole. The only question is in which order to take the delights. My preference would be to start with the interior, as we have just done, then to follow through with the Wagenburg (coach museum) which began life as the winter riding school of Empress Elizabeth, and brings more enlightenment about the quirks and fancies of the Habsburgs, as well as the discomforts of travel in those days!

The earlier carriage made up for any lack of modernity, like springs and rubber tyres, with lots of plush and tasselling, though the model for travelling through the mountains is thoughtfully provided with a discreet toilet. By 1800, the journey from Vienna to Paris took a mere 26 days, the men sleeping in inns overnight, and the ladies in the carriage, which converted into a sort of caravan. An inside panel lifted up to provide leg rests, there were shutters all round to provide privacy, a fitment for a washing bowl and a big box on top in which were stored the ladies' arrival dresses.

Of the royal examples, the diminutive ones for the young Habsburgs are irresistible. Marie-Louise's son, the Duke of Reichstadt, had a golden phaeton drawn by two white sheep, and as a child his mother was driven (ladies, even little ones, never drove themselves) in a cool pale green tiny coach lined with silk. Earlier in history Maria-Theresia's children had a little golden cart in which they raced around what is now the Spanish riding school.

Of the adult carriages, three are the most interesting: Franz Joseph's is predictably simple with its royal crown on the glass lamps, but it has touches which show his interest in gadgetry, like an ashtray (very daring) and rubber tyres (very unusual). His son, Rudolf, had a hunting sleigh with a swivel chair, reindeer horns to support his guns and servants to ride back and front.

Then there is the showpiece, the coronation coach, first used in 1711 for Charles VI, and last used for Charles in 1916 in Budapest. Its interior and exterior trimmings are gold and it had, incomprehensibly, an order of precedence for the horses: eight white ones for the emperor, six for the princes, four for the aristocracy and two for ordinary folk (though one cannot imagine a situation ever arising when only a pair of horses would be needed!).

Having strolled through an avenue of linden trees from the Wagenburg, there is still more of Schönbrunn to investigate, perhaps joining the natives on the terrace outside the zoo pavilion, Maria-Theresia's favourite breakfast spot. Her husband was greatly interested in animals and the ornamental cages of the menagerie were grouped like a star around the octagonal pavilion where visitors sat in comfort to view them. Nearly all were gifts, and, sadly, a number were killed during the second world war. Today's zoo has modernised quarters, but its personality as a plaything of the imperial court still lingers.

The flavour is even more tangible in the grounds, laid out in 1770-75, which are an open-air extension of the palace, dozens of flower beds copying the same baroque patterns as are on the gold-leaf walls inside Schönbrunn. From the house at diagonals run twin avenues of lime and ash, trimmed to form a solid wall of green, and a constant view back to the palace. Inset in these giant hedges are statues, Grecian and others, to improve the minds of the strolling archdukes and duchesses.

Like most French baroque gardens Schönbrunn includes the 'musts' of Roman ruins, an obelisk with fake Egyptian writing (the hieroglyphics were discovered to be pure nonsense years later), several fountains and the Neptune one in particular, a maze, the largest hothouse in Europe and an extraordinary renaissance-style temple, the Gloriette, looking down on the whole affair. No wonder the Viennese love to come here, and they have always been admitted to the largest part of the gardens, though the same rule did not apply in the riverside playground in the city.

It was the liberal son of Maria-Theresia, Joseph II, who opened the Prater (from Spanish prado, meaning meadow) to the public in 1776, retaining as imperial property only the deer meadow and the duelling rendezvous. But until then it had been a very exclusive area indeed. Ferdinand I thoughtfully planted the three-mile long chestnut avenue, Hauptallee (but not with the common people in mind), and then Maximilian II took over the Prater as an even more convenient hunting ground than Schönbrunn.

Rudolf II towards the end of the sixteenth century, was strangely worried that the wrong kind of people might get in, so made a rule that anyone wishing to visit the Prater must get permission from the imperial forester. This was a notoriously uncouth character called Hans Bengel and his memory lingers on, for the Viennese snarl 'bengel' today when they are describing a particularly rude person.

Today the Prater is a vast playground, combining in more than 1,000 acres everything from fun fair to sports stadium to that chestnut-tree walk. The Viennese eat in the emperor's hunting lodge or in another restaurant sitting atop the Prater's only high ground (and that artificially made from the earth-moving activity to produce the circular display hall for the world exhibition in 1873).

Businessmen head for the vast complex of buildings that make up the permanent international trade fair. Sports-lovers troop into the stadium, swimming pool or race course. Everyone visits the famous fun fair which a year or two ago celebrated its two-hundredth birthday. The most spectacular item is the 180-foot high ferris wheel, which takes ten minutes to make one turn and now only has half the number of wagons for which it was designed. They are replacements following a fire in 1945 which nearly destroyed this Viennese landmark.

In nearby Prater street is the little pink house in which Strauss composed the Blue Danube waltz in 1867, the tune still beloved by all, although its title is inaccurate. The river is not blue, and does not flow through the centre of the city.

It formerly had many arms (one of them is now a lake in the Prater parkland), and though the meadows are still retained on one bank to take the overflow, the precaution is no longer necessary, for the Danube was controlled and regulated 90 years ago. The river proper flows through the suburbs, the central 'Danube' is a canal, the whole complex best understood and seen from the top of the Danube tower, like London's G.P.O. tower, built a few years ago. It is a fitting beginning—or a sad goodbye—to Vienna. No, not a final goodbye, for you are bound to return to this city; you will not be able to resist it.

20 *Rein, near Graz: the monastery church*

21   Band playing in a small village near Velden

8 Burgenland

There is a giant of an old man with bristling moustache and voluminous breeches who speaks excruciating German to the visitors he shows round the little white bungalow at Raiding where Franz Liszt was born. He, more than the limitless plain stretching eastwards or the watch-towers down the long border, poignantly reminds us that this thin sliver of Austria was in Hungary until after the first world war.

Actually, the museum custodian with his uneasy German overlaid on native Hungarian, is more of a rarity than you might imagine. Of Burgenland's 270,000 population only 1½ per cent originate from the country over the border and you are more likely to run into Serbo-Croats, who number 11 per cent of the total inhabitants and cluster in their own villages, than the pure Hungarian remnants of the empire days.

The majority of the natives insist firmly on their Austrian heritage (gypsy bands in the hotels are there solely for tourists, the Croats have their own Tamburizza with tambourines, mandolines, accordions) and perhaps have forgotten how their province came to be named after the four main Hungarian towns which were in that part of the world.

They were Eisenburg, Odenburg, Wieselburg and Pressburg, so the original christening fell naturally into Vierburgenland, or country of the four towns. The 'vier' was dropped from the new name because, as it happened, none of the quartet eventually were part of the new province. Odenburg (now Sopron) would have been the obvious choice for the capital, but after the creation of the province by the treaty of St Germain in 1919 the natives of this town subsequently opted to remain Hungarian.

The decision forced Burgenland into a very odd shape. It is not more than 100 miles long from north to south, but has a nipped-in waist somewhere round its middle where its width is reduced to less than two miles. Left on the other side is not only Sopron, but the southern section of Burgenland's masterpiece, the Neusiedler-see.

An alternative capital had to be found and Eisenstadt, the largest town with 8,000 inhabitants, was chosen, not only for its size but because it had the imposing duke of Esterhazy's palace to give it authority. The duke lost much of his property to Hungary, escaped from there to Switzerland in the 1956 uprising and pays but occasional visits to see the vineyards and woods he owns in the northern part of Burgenland.

But his influence is considerable, he is in possession of what one Burgenlander described as 'most of the essentials in our province' and the regional authorities have to tread delicately to try and develop those amenities in Esterhazy's hands. Inexplicably, the little open-air café in the courtyard of the only intact castle was closed by ducal decree. The tourist office shakes its head sadly, tries not to count the Austrian schillings lost as a result, and hopes the decree may be reversed.

There are enough problems making ends meet in Burgenland. Something like 200,000 of the original natives have emigrated, 25,000 of them to Chicago alone, and a further 40,000 work and live in Vienna during the week returning home only for Saturday and Sunday. The pressing need is to augment agriculture with industry and tourism, but the pastoral flavour is the abiding memory the visitor takes away.

You will park your car outside a café and alongside it will come a horse and cart piled high with hay, waiting while the farmer has a quick drink. The same cart may be loaded with grapes in the lakeside vineyard district. In the fruit-growing area near Mattersburg the fields are full of pickers in the mornings and in the afternoon the women sit by the roadside selling their strawberries, apples, peaches and cherries. A few prosperous farmers can afford scooters to draw their carts.

The villages are so shuttered and quiet you wonder that anyone lives here at all, except the busy geese waddling in formation up the street or cooling their feet in the stream. But each and every village is a model example of the special Burgenland country architecture, the one-storey houses built in linked pairs all along the street, a courtyard with double doors between each. They are mostly painted white with a blue fringe round the bottom, but occasionally yellow and green is the colour scheme.

The only visible sign that this may be a Croatian village (like Trausdorf) is that it is maybe a little shabbier and lacks the gay window boxes that make the others look as though they are entering a competition for the best-kept village with the most flowers. The villages around the Neusiedler-see would surely carry off these floral trophies, Mörbisch, perhaps the gold-medallist with its series of narrow cobblestone alleys off the main streets, the flower-bedecked houses nodding to each other and yellow bunches of corn on the cob hanging up to dry.

Here, as in all the vineyard villages, are Heurigen and dozens of Flaschenweine where you can buy two-litre bottles of the really pure brew. The wine industry, third in importance after the Wienerwald and Lower Austria, depends entirely on the mysterious Neusiedler-see, about which many of the natives simply shrug their shoulders quizzically and point to heaven when asked for an explanation of how and why it stays as it does.

The lake not only regulates the climate for the vines, but provides Burgenland with its main tourist attraction, an expanse of water 2 miles long, from three to nine miles wide, never more than six feet deep so you could walk its length, though you are more likely to lie on its shimmering surface on an air bed. Why the water stays is the mystery, because it is fed by a ridiculously small creek that would not even account for evaporation, and in fact, horrifically, the entire lake disappeared for two years in 1865.

Its vital ingredient to the vines is that it retains the heat during the day and redistributes it at night. But it also has a belt of reeds, sometimes two miles thick, round almost the entire perimeter and unless the water is kept at a reasonable level the reeds would take over. Experts say that the water comes from underground springs, a theory confirmed in winter by mad fools who try to drive their cars across its frozen surface only to come unstuck in places where the ice is suddenly much thinner.

The modern safeguard against another total evaporation is a channel with lock gates to the Danube which was completed just before Burgenland became Burgenland and unfortunately left the lock gates in Hungary. So a careful treaty has been drawn up between the two countries to regulate the opening and closing of the lock.

It is not quantity, but quality of the vine that matters, and the climate provided by the elusive lake gives the grapes a high sugar content and consequently a high alcoholic content. The natives are proudest of three special kinds of grape which are left for a long time on the vine, resulting in something very golden, very thick, very sweet and very strong.

For large-scale consumption they concentrate on white wines like Rheinriesling, sparkling and medium dry; Traminer, which is sweet; Weissburgunder, fresh and sparkling; sweet Muskat Ottonel and others, all totally dependent on the natural phenomena. The Neusiedler-see is a tantalising Venetian-style illusion for the visitor. Almost the only panoramic view is just outside St Margarethen, where it appears as a shimmering shining line in the distance.

The nearer you get the less the view, striking first the vineyards and then the reed belt through which the road is cut. It is a sinister, closed-in feeling to drive to the lakeside seeing nothing of it and to have the reeds waving tall above the roof of the car. The Burgenlanders cut the reeds in winter when the lake is frozen, and pile them in wigwam shapes to dry before making mats and decorations.

For such a large expanse of water there are comparatively few places where the weeds, either artificially or naturally, have made room for humans. In half a dozen such places you can idle on grass or under trees, swim in the warm slightly salt, though not clear water, where live pike, carp and eel, sail its length or explore the reed inlets in row boats. Always there is a dreamy, heat-haze quality, rarely a view showing the enormous size of the Neusiedler-see except at Podersdorf am See.

But each plage, or lakeside village, provides at least one extra attraction, not the splendid and awe-inspiring monuments to be found in other Austrian provinces, but something of appeal and charm. Mörbisch, for instance, as well as its narrow cobblestones, has built an open-air theatre and every August puts on operetta with a Hungarian character.

Rust has an eye-opening flock of storks sitting in a dignified and statuesque way on top of the houses on specially built nests with a sort of barbecue grill for a base. How and why they chose Rust is as mysterious as the waters of the Neusiedler-see, but something like 150 of them arrive in late March, having wintered on the Nile and about eight weeks later the babies are born. The return trip to Egypt is at the end of August when the youngsters are strong enough to make the distance. Most of the birds have been ringed and return, like faithful family pets, to the house they occupied the year before.

The village which gives its name to the lake, Neusiedl am See, has made an artificial beach and in 1967 opened the first part of the See museum with, appropriately, stuffed birds, for it is reckoned there are more than 250 species living in the reed belt. The next museum section, to be built at Rust, will deal with the history of the lake.

Eastwards from the Neusiedler-see runs the seemingly limitless Hungarian plain and the best view of its enormity is further south in Burgenland, first taking the only main road north to south (all the other highways run west to east), which was built after the Russians left in 1955. Leaving the car above Rechnitz, it is a half-hour stroll through the woods, accompanied by a buzzing flotilla of insects, to the summit of Geschriebenstein, at 2,600 feet Burgenland's highest mountain, and a stone tower through the middle of which actually runs the frontier.

But Hungary kindly moved its border back a few yards, so the tower remains Austrian and from its top you look over into Hungary. Apart from the watch towers which mark, along about 150 miles, the division between the two countries, Burgenland has in common with other Austrian provinces the fortresses and castles which helped keep the Turks and other invaders at bay, but its original geographical position in the empire made it the most vulnerable to attack and only one of its castles remains intact.

It is the fourteenth-century Forchtenstein, bought by the Esterhazys in the early seventeenth century, and driving up to it you can see why the Turks never stormed it or wisely decided not to try. It sits in a pine forest, an open-air swimming pool just below, the open-air theatre in the moat a cheerful contrast to the sinister well inside the castle. It is a staggering 400 feet deep and is said to have been built by Turkish prisoners, 5,000 of whom would have taken 20 years to complete the job.

Castle-hunters can trace more history through Lockenhaus, another Esterhazy property, stopping at one of the 20 lidos opened in the last five years for natives not within travelling distance of the Neusiedler-see. Then drive on to Schlaining, a pretty hilly village with a castle that dates from the thirteenth century when it was owned by the Counts of Güssing. A big round tower was added during the sixteenth and seventeenth centuries and the castle is lived in during the summer by an Austrian minister, though it is open to the public.

Schlaining is south of Burgenland's nipped-in waist, but the same 'rules' apply here as in the lakeside villages in the way of little extra attractions. They have to be small-scale, for apart from Eisenstadt only a handful of towns in the province can boast as many as 4,000 inhabitants.

Raiding rightly collects its crop of tourists as Franz Liszt's birthplace. The question of whether the composer was Austrian or Hungarian was posed again when the village in which he was born changed nationalities—from Hungary to Austria. But his mother came from Krems in Lower Austria and the Austrians naturally claim him as their own. In fact Liszt did not spend much of his youth in Raiding. He went to Paris with his parents when he was 11 and by the time he was 20 years of age was so celebrated that fans were cutting strips off his coat as souvenirs. But he had his seventieth birthday in this sleepy village.

Bernstein makes a shiny grey-green stone called edelserpentin, a sort of cross between jade and marble, and though the stone is crude and the craft consequently so, too, the ornaments and statues and candleholders, necklaces and pipes are pretty souvenirs. Piringsdorf is the village of basket-makers, Bad-Tazmannsdorf has the proud title of the largest number of visitors because it is a spa with an all-year season.

In all these places the Burgenlanders are adept at making the most of what they have to offer, but without the sophistication and commercialism of the 'hard sell'. The necklaces and baskets are there, but not in overwhelming numbers and not so obtrusively that they repel visitors. You might pass right by the quarry at St Margarethen in the north of the province, for instance, and not realise this is a sort of sculpture museum. The original stones were used for building Vienna's cathedral; now there is an annual sculpture symposium when artists come from all over the world to collect a chunk of the rock. Their modern efforts look strangely anachronistic against the craggy, rather messy quarry background.

The quarry is owned by Esterhazy and is only a short drive out from Burgenland's capital, Eisenstadt, and Esterhazy's home when he visits the province. His castle here is more a great pile of stone than an elegant architectural structure, and certainly the interior is disappointing and shabby, very little of it to be seen as most is now occupied by government officials.

Perhaps it is best not even to drive into the courtyard, but to look at the faintly peeling exterior and imagine the glowing days when Haydn was here. He was musical director for the Esterhazys for nearly 30 years from 1760 and his house is a pretty pale blue with geranium window boxes and cool white courtyard. A bench has a musical stave motif, a modern embellishment, and upstairs the whole place is totally restored, but nicely done. There are old prints, musical scores, a hammerchord piano, busts of the master, all quite justified, for Haydn composed vigorously while he was here, including the Austrian national anthem.

Apart from the Esterhazy castle, Eisenstadt is really nothing more than a memorial to its favourite musician. Haydn's tomb is the only modest item in the church, whose exterior is strung about with angels perched on the stairs, the walls, in the grounds. Haydn is the native pride, but the visitor will remember the scenery and peace and dreamy atmosphere of slender Burgenland, the eastern foothills of the Alps nudging its long left side, the vast plain yawning away from its right.

Its appeal is not dramatic, its poverty more outspoken than elsewhere in Austria, yet its images remain, tiny cameos of gaggling geese, shuttered villages, modest but interesting things to see and absorb.

9 Styria

The prince who married a commoner, became a village mayor, and turned his house into a museum for the people is the nineteenth-century idol of Styria. His brother Franz II was emperor, but Johann had almost that stature in this province and the natives look back on him with affection and pride; rightly so, for the democratic prince not only gave an artistic lead but supported a number of crafts and industries which ensured the region's prosperity.

Whether they are conscious of it or not, the Styrians today have a similar enlightened attitude following Johann's example. Not that in the twentieth century they face the prince's premier problem—wanting to marry a commoner! He charmed everyone by secretly courting a postmaster's daughter and marrying her after a ten-year wait when she was graciously created a countess.

In the meantime, and afterwards, he looked about Styria to further develop its commerce, linking the southern climate to the vineyards, seeing the industrial value of the magical iron-ore mountain, a raw red rust wound in the green countryside. He also turned one of his houses in the capital, Graz, into a museum for his people, beginning the collection with his own paintings and minerals, and as mayor of a little village called Stainz, he made the abbey on top of the hill into his castle home in order to live on the spot.

To do all this and still remain popular needed a deal of diplomacy and tact, two qualities the Styrians have developed and certainly practise today. Frederick III built the fifteenth-century cathedral with gothic arches and baroque decoration and outside a grim reminder of life in the middle ages, a dimming fresco showing the old city and the four disasters of those days: war, plague, locusts and fire.

He also began the castle (now government offices) behind the cathedral, and its stone gate is one of the two still remaining entrances to the old city (the Paulustor is the other). Like everything else this emperor had a hand in, he left his signature on a plaque outside: the vowels of the alphabet. No-one is quite sure what they stand for, but a popular theory is 'Austria est in orbe ultima'—which in contemporary terms might be freely translated as 'Austria in all the world is the greatest'!

This did not, however, deter Napoleon from demolishing both the castle and other parts of the city. It suffered in World War II as well and afterwards was rebuilt in as near as possible the same style. What has survived intact from the late fifteenth century is a fascinating double spiral staircase with no pillars or supports except two sets of steps rising through four storeys. There is nothing spectacular about the reconstructed buildings themselves, irreverently christened the Ink Castle by the natives, who are not the white-collar workers inside.

Graz was the residence of the Habsburgs for 60 years and it was Archduke Charles who was 'given' Styria and Carinthia and chose the capital as his home. About this time, too, the breeding of the thoroughbreds began at Lipizza that was to lead to the Spanish riding school. The Jesuit college was also founded; today there are three universities and one-third of the students are foreign, an indication of Styria's position as a bridgehead between Germanic and Slavonic—the German-speaking world and Yugoslavia and the Balkans.

The next emperor to be interested in the province was Ferdinand II, who became so devoted to his Styrian heritage that he built himself a mausoleum in 1614 and became one of the very few Habsburgs not buried in the imperial vaults in Vienna. In those days the province was known as 'the strongest fortress in the Christian world' and 'the protective fence of the Holy Roman Empire and the German people'.

Today it has a different task, as delicate mediator between east and west. Graz is halfway between Vienna and Zagreb, a drive of about 125 miles to either, so it is no surprise to be lunching with a Yugoslav at the castle restaurant on the hill. But it is a surprise to see our hosts' chameleon character, very correct with the Englishwoman, very boisterous and Slavonic with the Yugoslav as we discuss the tourism possibilities of 're-routing' returning holidaymakers from Yugoslavia through Styria instead of Italy.

Afterwards the Styrians explain courteously to me the need to remain good friends and neighbours. South of the city is the enduring example of good neighbourliness, six miles of road which borders on to Yugoslavia. But it is a very special road, for on either side are vineyards cultivated by both nations and no matter how difficult the political situation became this Weinstrasse was never closed and retains its neutrality.

These southern vineyards, together with orchards and chestnut trees, are but a part of Styria's richness, scenically, historically and economically. Many of its castles and romanesque abbeys are in this region; in its central section are the hills and forests which give Styria its nickname the 'Green Province'; and in the north are the mountains and glaciers, including the Erzberg iron-ore mountain and the 9,840 feet Dachstein.

The countryside and towns have all the hallmarks of a prosperous upbringing, despite the wars—particularly the Napoleonic ones—that ravaged the province. The farmers have time and inclination to cultivate their window boxes; the shutters, usually green, are freshly painted, the wood building has a brick inset to take the stove. And up in the mountains their practical streak makes them add a covered corridor to the stable so that if the snow is very heavy the farmers still reach their animals.

In June they are harvesting the first hay crop, and exhibiting the same practicality coupled with old traditions, for how they dry the crop seems to depend not only on local climate, and whether you can spread the hay thin or need to bunch it together for protection, but on what your grandfather and his forbears did. Sometimes the hay is a wigwam shape; sometimes it is built into thin towers that stand like guardsmen in straight lines across the meadows; sometimes it is three-pronged like a tripod; sometimes it is a gate framework that forms the hay into a solid hedge.

Hard workers these countryfolk certainly are, but not over-earthy or rough. Near Stainz is a typical country restaurant called Engelweingarten (Angel's Vineyard), named after the surrounding area; one of the mountains nearby is called Rosenkogel (Rose Hill). They are picturesque names for a picturesque countryside.

In the cities and towns the earlier prosperity is very obvious, its result an elegance of style that makes Graz, with 250,000 inhabitants, a worthy number two to Vienna. It has none of the busyness and grandeur of Innsbruck, but a graciousness and spaciousness justifying its special nickname 'the garden city', for of its total area, only about a tenth is covered by houses: the remainder is set out in parks, meadows and woodland. They used to call it the city of pensioners. Now, with its 9,000 students, it is called the city of pensioners and students.

The visitors get little hint of its considerable area, unless they are looking down on it from the castle hill, and most people restrict themselves to a comfortable morning's stroll through the old city for a dip into renaissance history. Early merchants were prosperous enough to have Italians design their houses, so Graz is full of lovely courtyards, like the Keplerkeller where the astronomer Kepler lived while lecturing at the university.

Like Vienna, they fly flags (this time green and white) outside buildings of historic interest. The merchants provided the street names by the trades they practised; hence a painters' street, flour square, butchers' square and so on. Stempfergasse is a particularly fine example of sixteenth-century houses with ornate façades. The Sporgasse, going down to the main square, is wisely closed to motor traffic.

In the Hauptplatz, looking benignly down on the vegetable, fruit and flower market, stands a statue of favourite Prince

Johann, surrounded by women representing the four rivers of old Styria, one of which is now entirely in Yugoslavia. Neither of today's two rivers rise in the province, but in Land Salzburg. The Enns runs through the northern part; the Mur, which bubbles and flows fast through Graz but is badly polluted by industrial towns further upstream, flows into Yugoslavia. Both eventually join the Danube.

Graz's most impressive example of renaissance work is the sixteenth-century Landhaus, the provincial parliament, several storeys of elegant rounded arches and balustrades, each with its colourful window boxes. Down below, for one summer month, the courtyard becomes an open-air theatre, for the capital prides itself on being something of a musical and dramatic centre. Their version of the Vienna Boys' Choir is a grown-up Grazerdomchor which sings both locally and internationally.

The opera house and the playhouse are both heavily subsidised and operate for ten months of the year. Like the Vienna Opera House, the intimate 650-seat playhouse was also magnificently helped in its rebuilding by large contributions from the natives. It was originally built in 1820, rebuilt after a fire and completely run down and closed by the end of the second world war. When it was a question of pulling it down or reconstructing the people of Graz saw no choice: they raised money towards the cost and it reopened in 1963.

To one side of the elegant Landhaus and joined to it is Graz's most famous possession, the armoury, once used by the townsfolk, their soldiers and mercenaries as the weapon store. It is a unique arsenal which would have been pulled down had not the patriotic Styrians successfully petitioned Empress Maria-Theresia to keep it in place. Come the nineteenth century they catalogued the contents and counted more than 30,000 items. The building, four storeys high with timbered ceilings, dates from 1640, and very little except feeble electric light has been added to it since.

So because of poor lighting and no heating it is open only in summer, which gives the attendants the rest of the year to de-rust and clean everything. From the ceiling hang helmets, in endless racks are guns, pistols inlaid with cattle horn and ivory, powder horns, cannons, suits of armour, including some that are finely inlaid with religious motifs on the breastplates. The early weapons were made of iron, the later from steel.

The raw materials came, naturally, from Styria's iron-ore mountain, but it is not entirely a military inventory. They had time for play, too, with some examples of armour for tournaments and jousting showing the special device on which you could rest your lance between charges.

The Landhaus and armoury are clearly the focal points of the town, but the dominating geographical feature is the castle hill, the stronghold in the old days except when French troops occupied Graz during the Napoleonic wars of 1805-10 (the Turks despite several efforts in 1480, 1529 and 1532 had never managed to storm it). Napoleon destroyed almost the entire castle but the townsfolk paid up handsomely to leave one of the sixteenth-century bell towers just below it standing. It is called Lisl, short for Elizabeth after a chapel of that name, and strikes only three times a day, seven a.m., noon, and seven p.m.

Also still intact is a pretty clock tower, plus the castle bridge and the old dungeons, transformed by the artistic inhabitants into a summer theatre with the cells forming the boxes. The hill, Schlossberg, is reached by a funicular rising 350 feet in five minutes, and other hills on either side of the river restrict Graz's modern development, though there is a hideous 26-storey block of flats, the highest in Austria, sticking up in the centre of the panorama.

Now part of the suburbs, but out in the country when it was built in 1625, is Graz's answer to Schönbrunn, though it does not, of course, compare with the Viennese masterpiece. Nevertheless, Schloss Eggenberg was an elegant mansion for Prince Eggenberg. It has a tower on each corner, a courtyard in the middle, a moat with stags and deer, a front and back drawbridge and peacocks strutting about between the four warrior statues in front.

There are 12 entrances, 65 rooms and a window for each day

of the year, but its exterior looks much grander than this, and around the inner courtyard are the same Italian galleries and balustrades to be seen elsewhere in Graz, but this time hung with antlers and hunting gear—the prince and his successors were great hunters. The last Eggenberg, a boy of 13, died in 1707, so the place was taken over by the dukes of Herberstein and eventually acquired by the city of Graz.

The interior is disappointing, for though some treasures were removed during World War II the castle was occupied by the Russians until 1955 and the decorations have either disappeared or been crudely repainted. The state apartments on the second floor are still used for concerts and balls, but only one is really fine, the room with parallel rows of chandeliers, black and white floor, and paintings alternating with windows on either side. As you would expect, the museum on the first floor deals with hunting. The best part of Schloss Eggenberg for the natives is its park, a favourite with young mothers and children as a playground because it is closed to public traffic.

About 20 minutes' drive from Graz is one of the many pilgrim churches, Maria-Trost. It was originally a castle, became a Franciscan monastery from the late seventeenth century and is still operating. The style is not the best of baroque, but the hilltop setting is grand, and it is pleasing to see the monks pottering about in the garden.

As a provincial capital, Graz makes trading sense, sitting as it does in the commercially important area of Styria. But it is very isolated by mountains from its northern section, called Upper Styria, and it would be a rugged character indeed who expected to make day tours from here and cover the whole province.

It is better to use it as a base to cover nearby sights, making the same sort of excursions the natives themselves make at weekends. Only about half an hour or so north of the city is one of their favourite winter resorts, Semriach, which clearly at just over 2,000 feet cannot compare with Austria's famous ski resorts, but has a special place in their hearts because it is one of the 99 resorts in the entire country entitled to call itself tranquil.

In summer, visitors walk an hour from Semriach to take the chairlift up the Schökl mountain, then walk 1½ hours home; in winter there are several drag lifts to open up the skiing terrain. The village sits on a gentle rolling plateau, a sweet surprise after the usual snaky thin road to reach it. Down at the bottom, near the main road junction, is another surprise: hidden discreetly behind a dusty quarry is the entrance to Lurgrotte, the stalactite and stalagmite cave.

It is an unprepossessing beginning, not very well signposted, but worth soldiering on through the quarry buildings. The cave, at three miles long, is the largest of its kind in Austria, and cuts right through the mountain from Peggau to Semriach. Its name, Lur, means snail, after the fossilised snails that were found there. A tiny brook bubbles quietly through the cave and the complete conducted tour takes a couple of hours, with electric lights for a few hundred yards at either end, and a lantern to carry for the middle section.

All of this should put you in just the right pre-twentieth-century mood for Stubing, barely out of the quarry complex and on the way back to Graz, where they are building an open-air museum and transplanting items like a 400-year-old wine pressing barn to keep alive the old traditions.

It is a must on the curriculum for schoolchildren, as is another of the province's precious possessions, the Piber stud farm west of Graz where are bred the stallions for Vienna's Spanish riding school. My visit coincided with an en masse onslaught by coach-loads of youngsters, who hardly glanced at the elegant house with its Italian courtyard built in the eighteenth century and now the administration building, but made straight for the stables.

The director explained that the 1,400-acres farm was founded 'fairly recently' in 1798, but the district was always a horse-breeding one and before the Lipizzans arrived the stud farm kept the emperor's stables stocked with thoroughbreds. It soon becomes clear that the mares have the roughest life at Piber. The

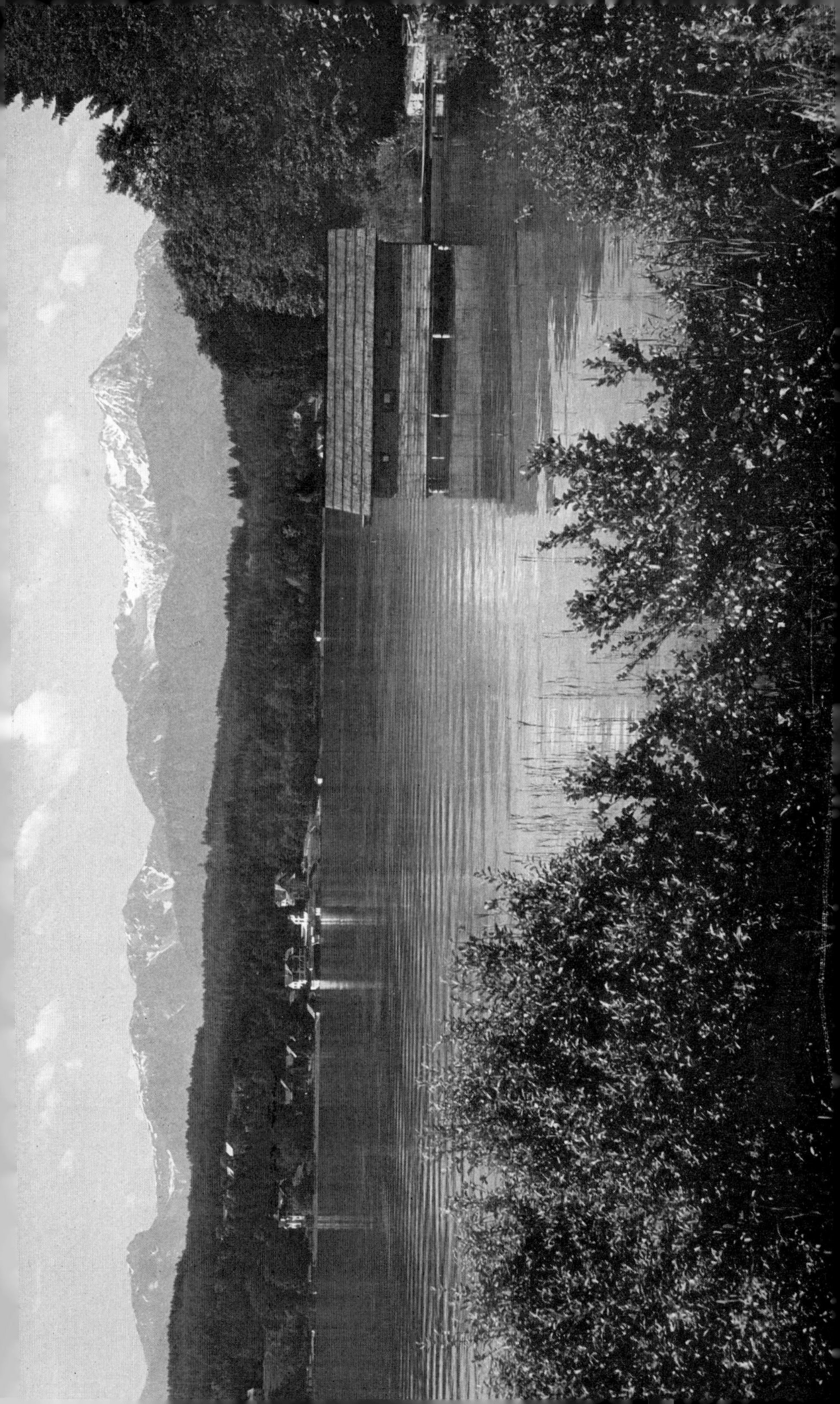

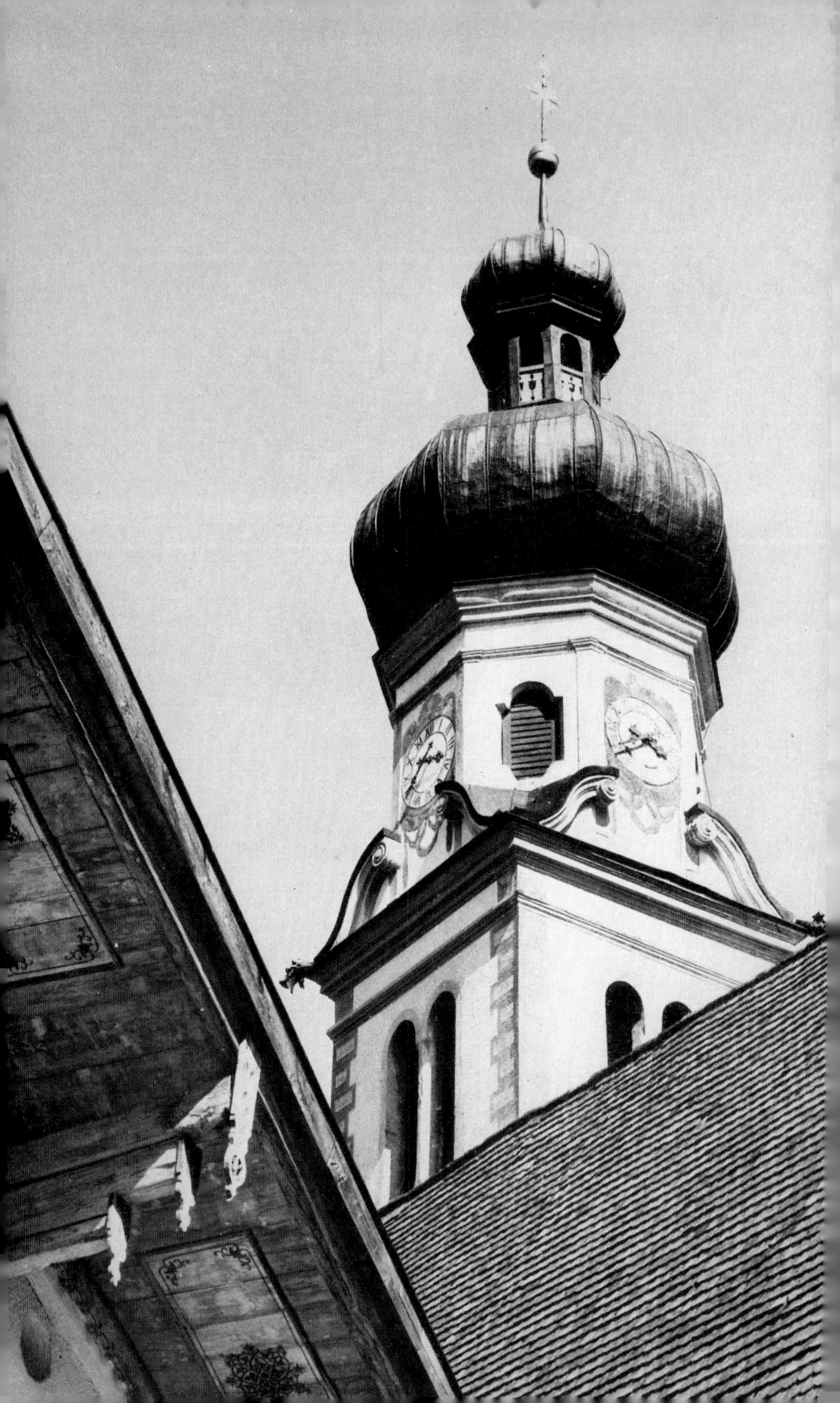

reason they are never used to perform at the Spanish riding school is not because they are unsuitable, but because in mediaeval days a knight would not be seen dead on a mare, and always rode a stallion. Tradition still holds good.

So the mares, while tenderly cared for, have only one purpose: to breed the new stallions, and after a one-year 'general education' course they are ready for the job of motherhood, which turns out to be an arduous one. Nine days after the birth of the foal they are put to the stallion (of whom there are always three on 'duty') again, so while suckling the new arrivals they are pregnant again.

They may bear up to 18 foals in their lifetime and the youngsters stay at Piber for their first $3\frac{1}{2}$ years, which is a great attraction for the visitors, gathered in the afternoons to watch mums and babies set off for their walk to the nearby Alpine meadows. When the young stallions are sent to Vienna they are absolutely unbroken, and their training at the school will take two or three years. Later, some will be brought back to Piber for a season or two to father the next generation.

East of Graz in an area not so well-known to visitors, lie the castles and fortresses which helped Styria live up to its 'protective fence' title; as elsewhere in the country, many of them are in ruins, but the thirteenth-century Riegersburg, not far from the border with Burgenland, still remains, famed for its seven arches and its size. They say you could build a small town on the space it occupies, and why not, when in the old days the entire town and outlying district inhabitants ran to it for shelter.

Also in this area is one of the few places in the world where they do ski-flying. It is at Kulm, which together with Mitterndorf in Upper Styria, Vikersond near Oslo in Norway, Planica in Yugoslavia and Obersdorf in Bavaria, Germany, takes turns to hold the world championships, an intimate affair with about 48 people competing over five days. There is no practising with this sport, just the annual get-together, and although the technique does not look very different from ski-jumping to the untuned and ignorant eye, the flyers cover about 450 feet in the air as opposed

23 *Natters church in Tyrol*

to under 300 feet in jumping, and take off at nearly 90 miles an hour.

Styria makes another claim to skiing fame at Mürzzuschlag, on the eastern exit of the province via the Semmering pass, where, it is said, two Styrians first introduced skiing, cross-country style, from Norway. It still remains more of a nordic than an Alpine sport in this region.

To reach Upper Styria it is a simple geographical switch of river valleys from the Mur, which you can hardly get away from in the south, to the Enns, which joins the Mur in a narrow valley, then slips right through the northern mountain chain to provide the valley westwards to Land Salzburg. There is only one other way to leave this part of the province and that is via Bad Aussee and the beginnings of the Salzkammergut.

The motorist heading north from Graz in search of adventure and sights will be tempted by several diversions before arriving anywhere near the Salzkammergut. The open-cast iron-ore mountain, Erzberg, near Eisenerz, may not be beautiful in an accepted sense, but it is a dramatic sight, divided up into about 40 rust-coloured ledges each from 75 to 100 feet high and placed one above the other like terraces. The mining goes back to at least Roman times, the Bavarians resumed the industry in the eighth century and by the late thirteenth it was world-renowned.

Not far from Eisenerz is a parting of the ways, where you need to toss a coin, not to make a final decision on whether to turn north or head west, but which direction to take first. The more northerly route goes into the Salza valley and finally to Mariazell, just in Styria, the largest shrine in Austria.

Its story began with a Benedictine monk who built a hermit's cell in the mid-twelfth century and not long afterwards one of the Margraves then ruling Styria was miraculously cured after visiting the monk. He put up a chapel in gratitude, which is still part of today's church, and Mariazell was launched on the pilgrim's way. Also still part of today's building is a gothic tower and a central nave built by King Ludwig of Hungary (very probably more gratitude) in the late fourteenth century and which somehow were not destroyed by a fire in 1474, nor by the Turks in 1529, nor by another fire in 1827.

Back to that junction near Eisenerz, the scenery turns highly dramatic in the Gesäuse gorge where road, railway and river clamour for room, criss-crossing each other below the sheer rock walls. The whirling river is a number one sport for canoeists; to the unathletic it is a little too sinister for comfort and they will reach with relief the next important stop on the tourist map, Admont, where if you ask the way to the library everyone knows you do not mean the place to borrow books but the baroque one at the abbey founded in 1074 by the archbishop of Salzburg.

Like Topsy, it just grew and grew and when finally completed in 1659 there were no less than seven courtyards, which made it one of the largest monasteries in Austria—until most of it burnt down and they wisely rebuilt on a smaller scale in 1865. Today you see a pale green building, almost rectangular, with one side including the church, which is a restful gothic after so much baroque, and in the centre of the inner courtyard is a rose garden.

First, though, there is the baroque library, finished in 1776, an endless length with about 130,000 books and manuscripts. Altomonte did the sham architectural ceiling and standing out in the centre of the long room are four wood carvings by Stammel which look much smaller in this setting than their 7½ feet high and depict death, the judgment, hell and heaven.

If you are there on a Sunday morning the experience can be rounded off by joining the local populace in the tree-filled park for the brass band concert, a good livener before heading further west along the Enns towards the Salzkammergut, divided between three provinces, Styria, Land Salzburg and Upper Austria (which has the largest bit).

Just on the outskirts of the area is one of the several mini-toll roads in this part of Styria. It is at Tauplitz (others are at Schladming, Gröbming and Ramsau) and up you drive round the hairpins, and through the pine trees with a flower carpet on which lounge dozy brown cows. At the top are guesthouses, seven little lakes, smaller brothers of the Salzkammergut, views of the mountains, including the Dachstein and the network of chairlifts and drag-lifts which in winter makes Tauplitzalm, at 5,000 feet, the premier skiing region in Styria.

A few miles down the road is one last pre-Salzkammergut stop, to take in some delightful folkloric stories at Mitterndorf, where, if you are not there in December for the St Nicholas procession, you can get a very good idea about what happens by a visit to a little museum in the centre of the village where the story is graphically told with the costume collection in the loft.

Like many old customs, its origin is almost certainly heathen, but today's celebrations have St Nicholas and his entourage followed by a team of straw-chasers (that is, men dressed in straw) carrying whips. They are, say some, heralding winter and the straw suits refer to the end of the harvest; or they are, because they carry whips, chasing out the evil spirits that winter may bring. It does not matter which variation you choose, the jollity comes out the same, St Nicholas followed by devils who kidnap teenagers, subsequently released by the 'bishop'.

It is not such a noisy affair as another custom in villages in the Upper Mur valley where every Shrovetide young men have a fancy dress race clad as road sweepers, mummers and hen-stealers (in which case they are covered in feathers). The objective of the race seems to be stealing eggs (which have been left in a prominent position by the farmer's wife who is attending the event with her husband), its purpose probably concerned with fertility of the soil during the coming year as well as again exorcising the spirits of the long hard winter. This is always a boisterous festival, with much clanking of chains and shouts and cries from the participants.

If you feel in need of a cure after all this, there is always Bad Heilbrunn, just outside Mitterndorf, where you can take the waters in modern comfort and luxury, the thermal machinery discreetly hidden behind brown doors and the thermal swimming pool overlooked by a gallery lounge.

Styria's contributions to the Salzkammergut are several little lakes and resorts, the most famous of which is Bad Aussee, not for its water but for Prince Johann's romance with the postmaster's daughter; the building is no longer the post-office, but a plaque proudly tells the story.

The resort is not actually on a lake, to find this you need to go as far as Altaussee, which has a different royal claim, as the place where Franz Joseph's wife, Elizabeth, had rooms. But like much of the Salzkammergut, you must not necessarily expect a lakeside view. Altaussee, for instance, is spread over wide open meadows and only one hotel and pension are actually lakeside, though there is a five-mile walk around the water, for pedestrians only.

The third member of the trio is Grundlsee, fairly sophisticated, a road running all the way along and clinging to its claim: the biggest lake in Styria. Its development is actually by the water, but to get this view you sacrifice a village centre and atmosphere, for it is basically ribbon development.

10 Carinthia

If you are crossing the Wörthersee by boat in the moonlight and hear church bells ringing beneath the waves no-one, but no-one, to whom you mention the matter will be surprised. For on the floor of this, the largest lake in Carinthia, and its number one tourist region, is supposed to be a church, a reminder of the decadence of earlier natives who are, presumably, repenting their sins in a watery way, too.

They were all drowned and the church submerged, so the legend goes, 1,000 years ago, after they had failed to heed the warnings of a little old fellow with a bell who kept turning up at their roisterous annual festivities to plead that they alter their ways. He could not have had much persuasion, for they got worse and worse and even closed the church. On his third visit he rang his bell, and the lake water rose and engulfed the church and the inhabitants of Maria-Worth.

The village today is the most peaceful tranquil spot here in which to ponder the more serious and far-reaching aspects of Carinthia's history before hurling yourself into the casino and other gaieties to be found at the bustling resorts. As a province, it lacks the corporate identity of other parts of Austria and even the churches are different, with the emphasis on romanesque and gothic rather than baroque. The dukes of Carinthia ruled from St Veit until in the sixteenth century it lost its title as provincial capital to Klagenfurt.

Much more recently part of the province suffered from the confusion of not knowing to whom she belonged, or even to whom she wished to belong. Yugoslavia made two attempts to annexe a section, after the first world war when the population voted to remain Austrian, and again in 1945 when the Yugoslavs hoped—and failed—to gain Klagenfurt and the Wörthersee as well as the few thousand inhabitants called Windisch who live in the southern mountain region. Though Austrian by choice, they speak a Slav dialect and run their own schools, radio and press.

Carinthia, with a population of half a million, has needed to develop a certain cosmopolitan flavour because of its position. The Tauern mountains form the northern border with Land Salzburg, the Julischen Alps with Italy, the Karawanken range with Yugoslavia. It takes half an hour to drive to the Italian border from Villach, an hour to the Yugoslav one, and it is not surprising there are strong commercial and cultural ties between this trio, with the Carinthians hoping, like the Styrians, that tourists will do more than pass through on their way elsewhere.

There is every reason to stop off, for the province is an amalgamation, in miniature, of the whole of Austria. Protected by its sheltering mountains north and south, it has the lakes, the woods, the abbeys and castles all in one area, not perhaps so awe-inspiring as elsewhere in Austria but appealing and not, with an occasional exception, so well-known or visited by masses of people. One of the exceptions in high summer is, of course, the lakeland district, for which they claim a better weather record than the more famous Salzkammergut.

The Wörthersee, it is said, is the warmest lake in Europe, no doubt helped by the hot springs that bubble beneath it, and at 10½ miles long it is a fair expanse of water with a consequent variety of activities and flavours. If you are still dreaming at Maria-Worth, you should be sitting in the cemetery, for that is the viewpoint, built out on a peninsula.

The church, basically gothic from the thirteenth century, looks much bigger from the outside, and its main altar is baroque. Like Hallstatt, graveyard space is limited and the skulls rest in the circular charnel house. The one day of the year when sleepy Maria-Worth, the road to it like a winding English country lane, comes to life is 15 August, St Maria's birthday, and cause for processions and fun.

Otherwise, the summer tourist life is to be found in Velden and Pörtschach, between them able to accommodate 24,000 visitors and provide enough entertainment to keep the crowd occupied and happy. Velden is a town of elegant, if somewhat old-fashioned hotels (the sort with turrets and embroidered drainpipes) and naturally has one that used to be a castle and is now haunted by celebrities. Its grounds are extensive and include a trout hatchery to which wire netting has regretfully been added to prevent the tame fish from sliding out of the water to receive titbits from the hotel guests.

No-one gets up particularly early in Velden, so a pre-breakfast stroll sees holidaymakers in their pyjamas and dressing gowns seated on their balconies watching the lakeside scene come to life. The high hour is around tea-time, after the afternoon open-air concerts, when everybody promenades down the main street to the tea dances and the policeman politely stops his car to allow lethargic visitors to wander across the road.

For a view over the lake, to see the pretty patterns made by the sailing school regatta, whose instructors are largely ski instructors doing this as a summer job, drive up the hill towards the Saisser See, almost through the farmyards on the way, and if it is evening, stop for a glass of wine at Am Heubad'n, an old barn turned into a restaurant.

There is little difference between Velden and Pörtschach, 15 minutes' drive away, except that the latter is built on a promontory stretching out into the lake which gives it a very long flower-bedecked promenade. It goes in for tennis and dancing tournaments, while Velden concentrates on horse riding. Pörtschach, too, has a castle turned into a hotel and, when it was a private home, Brahms was a guest at Schloss Leonstain. In fact he spent three consecutive summers here describing it as 'very beautiful scenery and the gateway to the most beautiful and splendid country of all' (meaning Italy).

Gustav Mahler, on the other hand, favoured the other side of the lake at Maiernigg. Schloss Leonstain keeps up its musical tradition, for in one exquisite courtyard are held chamber-music evenings, a quartet playing Haydn and Mozart. The players walk carefully round the pond in the centre with its tiny fountain to reach the raised dais in the corner, and there is room for not more than 100 in the audience. The lighting, apart from that on the musicians' stands, is real candles, hardly flickering in their silver candelabra, and the climbing plants that reach for the little first floor gallery tickle the cellist's ear.

At the opposite end of the Wörthersee from Velden is Klagenfurt, not quite on the lakeside, and though it has the title of provincial capital, this cosy town is overshadowed in importance by its commercial rival, Villach, so obviously the industrial master of Carinthia. Although two fires destroyed a greater part of Klagenfurt before and during the Napoleonic wars, it managed to retain some patrician sixteenth-century houses and two charmers: the Landhaus and the Dragon, building and statue both left to themselves on a Saturday afternoon when most of the 48,000 inhabitants are at their summer houses by the lake.

The sixteenth-century Landhaus was the setting for the legal sessions of the Dukes of Carinthia and the aristocracy. It is an elegant white renaissance building with a tower to one side, and on the first floor is, appropriately, the Wappensaal, a room showing the ducal coats of arms. The courtyard has an open-air theatre, which is in addition to Klagenfurt's other artistic ventures—its theatre, concert and city halls, museum and painting galleries.

The open-air museum, just out of town, is an unusual collection of buildings in miniature but, unlike many models of a similar kind which are a complete replica of their own town, this one travels the globe, its models showing some of the world's most famous buildings.

In a central position in the main square, Neuer Platz, sits the dragon, a splendid fiery creature with an equally dramatic story behind him. During the fifteenth century the area was a marsh and in its depths lived the monster, popping out when he was hungry to eat a few inhabitants. As his appetite grew larger the population's terror grew greater and they finally issued a proclamation that anyone who successfully slew the dragon would be rewarded by the hand of the duke's daughter (who else?). The young man who took up the challenge is standing triumphantly upon the dragon's back.

Just south of Klagenfurt are the Karawanken mountains that divide the province from Yugoslavia, and it was over this range that refugees fled into Austria after the first and second world wars, and were dismayed to discover that while the Yugoslav side of the range was gentle and easy, the Austrian face was forbidding and rugged. Today's road communications between the two are the Loibl tunnel and the Wurzen pass.

To see all of the sights Carinthia has to offer can easily be done from Klagenfurt by car. The road running almost directly northwards presents a pilgrimage church as its first showpiece, an enormous building dwarfing the tiny village around it. Maria Saal is gothic, there is a Roman basilica outside and the remnants of this era set into the walls of the church—a plaque showing Romulus and Remus, a Roman coach and so on.

They were found not far away at Magdalensberg where excavations of a Roman settlement have been going on for 15 years, and they are still finding items of interest. The settlement is believed to have been a health resort for rich Romans because its standard of houses is far too opulent to suit a military camp. History jumps disconcertingly from period to period on this same road, for near Maria Saal is Karnburg where Charlemagne spent Christmas in 800; and not far away is the imposing stone Herzogstuhl (duke's chair), where serfs swore allegiance to the dukes of Carinthia. The stone throne was built here because it was convenient for the dukes to travel to it from St Veit where they lived. Since this town lost its status as provincial capital it has gained a new commercial importance as centre of the timber industry.

Near St Veit is another of those fairy-tale castles which looks as if it was built as a film set. Hochosterwitz has 14 archways spiralling up the hill and is still owned by a member of the Khevenhüller family who built it in 1500. There were several takeover bids in its long history, the most well-known being that from the Tyrolean Countess Maultasch in 1600, who tried starving out the inmates, then fell for a similar 'confidence trick' as was put over in Salzburg.

The castle crowd were almost starved out, but when they had eaten their last bull they threw the skin down to the Countess's troops in a pretence that there were lots more; otherwise they could not, supposedly, have been so reckless with the remains. The troops below believed the bluff and retreated, defeated. Today's Count Khevenhüller lives in another castle at the bottom of the hill, and has turned over Hochosterwitz to the public, installing a restaurant to cater for the 3,000 visitors who arrive daily in summer.

From St Veit there are two possible routes back to Klagenfurt, either west along the Glantal, or still north through the Krappfeld region and little villages like Treibach to Zwischenwassern, to find a curtain-raiser for one of Carinthia's most famous sights. It is a beautiful country mansion which was formerly a bishop's palace and is now the administrative headquarters for Gurk Abbey, just down the road, whose twin towers with onion tops stand out in a homely sort of way amidst the meadows.

Gurk was founded by St Hemma, whose sons had been killed in local quarrels and whose husband, after taking an eye-for-an-eye revenge on the population, then repented and went on a pilgrimage to Rome never to return. Hemma built the Benedictine cloister, and the abbey in romanesque style dates from 1160-1200. There is a magnificent porch with frescoes, the colours remarkably retained, stained glass windows and a carved stone portal. Inside, the pews were originally divided into two sections, one for the populace, and one for the monks, and there is a warm feeling given by the pink chalkstone that looks like marble.

Three masterpieces command attention. Raphael Donner's pietà, from 1740, shows Mary holding the body of Christ. The carving was finished by one of his pupils for, tragically, Donner died of lead poisoning while he was working on it. The reliefs on the pulpit are by the same artist, also in lead, and depict the victory of the Christians over non-believers—these unfortunates being thrown head first from the top!

The high altar is the second showpiece. Made of linden, around 1626-32, by Michael Hönel, it almost disintegrated from woodworm, and only the gilt was holding it together. It has now been injected against the rot and they think it will last another 300 years as a result. The carving is a splendid panorama of figures and scenes; in all there are 72 sculptures including Mary on her way to heaven surrounded by angels and the four new testament apostles along the base.

The third item is the crypt, only 20 yards square and with 100 pillars so close together and so arranged that they form diagonal and square patterns throughout. It is impossible to put the architecture into words, but the visual impact is breathtaking. Here is the mausoleum of St Hemma and an Italian marble statue so realistic that you think you must be able to lift the veil from the woman's face.

The abbey sits in the middle of the Gurktal at its most gentle and open, with the little Gurk river jumping with trout: a non-fisherman claimed he had caught a couple of dozen one afternoon without really trying! A narrow-gauge railway runs through the valley, but its days are numbered and a bus service will take over eventually. The road drops quite steeply at one end to bring you to Feldkirchen, the makers of brandy (plum, raspberry, strawberry) and linen, and on to Moosburg, a dreamy little village with a large-size pond rather than a small lake and a little schloss perched on a little hill at which you can stay.

It is no distance from here back to Klagenfurt, and the scenery, undulating hills and farms, is remarkably anglicised except for the pine trees and the style of the houses. The Carinthian farmhouse has the hayloft in the middle and wings on either side, the ground floor occupied by animals and machinery. The hay is loaded from the carts directly at first-floor level, a sensible idea, and you can tell where the living quarters are in the building because the shutters are real, not merely wooden covers with air holes.

Having taken the country air on one day tour, it would be nice to vary the theme by driving west the following day, back to Velden and then on to see more of the province's lakeland. The Wörthersee may be the largest, but the little Faaker See is the only privately owned piece of water, looking across the Mittagskogel mountain with Three Lands Corner where Yugoslavia, Italy and Austria meet. In fact this part of Carinthia is very like Slovenia, the most northern province of Yugoslavia. The whole area is remote and quiet and wooded, and in the middle of the Faaker See is an island with an hotel upon it, for those who are in search of absolute solitude.

Villach is only four hours from Venice and sits firmly at the crossroads of the province. The place to grasp its geographical significance is at Landskron, ten minutes out of town, and so called because it is on the crown of the land, with views through the valleys and lakes and across the mountains. This castle's owners included the Habsburgs and the Knights of the Order of St George, but after the original building, some of it dating back to the fourteenth century, was destroyed by fire in 1848 it was left deserted, and even at one stage used as a quarry.

Its rebirth began in the 1950s when a local land owner (of the Faaker See among other things) bought it, and inside the shell put a restaurant decorated with chamois and stag shot on his own lands. Landskron is quite the best place to be at dusk, looking down on twinkling Villach—which at close quarters is something of a disappointment.

For 900 years the city commanded the important river Drau, which then circled the town, though now the inhabitants have spilled over on to the banks on the other side. But its industrial importance made it a target in World War II and it has been very much rebuilt inside the walls, with only a few relics remaining, like the monstrous gothic church, Stadtpfarrkirche, St Jakob, relieved inside by those warm pink chalkstone pillars.

Villach's 'home lake' is all of ten minutes' drive and at eight miles long, Ossiacher See is the second largest, though quieter and less developed than the Wörthersee. There is a ferry service to cross it and in it lots of fish, including the local speciality, carp. Part of the road runs through high maize fields, which is, along with corn, the major crop of the province, and the farmers make for themselves a famous dish called Sterz (maize meal). The maize, after the ears have been removed, is roasted in flat circular shapes and pork fat, fried in strips and basted in butter, is put on top. It is very cheap, filling and nutritious and, says my guide, his mother brought him up on it on the grounds that they would soon be bankrupt if they ate rolls and butter and jam!

On the shores of Ossiacher See is the little village of Annenheim, from where a cable railway leads up to the Kanzelhöhe plateau and several hotels. In winter this is a skiing region, with a couple of chairlifts and draglifts from the railway top terminal to bring you to the 6,300-foot summit of the Gerlitzen.

Diagonally across the lake is the resort which gives its name, Ossiach, to the water, and has a thirteenth-fourteenth-century Benedictine monastery transformed into a hotel after the first world war. On the courtyard walls are painted two marvellous old sundials and inside is the old staircase with sham marble pillars to adorn it. There are endless corridors, naturally, inlaid wooden doors and a lounge with a delicate stuccoed ceiling above modern furniture. You dine here surrounded by mediaeval noblemen striking poses in their portraits set into wall panels.

Next door is the enchanting Stiftskirche, restored quite recently, with a baroque altar and pulpit, stuccoed ceiling and pillars, glittering chandeliers and a black and white floor warmed by a red carpet. The dramatic legend behind church and monastery is that among its earlier monks was King Boleslav of Poland, but they only learned of his royal blood when he revealed it on his deathbed in 1089.

Before that the king was just an ordinary monk, and he had joined the Benedictines after he had been excommunicated by the pope for killing Bishop Stanislaw of Cracow in a church. He wandered the world before reaching Ossiach's monastery. If you continue north beyond the end of this lake, you will reach Feldkirchen.

West of Villach are two routes out of the province, either following the valley of the river Gail, or following the river Drau which leads eventually to Lienz in East Tyrol. The Drau valley is full of interest, and not far from Villach there is a lake on either side of the road, both worthy of a picnic lunch stop. Weissensee is proudly the highest lake in the Alps, at 7,874 feet, but they still swim in it from June to September. One end is very like a Norwegian fjord and narrow enough for a bridge across at Techendorf.

The most developed area for hotels is Neusach and here the road ends. It is also a fine region for mountain flowers like alpine roses, gentians, yellow daisies, primroses, and on one bank only of the nearby Drau grows the snow rose (the soil on the other side simply does not suit it!). To the right is the other lake, the Millstatter See, 7½ miles long, with views of the Tauern mountains. The resort of that name has a splendid swimming area with diving station, water chute, and so on, at which most of the inhabitants seem to be gathered on a fine Sunday.

But much more famous than the bathing is its Benedictine monastery dating from 1070. Part of the building is now the aptly named Lindenhof hotel, for in the courtyard is an incredible linden tree reckoned to be 1,000 years old. Wander through to the cloisters and you find a smaller brother to the linden, a mere 500 years old; despite its peaceful appearance with rounded arches and lots of flowers, the cloisters are part of today's working community, containing the offices of the police, post office, forestry commission, and so on. Through another archway is the twin-towered church, original date 800, and now with a very fine romanesque portal and lovely frescoes and columns inside.

At this end of the lake, from Seeboden, is the beginning of the Katschberg pass into Land Salzburg, but if you want to remain in Carinthia, Spittal is just round the next corner with the prospect of a cablecar up to the Goldeck for the panorama and a wander down below in a gentle park to find the sixteenth-century renaissance Schloss Portia.

It is rather austere and not particularly interesting from the outside, but you will catch your breath in the courtyard, which has been turned into a theatre (with a sliding roof in case of bad weather). There are tiers of soft pink galleries and balconies and the ostentatious coat of arms of the Portia family forms part of the proscenium.

Not far outside Spittal heading west there is another parting of the ways, either the Upper Drau valley to Lienz or change to the river Möll, with the same final destination. This latter is lovely scenery and you might happen, as I did, upon some fascinating local festival that is in none of the guidebooks. My chance, and it really was by chance, was at Obervellach, where the fire brigade was celebrating its hundredth birthday.

The Austrian idea of such a celebration is to start early in the afternoon with a parade, speeches and band (this one added carnations to their feathered hats), and continue through to an open-air concert and dance. Everyone is involved, the youngsters selling programmes, and one hopes fervently that there is no fire or theft or disorder to disturb the picturesque scene of the entire village population standing around in their Sunday best waiting patiently for the start.

Near here, by the way, is the Tauern tunnel which runs through to Land Salzburg. It has been open only a few years, you put your car on the train container and the journey from Mallnitz to Böckstein, near Bad Gastein, takes ten minutes. The natives are very proud of this quick method of getting north, and are slightly piqued when you choose to ignore it and insist on driving the fabulous Grossglockner instead, reached from Lienz in East Tyrol or from the Möll valley just west of Obervellach.

They say it is open from the beginning of May to early November, but it can be a much shorter season than that if the snow stays late. The pass was built over a five-year period from 1930 and stretches for almost 30 miles, the steepest ascent from Heiligenblut, with only the hairiest bends (26 of them) numbered, so you know how many more you and your car have to tackle.

Like the age of the road, the motoring matches it in flavour, with very much the adventurous feeling of the days when you were never certain of reaching your destination without a breakdown. The fear of being stuck behind someone going too slowly is so great that during one stretch I overtook a stream of traffic while I was in bottom gear! There are two cul-de-sac roads off the Grossglockner, the Edelweiss, which takes you by car to nearly 8,000 feet, and the longer route to Franz Joseph Höhe, 1,000 feet lower, which is the one with the glacier and the dramatic mountain.

It is also the one with loads of furry marmots, normally the shyest of creatures, happily begging food from the visitors. There is quite a contrast between the multi-storey car parks, hotels, cafés and souvenir shops and the creaking Pasterzen glacier below, a funicular thoughtfully provided for tourists who want to walk upon the grey ugly mass, brown at the edges, and very cracked. Apart from feeding the marmots and looking through binoculars at the climbers, crawling ant-like to the rocky Grossglockner summit at more than 11,000 feet, people take walks, the routes again thoughtfully marked out.

Most are a gentle, fairly short stroll, but you can embark on something a little more ambitious without realising it, as I did, in suede shoes and carrying a handbag. The sturdy walkers in boots with alpenstocks looked aghast at this innocent and her friend slithering about on a minor glacier at the Wasserfallwinkel. It is a sinister feeling to hear the water running beneath your feet and the roar of rocks throwing themselves off nearby mountains.

Once off the glacier, with frozen wet feet, it is a short scramble up to the Oberwalderhütte. The summit of the Grossglockner is less than 2,500 feet from here and a little silver plane is buzzing around its top, the passengers taking photographs of the black beetles who have nearly reached their goal. Lunch at the Oberwalderhütte is a splendid one of sausages and potatoes and a long draught of beer, afterwards writing a postcard with a special franking to prove you have actually been here, and watching the other walkers toiling across the snow and up the steep rocks.

The wander back to the car park seems very simple and less arduous, except that by the afternoon the snow has melted much more, the water is running in torrents down the hill and the shoes are a squelching mess, with still frozen feet inside them, by the time we reach the road.

All this has taken something like six hours, and we still have not 'done' the Grossglockner. The car is nursed gently over the top and down into the Salzach valley in Tyrol, passing the steaming radiators of the less fortunate motorists on the way. The view looking back is a perfect ending to an Austrian holiday, taking away with you the memory of one of its most dramatic sights.

Index

Abbey of Gurk, 29, 191
Abbey of Melk, 109, 115, 116, 117, 119, 121
Abtenau, 93
Achensee, 69
Admont, 183
Adriatic, 98
Aggstein, Castle of, 117
Aguntum, 76
Aicher, Anton, 83
Alemannic, 40
Alexander, Czar of Russia, 58
Allies, 20, 21
Alm, 24
Almatrieb, 65
Almeida, Duke of, 104
Alpenvorland, Salzburger, 88
Alpine, 22, 34, 39, 40, 43, 44, 62, 65, 67, 74, 98, 181, 182, 195
Alps, 22, 23, 24, 27, 58, 80, 121, 128, 170, 187, 195
Alps, Julischen, 187
Alps, Kitzbüheler, 74
Alt, Salome, 79
Altaussee, 185
Altenau, 79
Altmann, St, 120
Altomonte, 109, 123, 124, 183
Am Heubad'n, 188
Ambras, Schloss, 48, 49, 50
America, South, 113
American, 112, 152
Andech, Counts of, 45, 48
Anna, heiress to Hungary and Bohemia, 15
Anna, Queen of Hungary, 113
Annenheim, 194
Anschluss, 20
Antlasort, 105
Antlassritt, 65

Anton, St, 43, 67
Antwerp, 85
Arlberg, 44, 67
Arnsdorf, 88
Arthur, King, 47
Athens, 134
Attersee, 103, 104
Augsburg, 48
Augustines, 14, 119
Aussee, Bad, 182, 185
Austria, Emperor of, 16
Austria, Lower, 20, 23, 31, 32, 62, 106, 109, 114, 115, 121, 124, 127, 128, 165, 169
Austria, Upper, 20, 23, 24, 32, 98, 103, 104, 106, 111, 183
Austrian State Treaty, 21, 119
Austrian Succession, 16
Austro-Hungarian Empire, 19
Babenbergs, 13, 19, 20, 31, 105, 115, 116, 117, 118, 123, 127, 129, 139
Bacchus, Cult of, 49
Bad Aussee, 182, 185
Bad Gastein, 24, 33, 92, 94, 95, 96, 196
  Grüner Baum, 96
  Kaiser-Wilhelm Walk, 96
  Felsenbad, 96
  Hotel d'Europe, 95
  Kursaal, 95
  Straubinger Hotel, 95
  Schwaigerhaus, 95
  Villa Solitude, 95
Bad Hall, 111
Bad Heilbrunn, 184
Bad Ischl, 30, 98, 99, 101, 102, 103, 105
  Kaiservilla, 101, 102
  Zauner, 102
Bad-Tazmannsdorf, 169

Baden, 122
Balkans, 130, 172
Baltic, 98
Band'lkramerland'l, 121
Barbara, St, 67
Barokstrasse, Kleine, 122, 124
Baroness Marie Vetsera, 124, 142
baroque, 15, 29, 33, 39, 40, 55, 62, 68, 69, 83, 86, 87, 102, 103, 104, 109, 110, 116, 117, 119, 120, 124, 127, 128, 137, 151, 158, 159, 171, 177, 183, 186, 187, 194
Bavaria, 50, 57, 69, 80, 130, 181
Bavarians, 45, 55, 56, 57, 61, 69, 70, 73, 76, 78, 129, 182
Beethoven, 31, 113, 122, 136
Belgian, 124
Belvedere, Lower, 50, 150
Belvedere, Upper, 149, 150
Benedictines, 110, 115, 121, 182, 191, 194, 195
Bengel, Hans, 159
Bergisel, 45, 56
Bergputzer, 85
Bergtha, 94
Berlin, 103
Bernstein, 169
Bezau, 40, 41
Bezegg, 40
Biedermeier, 29
Bieler Höhe, 44
Birgitzköpfl, 59
Bischofshofen, 93, 94
Bismarck, 95
Black Sea, 19
Blondel, 118
Bludenz, 42, 43, 44
  Frederick Tor, 43
'Blue Danube', 160

200 Index

Böckstein, 97, 196
  Stollenkurhaus, 97
Bohemia, 14, 15, 16, 49, 141, 146
Bohemia, heir to, 15
Bohemia, heiress to, 15
Bohemian, 46, 156
Bohemian, King Ottakar, 14
Boleslav, King, 194
Bolzano, Italian province of, 22
Bonn, 136
Bosnia, 19
Bourbons, 16
Bozen, 58
Brahms, 137, 188
Brandenburg, Ludwig of, 46
Brandnertal, 43
Brass Bands, 65
Bregenz, 23, 37, 38, 39, 41
  Gebhardsberg, 38
  Hohenbregenz, 38
  Kolumban Kirche, 39
  Martinsturm, 38
  Pfaender, 38
  St Gallus, 39
  See Kapelle, 38
Bregenz, Counts of, 37
Bregenzernach, 39
Bregenzerwald, 38, 40
Brenner Pass, 21, 23, 34, 45, 58, 59, 75, 127
Brennersee, 59
Brigantium, 37
Britain, 20, 21, 114
British, 19, 34, 118, 156
Bruck, Castle of, 76, 77
Bruckner, Anton, 109, 110, 113, 137, 150
Brueghel, 134
Brunnen, Simandl, 120
Budapest, 19, 141, 158
Bulgaria, 19
Burgau, Charles of, 49
Burgenland, 20, 24, 31, 136, 163, 164, 165, 166, 167, 168, 169, 170, 181
Burgtheatre, 134
Burgundy, 15, 123, 146
Burgundy, Maria of, 15, 146

Candlemas, 66
Canova, 133
Capriole, 149
Capuchins, 30, 57, 153
Carinthia, 16, 20, 23, 24, 29, 32, 33, 75, 87, 92, 97, 172, 186, 187, 189, 190, 191, 192, 193, 195
Carinthia, Dukes of, 186, 189, 190
Carinthian, 30
Carlone, 109
Carmelite, 124
Carnuntum, 129
Castle of Aggstein, 117
Castle of Bruck, 76, 77
Castle of Orth, 105
Castle of Tyrol, 58
Cellini, 134
Celts, 13, 37, 78, 98, 104
Charlemagne, 15, 93, 147, 190
Charles, Archduke, 149, 172
Charles, the Bold, 15
Charles, of Burgau, 49
Charles, last Habsburg Emperor, 19, 20, 115, 155, 158
Charles Louis, brother of Franz Joseph, 50
Charles, St, 151
Charles V, of Lorraine, 51
Charles VI, 16, 109, 135, 147, 151, 158
Chicago, 164
China, Emperor of, 102
chinchillas, 76
Christendom, 15
Christian Socialists, 20
Christianity, 37, 63
Christkindl, 65, 112
Christmas, 65, 190
Christoph, St, 43, 44, 67
Cistercians, 29, 39, 123
Columbine, 37
Communists, 21
Congress of Vienna, 16, 155
Constance, Lake, 24, 37, 39, 40, 43, 44
Constantinople, 14
Co-operative Winegrowers' Society, 119
copper mines, 68, 73, 78
Corpus Christi, 65, 106
Counter-Reformation, 15, 112
Count Schurff, 70
Count Starhemberg, 130
Countess Fuchs-Mollard, 154
Countess Margaretha Maultasch, 46, 62, 191
Counts of Bregenz, 37
Counts of Güssing, 168

Counts of Harrach, 136
Counts of Khevenhüller, 191
Counts of Montfort, 37, 38, 40
Courbette, 149
Cracow, 194
Cranach, Lucas, 55
Croatian, 163, 165
Czar Alexander, of Russia, 58
Czechoslovakia, 20, 149

Dachstein, 100, 173, 184
Damüls, 41
Danish, 134
Danube, 19, 20, 22, 23, 32, 98, 110, 113, 114, 115, 117, 118, 120, 121, 129, 132, 133, 134, 160, 166, 175
Demel, 102, 131
Deutsche, Eck, 88
'Die Fledermaus', 137
Diesbach, 91
Dietmayr, Berthold, 115
Dietrich, Wolf, 33, 79, 80, 85, 86
Dollfuss, Engelbert, 20
Dolomites, Lienzer, 75
Donner, Raphael, 83, 191
Dornbirn, 38, 41, 42
  The Red House, 41
Drachenwand, 104, 105
Drau, 23, 193, 195, 196
Duchess of Mantua, 49
Duke of Reichstadt, 146, 157
Duke of Tassilo, 110, 111
Dukes of Almeida, 104
Dukes of Carinthia, 186, 189, 190
Dukes of Herberstein, 177
Dürnberg, 78, 81
Dürnstein, 118, 119, 120
  Co-operative Winegrowers' Society, 119
  Keller Schlossl, 119
Dürnsteiner Katzensprung, 119
Dutch, 85, 91, 133, 153

East Tyrol, 20, 34, 65, 66, 75, 76, 87, 91, 195, 196
Eben, 93
Ebensee, 106
Edelweiss, 197
Edward VII, 102

Index

Eggenberg, Prince, 176, 177
Eggenberg, Schloss, 176, 177
Egypt, 167
Egyptian, 159
Ehrwald, 61
Eisenburg, 163
Eisenstadt, 136, 164, 168, 169, 170
Eisernerz, 111, 182, 183
Eisriesenwelt, 93
Elizabeth, Empress, 102, 114, 141, 142, 145, 148, 157, 185
Emperor of Austria, 16
Emperor of China, 102
Emperor Matthias, 154
Emperor of Mexico, 142, 150
Emperors, Holy Roman, 47, 141
Empire, Austro-Hungarian, 19
Empire, Holy Roman, 15, 16, 58, 141, 147, 172
Engelweingarten, 174
England, 16, 118
English, 63, 118, 140, 173
Enns, 16, 23, 92, 109, 111, 175, 182, 183
Erlach, Fischer von, 83, 84, 88, 151, 155
Erzberg, 173, 182
Esterhazy, 135, 136, 164, 168, 169, 170
Eugene, Prince, 52, 109, 130, 149, 150, 153
Europe, 13, 14, 16, 21, 83, 86, 98, 100, 112, 123, 133, 146, 153, 154, 159, 187
'Everyman', 86

Faaker, See, 193
Falkenstein, 103
Fasching, 138
Felbertauern, 75, 91
Feldkirch, 42, 43
 Katzenturm, 42
 Schattenburg, 42
 St Nicholas, 42
Feldkirchen, 192, 195
Ferdinand, 148
Ferdinand, Archduke, 15, 113
Ferdinand I, 16, 48, 159
Ferdinand II, 172
Ferdinand III, 135

Ferdinand of Tyrol, 48, 49, 50, 51, 52
Fernpass, 61
Festnung Kniepass, 88
Festpielhaus, 85
Firmian, Archbishop von, 88
Fine Arts Museum, 133
Flachau, 92
Flaschenweine, 165
Fleece, Golden, order of the, 146, 150
Flemish, 48
Flexenstrasse, 43
Florentine diamond, 147, 148
Florian, St, 106, 109, 110
Flügel, 100, 103
Forchtenstein, 168
France, 14, 20, 21, 102
Franciscans, 79, 86, 177
Franco-Prussian war, 19
Franconia, 130
Franz Ferdinand, 19
Franz I, 135
Franz II, 16, 58, 171
Franz Joseph, 16, 19, 30, 50, 95, 98, 101, 102, 114, 122, 124, 127, 131, 132, 133, 138, 141, 142, 145, 150, 152, 155, 156, 158, 185
Franz Joseph Höhe, 197
Franz Stephan, of Lorraine, 16, 50, 61, 141, 154
Frederick III, 113, 119, 153, 171
Frederick, the Quarrelsome, 14
Frederick, von Tyrol of the Empty Purse, 43, 48
Frederick Tor, 43
French, 16, 57, 58, 115, 129, 133, 150, 159, 176
Frigga, 94
Fuchs-Mollard, Countess, 154
Fugger, 69, 73

Gail, 195
Gaisberg, 87
Gaislachkogel, 63
Gallus, 37
Gallus, St, 39
Galtür, 67
Gargellen, 44
Garmisch-Partenkirchen, 61
Gastein, Bad, 24, 33, 92, 94, 95, 96, 196

Gastein, valley, 91
'Gasteiner' Symphony, 95
Gauderfest, 64
Gebhard, St, 38
Gebhardsberg, 38
Geneva, 142
George, St, 64, 127, 193
George V, 19
Gerlitzen, 194
Gerlospass, 92
Germain, St, treaty of, 163
German, 19, 21, 22, 38, 62, 68, 70, 114, 134, 163, 172
Germanic, 31, 33, 45, 48, 172
Germans, 37, 58, 68, 123, 134, 138
Germany, 13, 16, 19, 20, 22, 24, 37, 38, 61, 64, 78, 88, 102, 172, 181
Germany, Wilhelm of, 102
Gesäuse, 183
Geschriebenstein, 167
Gestapo, 20
Ghega, Karl Ritter von, 127
Gibraltar, 19
Gilgen, St, 102
Giuliani, 123
Glantal, 191
Glemm, valley, 91
Gloggnitz, 127
Gmunden, 105, 106
Gobelin, 148
Godl, Stephan, 47
Goering, Hermann, 97
gold mines, 78, 97
Goldeck, 195
Golden Fleece, order of the, 146, 150
Goldenes Dachl, 48, 52
Gorz, 16
gothic, 29, 33, 41, 42, 51, 52, 55, 56, 61, 68, 69, 86, 100, 104, 110, 112, 117, 119, 120, 121, 152, 171, 182, 183, 186, 187, 190, 193
Göttweig, 120, 121
Grand Chamberlain, 148, 153
Graz, 32, 149, 171, 172, 173, 174, 175, 176, 177, 178, 181, 182
 Armoury, 175, 176
 Hauptplatz, 174
 'Ink' Castle, 172
 Keplerkeller, 174
 Landhaus, 175, 176

202 Index

Hauptplatz—cont.
  Lisl, 176
  Paulustor, 172
  Schloss Eggenberg, 176, 177
  Schlossberg, 176
  Sporgasse, 174
  Stempfergasse, 174
Grazerdomchor, 175
Great Britain, 20, 21, 114
Grecian, 134, 158
Grins, 65
Gröbming, 183
Grossglockner, 33, 44, 75, 91, 196, 197, 198
Grosswalsertal, 43
Gruber, Franz Xavier, 88
Grünberg, 106
Grundlsee, 185
Gurk, Abbey of, 29, 191
Gurk, river, 192
Gurktal, 192
Güssing, Counts of, 168
Gustav, King of Sweden, 52
Gutenstein, 128

Habsburgs, 13, 14, 15, 16, 19, 20, 29, 30, 33, 38, 46, 48, 57, 116, 119, 127, 140, 146, 148, 153, 155, 156, 157, 172, 193
Haflinger, 91
Hafnerberg, 124
Hall, 57, 76
Hall, Bad, 111
Hallein, 88
Hallstatt, 98, 99, 100, 101, 103, 187
Harrach, Counts of, 136
Haspinger, Joachim, 57, 58
Haydn, 135, 136, 169, 170, 189
Heilbrunn, Bad, 184
Heiligenblut, 196
Heiligenkreuz, 29, 123, 124
Hellbrunn, 80, 81, 85
  Neptune grotto, 81
  Stein Theatre, 81
  Wasser-spiele, 81
Hemma, St, 191, 192
Herberstein, Dukes of, 177
Herod, King, 93
Herzogstuhl, 190
Heuharpfen, 76
Heurigen, 32, 124, 165
Hildebrandt, Lucas von, 83, 120, 121, 149, 151
Hinterbrühl, 123
Hintertux, 69

Hitler, 20, 21, 148
Hoadl, 59
Hoch-gurgl, 63
Hochosterwitz, 190, 191
Hochsölden, 62
Hochtannberg, 40
Hofburg, 139, 141, 145, 148, 149
Hofer, Andreas, 52, 56, 57, 58
Hofgastein, 95
Hofkirche, 47, 48, 50, 55, 58
Hofmannsthal, 86
Högl, 73
Hohenbregenz, 38
Hohensalzburg, 79, 82
Höllental, 128
Holy Alliance, 133
Holy Roman Emperors, 47, 141
Holy Roman Empire, 15, 16, 58, 141, 147, 172
Hönel, Michael, 192
Hönigkogel, 92
Horn, 74
Hötting, 52
Huber, Wolf, 42
Hungarian Crown, 19, 148
Hungarian Plain, 22, 31, 167
Hungarians, 76, 141, 148, 163, 167
Hungary, heir to, 15
Hungary, heiress to, 15
Hungary, King of, 182
Hungary, Queen of, 113
Hungary, 14, 15, 16, 21, 24, 113, 124, 136, 141, 163, 164, 166, 167, 168
Hungerburg, 59
Huns, 129

Igls, 59, 60
Ill, 39
Imst, 63, 64, 67
Indian, 157
Inn, river, 34, 45, 52, 60, 68
Inn, valley, 59, 61, 62, 67, 74
Innsbruck, 30, 34, 42, 45, 46, 47, 48, 49, 50, 51, 52, 55, 56, 59, 60, 62, 63, 64, 65, 66, 67, 68, 74, 75, 174
  Bergisel, 45, 56
  Boznerplatz, 55
  Burg Graben, 52
  Goldener Adler, 52

Goldenes Dachl, 48, 52
Helbling House, 52
Herzog-Friedrichstrasse, 52
Hofgasse, 55
Hofkirche, 47, 48, 50, 55, 58
Hötting, 52
Hungerburg, 59
Imperial Palace, 51, 52
Landhaus, 55
Leopold fountain, 52
Maria-Theresienstrasse, 55
Markt Graben, 52
Nordkettenbahn, 59
Riesensaal, 51
Rudolph's fountain, 55
St Anna's Column, 55
St Jacob's, 52
Tiroler Volkskunstmuseum, 55, 56, 66
Wilten, 45
Ireland, 13, 145
Irish, 58, 110, 151
iron and steel, 111, 112, 113, 173, 182
Ischgl, 67
Ischl, Bad, 30, 98, 99, 101, 102, 103, 105
Islam, 130
Italian, 16, 33, 49, 50, 51, 59, 63, 78, 83, 84, 110, 133, 155, 174, 177, 178
Italians, 21, 29, 120, 123, 134, 187, 192
Italy, 14, 19, 21, 22, 34, 45, 57, 75, 83, 102, 129, 148, 149, 173, 187, 188, 193

Jenbach, 69
Jesuits, 172
Joanna, of Spain, 15
Johann, 43
Johann, Prince, 171, 174, 175, 185
Johann, St, 70, 92
Joseph I, 135
Joseph II, 30, 61, 76, 115, 123, 135, 148, 151, 154, 156, 159
Julischen Alps, 187

Kahlenberg, 130
Kaiservilla, 101, 102
Kanzelhöhe, 194
Kaprun, 92
Karajan, Herbert von, 85, 139

Index

Karawanken, 187, 190
Karnburg, 190
Karwendel, 50, 57, 59, 69
Katschberg, 92, 195
Katzensprung Dürnsteiner, 119
Keller Schlössl, 119
Kepler, 113, 174
Khevenhüller, Counts of, 191
King Arthur, 47
King of Bohemia, 14
King Boleslav, 194
King Gustav of Sweden, 52
King Herod, 93
King Ottakar, 14
King of Rome, 146
Kirchtag, 66
Kitzbühel, 56, 70, 73, 74, 75
  Our Lady's, 73, 74
  St Catherine's, 73
  Schwarzsee, 74
Kitzbüheler Alps, 74
Kitzsteinhorn, 92
Klagenfurt, 186, 187, 189, 190, 191, 192
  Dragon, 189, 190
  Landhaus, 189
  Neuer Platz, 189
  Wappensaal, 189
Kleine Barokstrasse, 122, 124
Kleine Mariazell, 124
Klosterneuburg, 14
Klostertal, 43
Kohlmaiskopf, 91
Krain, 16
Krappfeld, 191
Krems, 119, 120, 169
  Piaristenkirchen, 120
Kremser-Schmidt, 120
Kremsmunster, 106, 110, 111
Kreuzkirchlein, 68
Kreuzstein, 105
Krimml, 92
Kuenringers, 117
Kufstein, 70
Kulm, 181
Kunsthistorisches Museum, 133

Lake Constance, 24, 37, 39, 40, 43, 44
Lammer, 93
Lamprechtsofen, 88
Land Salzburg, 20, 23, 33, 34, 37, 75, 78, 87, 92, 103, 175, 182, 183, 187, 195, 196
Landeck, 63, 65, 67
Länder, 31
Landestheatre, 113
Landlibell, 45, 46, 56, 57
Landskron, 193
Lanersbach, 69
Längenfeld, 62
Lanser, See, 60
Lech, 43
Lechfeld, battle of, 147
Lechtal, 61
Lehar, Franz, 137
Leitha, battle of, 14
Leonstain, Schloss, 188
Leopold I, 49, 115, 130, 135, 155
Leopold II, 50, 115
Leopold III, 14, 115
Leopold IV, 118
Leopoldsberg, 130
Lermoos, 61
Leutasch, 61
Liechtenstein, 37, 42
Lienz, 65, 75, 76, 195, 196
  Bruck Castle, 76, 77
  Tristachersee, 76
Lienzer Dolomites, 75
Lilienfeld, 124
Linz, 32, 87, 98, 106, 109, 111, 112, 113, 114, 152
  Landestheatre, 113
  St Ignatius, 109
  St Martins, 113
Lipizza, 149, 172, 178
Liszt, Franz, 163, 168, 169
Lizum, 59
Lockenhaus, 168
Lodron, Paris, 82
Loeffler, Peter, 47
Lofer, 88, 91
Loibl, 190
Lombardy, 16, 19
London, 21, 160
Lorraine, Charles V, of, 51
Lorraine, Franz Stephan of, 16, 50, 51, 141, 154
Louis, heir to Hungary and Bohemia, 15
Low Countries, the, 15
Lower Austria, 20,23,31,32
Lower Austria, 20, 23, 31, 32, 62, 106, 109, 114, 115, 121, 124, 127, 128, 165, 169
Lower Belvedere, 50, 150
Lucca, 113
Ludesch, 43

Ludwig, of Brandenburg, 46
Ludwig, King of Hungary, 182
Lungau, 92
Lurgrotte, 178
Lutheran, 128
Luxembourg, 46

Madeira, 19, 20
Magdalensberg, 190
'Magic Flute', the, 137
Magyars, 110, 130, 147
Mahler, Gustav, 137, 139, 188
Maiernigg, 188
Maisäss, 40
Maishofen, 91
Mallnitz, 196
Mantua, 58
Mantua, Duchess of, 49
Marchfeld, battle of, 14
Marcus Sitticus, 33, 80, 81, 82
Margarethen, St, 166, 169
Margraves, 13, 182
Maria, of Burgundy, 15, 146
Maria Bianca Sforza, of Milan, 48, 62
Maria Kirchental, 88
Maria Lanzendorf, 123
Maria Louise, of Spain, 50
Maria, Maximilian I's grand-daughter, 15
Maria Plain, 87
Maria Saal, 190
Maria, St, 187
Maria Schutz, 127
Maria-Theresia, 16, 30, 50, 51, 57, 58, 109, 122, 127, 133, 140, 141, 145, 146, 147, 153, 154, 155, 156, 158, 159, 175
Maria-Trost, 177
Maria-Worth, 186, 187
Mariahilfberg, 128
Mariastein, 70
Mariazell, 122, 182
Mariazell, Kleine, 124
Marie-Christine, Maria-Theresia's daughter, 140
Marie-Louise, Napoleon's wife, 16, 146, 157
Martin, St bei Lofer, 88
Mattersburg, 164
Matthias, Emperor, 154
Mattsee, 88

Index

Maultasch, Countess Margaretha, 46, 62, 191
Maurach, 62
Maximilian, governor of Tyrol, 82
Maximilian, I, 15, 30, 45, 46, 47, 48, 50, 52, 62, 69, 94, 127, 146
Maximilian II, 154, 159
Maximilian, Prince, 140
Mayerling, 124, 142
Mayr, Peter, 57, 58
Mayrhofen, 69
Mehrerau, 39
Melk, Abbey of, 109, 115, 116, 117, 119, 121
Meran, 46
'Merry Widow', the, 137
Metternich, Prince, 16
Mexico, Emperor of, 142, 150
Michael, St, 117, 118
Milan, 48
mines, copper, 68, 73, 78
mines, gold, 78, 97
mines, salt, 67, 73, 78, 98, 99, 100
mines, silver, 68, 73
Mirabell Palace, 79, 80, 82, 83, 84
Mittagskogel, 193
Mitterndorf, 181, 184
Millstatter, See, 195
 Lindenhof, 195
Mödling, 123
Mohacs, battle of, 15
Mohr, Rev Joseph, 88
Möll, 196
Monats-Schlösschen, 82
Mönchsberg, 84, 87
Mondsee, 104, 105
 Rauchhaus, 104
Montafon, 38, 43, 44
Montfort, Counts of, 37, 38, 40
Moosburg, 192
Mörbisch, 165, 167
Moslems, 118
Mozart, 23, 33, 83, 84, 85, 86, 87, 103, 113, 133, 135, 136, 137, 153, 155, 189
Mozarteum, 85
Mühlbach, 78
Mullerlaufen, 64
Munich, 47, 73
Mur, 23, 175, 182, 184
Mürzzuschlag, 127, 182
Musikverein, 139

Muskat Ottonel, 166
Mussolini, 21
Mutterer Alm, 59
Mutters, 59

Nancy, battle of, 15
Napoleon, 16, 56, 57, 88, 102, 104, 115, 133, 141, 146, 148, 149, 155, 157, 172, 176
Napoleon, Franz Karl, 146
Napoleonic, 61, 120, 173, 176, 189
Nassereith, 64
Nassereither Schellenlaufen, 64
Nassfeld, 97
Natters, 59
Natural History Museum, 133
Nazis, 22
Netherlands, the, 14, 16
Neunkirchen, 127
Neusach, 195
Neusedl am, See, 167
Neusiedler-see, 24, 41, 164, 165, 166, 167, 168
Ney, Marshal, 61
Nicholas, St, 65, 184
Nikola, St, 88
Nile, the, 167
Ninth 'Choral' Symphony, 122
Nordkettenbahn, 59
Noriker, 91
North Tyrol, 57, 76
Notre Dame, 151
Norway, 74, 181, 182, 195
Nüll, Eduard van der, 138
Nuremberg, 45, 47, 141, 145, 148

Ober-gurgl, 63
Oberndorf, 88
Obersdorf, 181
Obertrumer, See, 88
Obervellach, 196
Oberwalderhütte, 197
Odenburg, 163
Olympics, Winter, 59
Opera House, 132, 137, 138, 152, 175
operetta, 23, 39, 137, 142, 167
Orpheus, 81, 99
Orth, Castle of, 105
Oslo, 181
Ossiach, 194, 195
Ossiacher, See, 194

Ostmark, 14, 20
Oswald, 61
Ottakar, 14
Otto the Gay, 153
Otto the Great, 147
Ottonel, Muskat, 166
Ötz, 62
Ötztal, 56, 62, 63
Our Lady's Day, 65

Pannonia, 129
Paris, 157, 169
Paris Lodron, 82
Partenen, 44
Passau, 114
Passau, Bishop of, 120
Passeier, 57
Pasterzen, 197
'Pastoral' Symphony, 137
Patscherkofel, 60
Patton, American General, 149
Paznaun, 44, 67
Peggau, 178
Perchtoldsdorf, 124
Perchts, Run of the, 93, 94
Persenbeug, 115
Pertisau, 69
Pfaender, 38
Philip, the Handsome, 15
Philippine Welser, 48, 49, 50
Phillip the Good, 146
Piber, 149, 178, 181
Piburger, See, 62
Pill, 68
Pinswang, 65
Pinzgau, 88, 92
Piringsdorf, 169
Piz Buin, 44
Planica, 181
Podersdorf am, See, 167
Poland, 20, 130, 194
Polish, 131
Pongau, 88, 92, 93
Pope Pius VI, 109, 148, 151
Portia, Schloss, 196
Pörtschach, 188
pragmatic sanction, 16
Pragraten, 65
Prague, 48, 147
Prandtaur, 109
Pressburg, 163
Prater, 30, 159, 160
Prince Eggenberg, 176, 177
Prince Eugene, 52, 109, 130, 149, 150, 153
Prince Johann, 171, 174, 175 185

Index

Prince Maximilian, 140
Prince Metternich, 16
Prussia, 16, 95
Prussia, Wilhelm I, of, 95

Radetzky, field marshal, 132, 142
Radhausberg, 97
Radstadt, 88, 92
Raggal, 43
Raiding, 163, 168, 169
Ramsau, 183
Rankweil, 42
Liebfraven, 42
Räthla, 37
Rattenberg, 69
Rauheneck, 122
Rauhenstein, 122
Rauchhaus, 104
Rax, King of the, 128
Rax-Alpe, 128
Rechnitz, 167
Red House, 41
Regent, 19
Reichstadt, Duke of, 146, 157
Reinhardt, Max, 86
Reisch, Franz, 74
Remus, 190
renaissance, 39, 86, 110, 112, 124, 134, 145, 174, 175, 189, 196
Renner, Karl, 19, 21
Reuthe, 40
Reutte, 61, 62
Rheinriesling, 166
Rhine, the, 39, 41
Richard, the Lion Heart, 114, 118, 119
Riegersburg, 181
Ringstrasse, 132, 133, 134
Rinn, 57
Rohr, 128
Rohrau, 136
Roller, 63, 64
Roman, 38, 58, 76, 81, 110, 151, 190
Roman Catholic, 14, 79, 140
romanesque, 29, 33, 79, 86, 110, 115, 123, 124, 173, 186, 191, 195
Romans, 13, 37, 45, 78, 109, 110, 113, 129, 131, 134, 138, 159, 182
Rome, 15, 146, 191
Rome, King of, 146
Romulus, 190
Rosenbergs, 73

Rosenkogel, 174
Rubens, 134
Rudolph, Crown Prince, 19, 124, 142, 158
Rudolph I, 14, 140
Rudolph II, 49, 140, 147, 159
Rudolph IV, 46
Rumania, 20
Rupert, St, 78, 79, 86
Russia, 16, 20, 21, 58, 113, 122, 149
Russia, Czar Alexander of, 58
Russians, 167, 177
Rust, 167

Saalach, 88, 92
Saalbach, 27, 88, 91
Saalfelden, 91
Saiser, See, 188
Salome Alt, 79
salt mines, 67, 73, 78, 98, 99, 100
Salurn, 21
Salza, 182
Salzach, 23, 92, 93, 198
Salzburg, 23, 33, 78, 79, 82, 83, 84, 85, 86, 87, 88, 136, 183, 191
Cafe Mozart, 80
Cathedral, 79, 80, 82, 86
Festspielhaus, 85
Festungsgasse, 87
Fransican church, 79, 86
Gaisberg, 87
Getriedgasse, 84
Glockenspiel, 85
Hohensalzburg, 79, 82
Holy Trinity church, 84
Kurgarten, 84
Linzer gasse, 86
Makart Platz, 83, 84
Mirabell Palace, 79, 80, 82, 83, 84
Mönchsberg, 84, 87
Residenzplatz, 85
Sigmund Haffnergasse, 79
St Gabriel's, 79
St Peter's, 78, 79, 85
St Sebastian, 79, 84, 85, 86
University church, 86
Untersberg, 87
Salzburg, Archbishop of, 183
Salzburg, Land, 20, 23, 27, 33, 34, 75, 78, 87, 92, 103, 175, 182, 183, 187,

195, 196
Salzburger Alpenvorland, 88
Salzburger Stier, 82
Salzburgers, 33, 87
Salzkammergut, 24, 32, 33, 98, 99, 100, 103, 104, 105, 106, 182, 183, 184, 185, 187
Samnaun, 67
Sarajevo, 19
Saturnalia, 138
Saxony, 130
Schattberg, 91
Schattenburg, 42
Schatzkammer, 145, 147, 148
Scheibenschlagen, 65
Schellenlaufen, 64
Scheller, 63, 64
Schemenlaufen, 63, 64
Schikaneder, Emanuel, 137
Schladming, 183
Schlaining, 168
Schleicherlofen, 64
Schloss Ambras, 48, 49, 50
Schloss Eggenberg, 176, 177
Schloss Leonstain, 188
Schloss Portia, 196
Schlossberg, 176
Schlösschen, Monats, 182
Schlossl, Keller, 119
Schmittenhöhe, 92
schnapps, 28, 40
Schneeberg, 128
Schökl, 178
Schönberg, 137
Schönbrunn, 19, 102, 136, 141, 145, 149, 154, 155, 156, 157, 158, 159, 176
Schottwien, 128
Schratt, Katharina, 101, 145
Schruns, 44
Schubert, 95, 137
Schuplattler, 93
Schurff, Count, 70
Schwarza, 128
Schwarzach, 95
Schwarzsee, 74
Schwaz, 68, 69
Schwechat, 122
Schwedentracht, 41
Scotos, 61, 151
Sebastian, 110
Seeboden, 195
Seefeld, 60, 61
Klosterbrau, 61
Wildsee, 60
Seegrotte, 123
Seegrubbe, 59

206 Index

Semmering, 127, 128
Semmering Pass, 23, 127, 182
Semriach, 177, 178
'Seraglio, Abduction from the', 136
Serbia, 19
Serbo-Croats, 31, 163
Sesselscreiber, Master Gilg, 47
Sforza, Maria Bianca, 48, 62
Siccardsburg, August Siccard von, 138
Sigismund, Archduke, 46, 67
'Silent night, Holy Night', 88
silver mines, 68, 73
Silvretta, 39, 43, 44, 67
Simandl Brunnen, 120
Sitticus, Marcus, 33, 80, 81, 82
skiing, 27, 28, 34, 43, 44, 59, 60, 63, 67, 70, 74, 75, 88, 91, 92, 96, 104, 127, 177, 178, 182, 184, 194
ski-flying, 92, 181
ski-joring, 104
ski-jumping, 91, 181
Slovenia, 193
Slavonic, 31, 172, 173
Slavs, 76, 187
Social Democrats, 19
Solari, Santino, 80, 82
Solbad Hall, 67, 68
Sölden, 62
'Son et Lumière', 119
Sonnwendstein, 127, 128
Sopron, 163, 164
'Sound of Music', 104
South America, 113
South Tyrol, 21, 22, 57
Spain, 14, 15, 50
Spain, Joanna of, 15
Spain, Maria Louise of, 50
Spanish, 133, 134, 159
Spanish Riding School, 140, 149, 158, 172, 178, 181
Spanish Succession, 16, 68
spas, 24, 30, 33, 94, 95, 96, 98, 106, 111, 184
Speckbacher, Joseph, 57
Spittal, 195, 196
Spitz, 117
Stainz, 171, 174
Stammel, 183
Stams, 61, 62

Stanislaw, Bishop, 194
Starhemberg, Count, 130
State Treaty, Austrian, 21, 119
steel and iron, 111, 112, 113, 173, 182
Stein Pass, 88
Stein Theatre, 81
St Altmann, 120
St Anton, 43, 67
St Barbara, 67
St Christoph, 43, 44, 67
St Gallus, 39
St Gebhard, 38
St Germain, 163
St Gilgen, 102
St Hemma, 191, 192
St Johann, 70, 92
St Margarethen, 166, 169
St Maria, 187
St Martin bei Lofer, 88
St Michael, 117, 118
St Nicholas, 65, 184
St Nikola, 88
St Rupert, 78, 79, 86
St Stephens, 123, 130, 135, 152, 153, 154
St Veit, 95, 186, 190, 191
St Wolfgang, 103
Steyr, 111, 112
Sterz, 194
Stierwascher, 83
Stiftskirche, 194
Stollenkurhaus, 97
Strauss, Johann, 31, 132, 137, 138, 160
Strauss, Joseph, 137
Strauss, Richard, 86
Stuben, 43, 44
Stubing, 178
Stubnerkogel, 96
Styria, 14, 16, 20, 23, 32, 87, 92, 122, 124, 171, 172, 173, 175, 176, 177, 181, 182, 183, 184, 185
Styria, Upper, 32, 177, 181, 182
Styrian, 30, 127, 153, 171, 172, 173, 175, 182, 187
Succession, Austrian, 16
Swabian, 48
Sweden, 16, 38, 113
Sweden, King Gustav of, 52
Swedes, 38, 41, 42, 56, 117, 129
Swedish, 15, 65
Swiss, 37, 38, 41, 67, 140

Switzerland, 20, 21, 24, 37, 39, 67, 140, 164

Tamburizza, 163
Tartars, 130
Tassilo, Duke of, 110, 111
Tauern mountains, 78, 87, 92, 187, 195
Tauern pass, 92
Tauern tunnel, 97, 196
Tauplitz, 183
Tauplitzalm, 184
Tazmannsdorf, Bad, 169
Techendorf, 195
Telfs, 62, 64
Tennengebirge, 93
Thaur, 64, 65
Theater an der Wien, 137
Thirty Years War, 15, 38, 82, 116, 129
Three Lands Corner, 193
Thumersbach, 91
Thurn, 75, 76
Thyrsus, 60
timber, 22, 40, 68, 128
Timmelsjoch, 63
Tiroler Volkskunstmuseum, 55, 56, 66
tourism, 22, 31, 68, 98, 164, 188, 197
Traminer, 166
Traunsee, 105
Traunstein, 106
Trausdorf, 165
Treaty, Austrian State, 21, 119
Treaty, of St Germain, 163
Treibach, 191
Trieste, 149
Tristachersee, 76
Troger, Paul, 121
Turkey, 19
Turkish, 15, 29, 116
Turks, 14, 15, 94, 109, 115, 116, 122, 124, 129, 130, 131, 152, 155, 168, 176, 183
Turnitz, 124
Tyrol, 16, 20, 27, 33, 34, 37, 40, 43, 44, 45, 46, 47, 48, 49, 50, 51, 55, 56, 57, 58, 60, 62, 64, 65, 67, 68, 69, 70, 75, 82, 87, 92, 198
Tyrol, Castle of, 58
Tyrol, East, 20, 34, 65, 66, 75, 76, 87, 91, 195, 196
Tyrol, Ferdinand of, 48, 49, 50, 51, 52

Index

Tyrol, governor of, 47, 48, 82
Tyrol, North, 57, 76
Tyrol, South, 21, 22, 57
Tyrolean, 30, 46, 48, 58, 67, 69, 191
Tyrolese, 46, 56, 57, 64, 69, 70, 75

United States, 20
Unken, 88
Untersberg, 87
Upper Austria, 20, 23, 24, 32, 98, 103, 104, 106, 111, 183
Upper Belvedere, 149, 150
Upper Styria, 32, 177, 181, 182

Valais, 41
Vebelbacher, Hienonymus, 119
Veit, St, 95, 186, 190, 191
Velden, 188, 189, 193
Venetia, 16, 19
Venetian, 59, 166
Venice, 45, 193
Vent, 63
Venus von Willendorf, 133
Vermunt, 44
Vetsera, Baroness Marie, 124, 142
Victoria, Queen, 102
Vieldidena, 45
Vienna, 14, 15, 16, 19, 20, 21, 23, 29, 31, 45, 49, 50, 51, 78, 85, 102, 104, 109, 114, 115, 118, 121, 122, 123, 127, 128, 129, 130, 131, 132, 135, 136, 139, 141, 142, 148, 149, 150, 151, 152, 153, 154, 156, 157, 160, 164, 169, 172, 173, 174, 175, 178, 181
 Blue Bottle, 131
 Burggarten, 132
 Burgring, 133
 Burgtheatre, 134
 Chinese cabinet room, 155
 Chinese lacquer room, 156
 Church am Hof, 151
 Demel, 102, 131
 Dr Karl-Lueger Ring, 134
 Dr Karl-Renner Ring, 134
 Deutschordenkirche, 151
 Fine Arts Museum, 133
 Figarohaus, 136
 Gloriette, 155, 159
 Goddess of Wisdom, 134
 Hauptallee, 159
 Hausmutter, 153
 Hofburg, 139, 141, 145, 148, 149
 Josefplatz, 140
 Kaisertor, 148
 Karlskirche, 151
 Kartner Ring, 132
 Kunsthistorisches Museum, 133
 Lower Belvedere, 50, 150
 Million's Room, 157
 Musikverein, 139
 Natural History Museum, 133
 Neptune fountain, 159
 Opera House, 132, 137, 138, 152, 175
 Opernring, 132
 Parkring, 132
 Parliament, 134
 Prater, 30, 159, 160
 Pummerin, 152
 Rathaus, 134
 Rathauspark, 134
 Ringstrasse, 132, 133, 134
 Rooseveltplatz, 150
 Sacher Hotel, 131
 Schatzkammer, 145, 147, 148
 Schönbrunn, 19, 102, 136, 141, 145, 149, 154, 155, 156, 157, 158, 159, 176
 Schottenkirche, 151
 Schottenring, 134
 Schubertring, 132
 Spanish Riding School, 140, 149, 158, 172, 178, 181
 St Catherine's, 152
 St Peter's, 151
 St Rupert's, 151
 St Mark's, 136
 St Stephens, 123, 130, 135, 152, 153, 154
 Stadtpark, 132
 Stock Exchange, 134
 Stubenring, 132
 Theater an der Wien, 137
 University, 134
 Upper Belvedere, 149, 150
 Wagenburg, 157, 158
 Volksgarten, 132
Votiv Church, 150
Wurstelstand, 131
Vienna Boys' Choir, 139, 175
Vienna, Congress of, 16, 155
Vienna Philharmonic, 139
Viennese, 30, 31, 39, 124, 127, 131, 135, 137, 138, 139, 142, 145, 150, 151, 152, 154, 159, 160, 176
Vierburgenland, 163
Vikersond, 181
Villa Solitude, 95
Villach, 187, 189, 193, 195
 St Jackob, 193
Volders, 59
Volkskunstmuseum, Tiroler, 55, 56, 66
Vorarlberg, 16, 20, 27, 34, 37, 38, 39, 41, 43, 44, 48, 55, 62, 67
Vorlande, 48
Vindobona, 129

Wachau, 114, 115, 117, 118, 121
Wagner, 52, 85
Wagrain, 92
Waldviertel, 121
Walgau, 43
Wallersee, 88
Warth, 40, 62
Wasserfallwinkel, 197
Wasser-Spiele, 81
Wattens, 68
Weer, 68
Weinstrasse, 173
Weinviertel, 121
Weissbach, 91
Weissburgunder, 166
Weissenkirchen, 118
Weissensee, 195
Welser, Philippine, 48, 49, 50
Wenia, 129
Werfen, 93
Werndl, Joseph, 112
Westminster Abbey, 151
White Horse Inn, 103
Wien, 129
Wienebecken, 121
Wiener-Neustadt, 47, 127
 St George's, 127
Wienerwald, 31, 121, 122, 165
Wienne, 129
Wieselburg, 163
Wildsee, 60

Index

Wilhelm, of Germany, 102
Wilhelm I, of Prussia, 95
Willendorf, Venus von, 133
Wilten, 45
Windisch, 187
wine, 31, 32, 117, 119, 171, 173
Winegrowers' Society, Cooperative, 119
Winter Olympics, 59
winter sports, 27, 28, 34, 43, 44, 59, 60, 63, 67, 70, 74, 75, 88, 91, 92, 104, 127, 177, 178, 181, 182, 184, 194, 196
Wodan, 94

Wolfgang, St, 103
Wolgangsee, 103
Wörgl, 70
World War I, 110, 149, 163, 186, 190, 194
World War II, 84, 116, 120, 127, 149, 152, 155, 158, 172, 175, 177, 190, 193
Wörthersee, 33, 186, 187, 189, 193, 194
Wurmkogel, 63
Wurzen, 190

Ybbs, 115
Yugoslavia, 20, 32, 172, 173, 175, 181, 186, 187, 190, 193
Yuvavum, 78

Zagreb, 173
Zauner, 102
Zell am, See, 64, 88, 91, 92
Zielstätten, 58
Zillertal, 64, 69
Zirl, 68
Zita, Empress, 20
Zugspitze, 61
Zurs, 43
Zwieselstein, 63
Zwischenwassern, 191
Zwölferhorn, 103